THEOSONY

Nóirín Ní Riain

Theosony

TOWARDS A THEOLOGY OF LISTENING

the columba press

First edition, 2011, published by
The Columba Press
55A Spruce Avenue, Stillorgan Industrial Park,
Blackrock, Co Dublin

Cover by Bill Bolger
Origination by The Columba Press
Printed in Ireland by
Brunswick Press Ltd, Dublin

ISBN 978 1 85607 723 1

Contents

Foreword

Andrew Cyprian Love OSB

Dr Nóirín Ní Riain is acclaimed internationally as a singer in the traditional Irish style. More than a performer of music, however, she places her unique vocal art at the service of others' spiritual awareness and inner healing. This naturally tends to make Dr Ní Riain a highly conscious artist, who is not merely creative in music, but also reflects in depth upon the meanings and message of music and sound. Further still, the present book performs a valuable service to the theological and artistic communities by broaching some wide-ranging issues which arise from examining the interconnection of Christian theology and sound. It is both an intellectually stimulating, and a deeply intuitive book. This is because it flows from rational reflection about sound, music and the Christian faith, yet is at the same time rooted in the subtle instincts and discernments of a practising musician and Christian believer.

The author argues that God communicates himself to humans primarily and primevally through the aural sense. God's entire creation lives, moves and has its being in the fullness of the grace of sounds. It is the providential destiny of humans to experience this fact and to reflect upon it. This overall proposal is gathered up under a term the author has coined: *theosony*. Theosony is both a practice and a theory. As a practice, it is God's revelation considered both from the standpoint of the sounds (and silences) in which he reveals himself to humanity, and the act of listening to God required by humans in order to receive this revelation. As a theory, it is the task of reflecting theoretically on these matters, so that they find definition consciously and rigorously in a new domain of theological discourse.

'In the beginning was the Word' (John 1:1). The Second Person of the Trinity is here called the Word or, in Greek, the *Logos*. But what is a word? We sometimes forget that a word is a thing of sound as well as of rational content. In this famous gospel opening, John is therefore using an image of sound as well as of rationality to designate the Second Person of the Trinity, the Person who, according to theological tradition, additionally exercises a special role in the creation of our world. What is this if not an imagery of sound poised at the very heart of our understandings both of the Trinity and of the origin of created things? If our understandings of Trinity and of creation encompass imagery of the sonic in this way, who would dare to assert that sound has no significance for theology? Yet, before Nóirín proceeded with her work, the theological significance of sound remained, if not wholly, at least largely unexplored. The work of theology is a work of development. Christians believe that there is always more meaning waiting to break forth from God's revelation, and the author has wagered, powerfully and plausibly, on a fuller theological meaning for sound, and believes its time has come.

As we read the writer's compelling text, it gradually emerges how the idea of sound resounds behind all theology. Sound is seen to reverberate insurpressibly through the halls of theology and now, thanks to the author, sound is able to recast the existing lineaments of our orthodox Christian faith into new, theosonic configurations, theology different yet the same. As we read, we recognise things we have already deeply sensed about the salience of sound in Christian life and thought, but which we had never brought to conscious awareness. Paradoxically, this makes even what is new in Nóirín's vision strangely familiar, so that the experience of reading this book is an experience of coming home to ourselves. If what this book says about the nature of Christian experience is true, then by definition what it says will be not merely understood, but recognised. And it is recognised. Such a recognisability of the role which the author proposes for sound suggests the authenticity of theosony, just as much as the intellectual cogency of her arguments suggests it. For the writer is making explicit what Christianity has always somehow known about sound with a subtle, informal kind of knowledge embedded in the heart of the tradition. Christian tradition has universally acknowledged a theosony of the heart. What Nóirín has done is to give her fortunate readers a theosony of the intellect.

Introduction

The immediate person thinks and imagines that when he prays, the important thing, the thing he must concentrate upon, is that *God should hear* what HE *is praying for*. And yet in the true eternal sense it is just the reverse: the true relation in prayer is not when God hears what is prayed for, but when the *person praying* continues to pray until he is *the one who hears*, who hears what God wills. The immediate person, therefore, uses many words and, therefore, makes demands in his prayer; the true man of prayer only *attends*.[1]

This book is an attempt to argue that, of all the existential sites where nature prepares for the event of revelation, the human ear is the most sensitive and theologically attuned. The foundation stone of this work is that the encounter with the incarnate Word of God through the Holy Spirit takes place primarily, although not excepting other media, through the human sense of hearing, listening and its associate silence. From Abraham to the incarnate Son of God, the connection between humanity and God was through the ear. God taught and continues to teach the universe to listen. Any listening, therefore, is, in itself, the voice of God in the transcendental ear of the listener. It is a dialogue between partners and friends.

Such acts of listening to the Spirit of God are undervalued, un-

---

1. Søren Kierkegaard, *The Journals of Kierkegaard*, trs Alexander Dru, Harper & Row, 1959, p 97.

I have taken a deliberate decision, after consulting the publisher and others, not to interfere with the flow of the quotations by inserting (*sic*) where overtly male terminology appears. Suffice it to say that these writings are from an era when 'he' embraces 'she' and 'man' also refers to 'woman'.

explored and unappreciated in Western Christianity. That sound preceded sight is a fact of the Christian narrative, yet the Christian tradition has made little effort to develop a methodology to explore such an aural concept of God's self-disclosure. It is my intention to propose and sketch one possible methodology in order to begin to address this absence.

The event of listening for the sound of God is expressed in a new word: 'theosony'. This neologism will be defined broadly, etymologically and linguistically. This word, 'theosony', brought into being here, has a twofold task in this book. It presents the current theological debate, scant as it is, on aural religious experience. The second point here concerns the eclectic scope of the research. The methodology of this work relies more on an initial presentation of diverse seedlings of possibility rather than on one reflection on a mature tree of life. Of its very nature, therefore, the analysis and evaluation of the word is elusive and shifting in its developing epistemology. 'Theosony' cannot be exhaustively defined in this study, as it is, by its nature, open-ended.

God provides both the faculty of hearing and the content of what is heard as prevenient, antecedent grace. Such aural grace is ubiquitous and indiscriminate; it precedes all human experience in and of the world. 'Theo' in theosony evokes this graced Christian experience.

At least four branches of learning – theology, biology, philosophy and phonetics – prompt questions with which this theological book on the theory of auditory Christian belief begins. It may appear that there is a lacuna here in the omission of musicology as a disciplinary partner. However I argue that much of the debate between musicology and theology is initiated by the musicologist. The thrust of the debate is more often on what musicology has to offer to theology, particularly through the phenomena of music timing and more importantly, improvisation. The first words rest in the area of theology itself.

Many insights from contemporary philosophy have been used to develop this aural existence. For the most part, this work could be described as an experience of hearing as the basis for human interconnectedness, including our relationship with God.

It describes the human ear as the heart of human being: the membrane which allows access to all that is beyond ourselves and, therefore, one of the most privileged inlets to God.

Secondly, this work must consider the biological reality of the sense of hearing, exploring the two interconnected areas of aural physiology and psychological listening, and asking what happens when a God-made earthly sound travels the birth canal from the ear lobe, through the inner ear and to the brain.

Thirdly, a definition of the truth of the divine / human conversation looks to phonetics – the science of speech, sounds and their production. Combined with semiology – the science of signs by which people communicate with one another – phonetics embraces the subjective amalgam where language and body interact. Indeed, the French literary critic and semiologist, Roland Barthes, holds that 'if contact with the music and phoneticism of one's own language is lost, the relationship between language and the body is destroyed.'[2] On the other hand, literary historian Robin Flower holds that it is in the very act of sounding language that the music of the word is heard: 'If the spoken Irish of today is … the liveliest, the most concise, and the most literary in its turns of all vernaculars of Europe, this is due in no small part to the passionate preoccupation of the poets … restlessly seeking the last perfection of phrase and idiom.'[3]

Before we embark on this theology of listening, there are some people that I must thank in deepest respect and admiration, le mórmheas agus cion. Go raibh míle maith agat – (literally, 'may thousands of good things be showered upon you) - is our Irish way of saying 'thank you' from the deepest recesses of the heart and no better blessing can I can shower upon all of you out there, too numerous to mention, who have been and are so much part of my life, let alone this book.

First, míle maith agat to Dr Eamonn Conway for agreeing to supervise a doctoral thesis on Theosony and bringing it to completion in 2003 marking the first Doctorate in Theology to be awarded

2. Roland Barthes, *The Grain of the Voice: Interviews 1962-1980*, trs Linda Coverdale, London: Jonathan Cape, 1985, p 185.
3. Robin Flower, *The Irish Tradition*, Oxford: OUP (1947), 1979, p 106.

by his department of Theology at Mary Immaculate College, University of Limerick.

Míle buíochas to my lovely friend, Gregory Collins OSB, who has always been a wonderful inspiration, not just academically but, more importantly, personally and spiritually.

Another Benedictine genius, Andrew Cyprian Love OSB, often fine-tuned my 'strae' (Irish: 'stray') thoughts and writes a foreword to this book.

Céad míle maith agaibh to four Abbots, wonderful custodians of Glenstal Abbey who, through their individual visions, have created a lighthouse here that will shepherd the people of Ireland home: Augustine (RIP), Celestine, Christopher and Patrick. This abbatial quartet welcomed us into the Abbey over the years and I will always be grateful to them for granting me the honour of living here, praying, gently singing daily and working alongside the community in this very sacred space, all 'for the glory and praise of the triune God.'

Céad míle, míle maith agaibh freisin to two fine sons, Moley and Eoin (including dear Andrea); to their artistic musician-father, Mícheál with whom I was blessed to spend so much of my life; to soul sisters, Carmel Sheridan, Anne Harris, Loretta Brennan-Glucksman, Fanny Howe, Marie Richardson and Sheila Grassick; to my siblings, Noel and Marion and all of their angelic families; to so many members of the Glenstal Benedictine community for their friendship and support over the years and looking forward to more of that in the future! You know who you are without me having to name you all here.

Finally, to you the reader / listener, may you be showered with every good blessing and may every word be a prayer as you read – aloud if you can!

Nóirín
Centenary of International Women's Day/
Shrove Tuesday, 8 March 2011

CHAPTER ONE

Theosony and Theology

Two intentions and two premises

God's self-disclosure can occur through a certain kind of *listening*. Such listening is an aural understanding that involves hearing, obedience and silence. The English term 'obedience' is derived from the Latin 'ob-audire'; the Hebrew and Greek words meaning 'to obey' are also connected with the verb 'to hear'. The first intention, therefore, is to present a taxonomy, i.e. a classification, of the human listening experience which can be taken up into a Christian sensibility.

The second is to argue for the recovery of the aural / oral experience which itself was an integral component of the earliest Christian tradition and transmission. Bonding both aims is the fact that divine auditory perception has been neglected in Western theology; how and why this is the case is the *leit-motif* of the work. In this text, 'aural' refers to what is heard and relates to the sense of hearing; 'oral' is what is spoken, uttered and also heard; 'verbal' specifically relates to the inherent meaning or feeling communicated through words. 'Oral' and 'verbal' do not carry the same meaning.

This listening theology, on the other-hand, begins from two premises: firstly, that the aural was and still remains crucial in the full realisation of God's grace in humanity. This does not exclude those who lack or are deprived of the sense of hearing either totally or partially. The fundamental hypothesis in no way excludes the deaf person from the metaphorical, religious, aural, graced experience proposed here. For the Christian, Christ voices the ultimate word of God's self-communication; he, through the human spoken word, is the supreme human spokesperson for divine revelation.

This book is biased in favour of the value and consequences of the actual heard sound of God, which is to be listened to in non-human, cosmic form, in linguistic concepts and in silence. Yet, as Karl Rahner points out, 'Christianity ... needs practice in learning

to hear such words.'[1] The gospel according to John has been a particular yardstick in this research. The evangelist brings the reader
to the recurring awareness that, as Paul also believes, 'faith comes
from what is heard (Rom. 10:17). But for John this is 'that you may
believe that Jesus is the Christ, the Son of God, and that believing
you may have life in the name' (Jn 3: 18).

The second premise is that this aural/oral aspect of religious
experience, which embraces silence, is neglected in the practice
and theology of contemporary Western Christianity. This neglect
is apparent not only in religion. Throughout Western culture it is
an all-pervasive trait to bypass the ear in favour of the eye. In every
discipline throughout Western history, the ear has taken second
place. 'Ever since the age of Newton and Descartes we have existed
in a culture that put excessive emphasis on the eye.'[2]

Such neglect of the aural must affect the spiritual climate also.
According to Søren Kierkegaard, the ear 'is the most spiritually
determined of the senses.'[3] Favouring the visual and the visible in
all areas of life has, in the words of Joachim Ernest Berendt, generally 'despiritualised our existence'.[4] Hearing, he concurs with
Kierkegaard, 'is none the less the most spiritual of all our senses.'[5]
Through learning and practising hearing, not only is one's quality
of life enhanced but God's self-revelation is more readily and
obediently received.

Western theology has investigated the nature of God primarily
from a visual perspective, largely ignoring the transcendent possibilities of the sense of hearing. The ways in which such possibilities have been experienced in some eastern traditions will be dis-
cussed later here. The religion of the Hebrews valorised the ear in
revelation. Hellenist and Greek culture favoured the eye over the
ear. The Greek noun for an eye, *ophthalmos*, occurs over a hundred

1. Karl Rahner, *Theological Investigations*, Vol 4, London: DLT, 1966, p 359.
Italics mine.
2. Joachim E. Berendt, *The Third Ear: On Listening to the World*, 1985,
Dorset: Element Books, 1988, p 32.
3. Søren Kierkegaard, *Either/Or*, Vol 1, trs David F. Swenson/Lilian
Marvin Swenson, NJ: Princeton University Press, 1944, (1959), p 66.
4. Berendt, *The Third Ear*, p 23.
5. Ibid, p 24.

times in the New Testament; the aural equivalent, *akoè*, is used
only thirty six times. The abundance of phrases such as, 'thus says
the Lord' and 'the word of the Lord came', in the Hebrew scriptures is a testimony of this point.

For its future survival, Christianity must address the function
of the auditory sense, indeed all sensory functions, in revelation
and religious experience. Western Christian theology can do this
by showing both how the aural conveys the revelation of God to
the human subject, and how the aural holds open the space
wherein the world can awaken to the graced presence of God.
This requires a new kind of listening to the word of scripture. The
original meaning of the Hebrew *däbär* and the Greek *logos* embod-
ied an understanding ('theosony' in the context of this book) and
a reciprocated effectiveness (the effect of the sounding of a word
on both the speaker and the listener). The divine Logos, in its
sounding and in its hearing, *releases* an understanding of oneself,
of the universe and of God. Before a discussion on the neglect of
attention to the auditory sense in theological scholarship, a word
about the current heightened awareness of the significance of
hearing and listening in contemporary thought is called for.

As early as 1985, Berendt highlighted an interdisciplinary
obsession with hearing, although he excludes the discipline of
theology. 'Hearing and listening are suddenly "in",'[6] he wrote.
This interdisciplinary interest in the sense of hearing makes it
exciting to research the theological implications. The term
'theosony' carries a multiplicity of meanings. All relate to the listening functions of the ear in the particular event of intimate
prayer, scripture and divine revelation. It is not a clear-cut system
of theology, nor is its uniqueness as yet obvious.

---

6. Berendt, *The Third Ear*, p 6.

The Cinderella of the Senses

It is important to chart a brief outline of the neglect of the aural in Western theology. *The Encyclopedia of Religion*, still a classic theological and anthropological resource and edited by Mircea Eliade in 1987, for example, has no entry under 'hearing', 'listening' or 'the ear', yet it includes articles on the 'human body', the 'head', the 'heart', the 'eyes', the 'hair', the 'hands', the 'knees', the 'feet' and the 'phallus'. There is an entry on 'silence' by Elizabeth McCumsey and, in the course of this short article, she refers to the paucity of scholarship on silence.[1]

The second edition of the Roman Catholic equivalent, the *New Catholic Encyclopedia* has entries on 'sensation', 'sense knowledge', 'senses' and 'sensibles'. These are exact reprints of the 1967 edition of the *Encyclopaedia*. All four bibliographies to these articles remain unchanged in this 2003 edition except for one new text, which is added to the 'sense knowledge' bibliography.

There are three further points here: the 1967 edition's entry on 'sensation' incorporates an article on 'physico-chemical factors in sensation' by R. A. Wunderlich. The auditory is considered only on the physical characteristics of the ear and its functions and, as is also the case with the other sensations biologically described here, makes no reference whatsoever to the theological implications of hearing. This article is omitted from the 2003 publication. Secondly, there is an entry for 'sound' in the 1967 edition which is again scantily scientific, ignoring the theological context. Furthermore, its bibliographies recommend only scientific, acoustic titles. There is no entry under 'sound' in the most recent second edition. Finally, there is an entry under 'deaf' in the first edition that deals only with the education and social rehabilitation

---

1.See Elizabeth McCumsey, 'Silence' in *The Encyclopedia of Religion*, Vol 13, pp 321-324.

of deaf people; there is no biblical or theological discussion. The 2003 edition has eliminated this article altogether. (A black-and-white cartoon entitled 'Humourous illustration of The Five Senses' appears on the 'senses' article page of the 2003 edition which in ways highlights the frivolous manner in which the senses are regarded in this most recent *New Catholic Encyclopaedia*.)

The six-volume theological encyclopaedia, published simult-aneously in six languages, *Sacramentum Mundi*, has no entry on hearing, listening or the ear. *The Dictionary of Fundamental Theology*, which includes an excellent article on silence, makes no specific reference to hearing, listening or the ear. *The New International Dictionary of the New Testament*, Vol 2, does provide an article entitled, 'Hear, Obey' by W. Mundle, referred to above. The equivalent visual entry is relevant because it makes an argu-ment for the primacy of the eye and the ear in the reception of God's revelation.[2] This three-volume dictionary includes a short entry on deafness and dumbness, which in classical Greek and New Testament usage are embraced by the one word, *kophos*. *Eerdmans Dictionary of the Bible* has two brief entries under 'ear' and 'voice' by William Domeris. In short, of the twenty-three major reference sources consulted, only three find the auditory sense worth mentioning regarding God's self-revelation. One of these references is out of date.

Consultation of concordances to the Old and New Testaments for references to the sense of hearing makes interesting reading. One such index[3] has four full pages citing biblical references to hearing and two pages on voice. In contrast, there is about one page of citations on seeing. Specific references to the eye and ear are similar in number. Berendt finds hearing referred to no less than ninety-one times in the first five books of the Old Testament.[4]

The Christian tradition has failed to penetrate the depths of mystery in a listening relationship with the triune God. One of the

2. See K. Dann, 'See, Vision, Eye' in Ibid, Vol 3, pp 511-518.
3. *Cruden's Complete Concordance to the Old and New Testaments*, Revised Edition, Guildford / London: Lutterworth Press, (1930), 1982. 'Hear' cita-tions, pp 286-290; 'voice' pp 724-725; 'see' part of 576, 577, 578.
4. Berendt, *The Third Ear*, p 24.

reasons for this is arguably that many theologians have been provided with a professional vocabulary which is as intricate as it is scientific. As Paul Newham, suggests: 'The more scientifically orientated one is, the less one's voice uses the affective undulation of music.'[5] Theology may have suffered from an equivalent desiccation. René Fisichella criticises theologians' neglect of silence for similar reasons.[6]

Theology's failure to understand the 'most spiritual'[7] of all senses is a major lacuna, leading to Western theology's failure to understand the power and the virtuosity of the aural. Such failure has important implications. The reliance upon language as a trustworthy and self-contained vehicle leads to the adoption of a particular language style. Much theological scholarship, and indeed much preaching, still revolves around stilted, technical, Greco-Roman vocabulary, far removed from everyday prayer and conversational language. Donald Cozzins summarises the listening experience well: 'They [priests] may preach the gospel, but the assembly senses that they have yet to live it.'[8] This is not to acknowledge and respect theological language as a particular 'language system' in itself. The failure to recognise the transmission of mystery in the space between the words has resulted in a fetishistic obsession with precision and perfection in the words themselves. Whether from the pulpit or between doctrinal book covers, God's grace has sometimes been smothered in verbose abstractions and dogmatic tracts. The intimations, the whispering breath of the Spirit, have been eliminated. The fundamental elements of the music – the melody, the rhythm and the harmony of the triune God – have been lost. Much theological speculation has been dominated by highly technical, formal language, closely allied to seminary training and a particular sacerdotal culture. This genre of linguistic expression emanates from a left-brain, rational source

5. Paul Newham, *The Singing Cure: An Introduction to Voice Movement Therapy*, Boston: Shambala Publications, 1993, p 221.
6. René Fisichella, 'Silence' in *The Dictionary of Fundamental Theology*, p 1001.
7. Ernst Berendt, *The Third Ear*, p 24.
8. Donald B. Cozzens, *The Challenging Face of the Priesthood*, Collegeville MN: The Liturgical Press, 2000, p 16.

and largely ignores the personal, emotional, experiential, listening, religious experience. Such speech, it could be argued, is primarily a stylistic, literary genre, to be read and not heard. One-
sided as this stance might seem, it is important to state that the language system of most Western theology does not intend to be either musical or poetic and is most definitely intended to be read
rather than spoken or heard. The traditional language game of
Western Christian theology is a stiffly formal mode of the eye and
not of the ear. Words should be heard and listened to; spoken
aloud and responded to. This is particularly true in the transmission of scripture in antiquity and the oral and aural historical aspect of this will be presented and developed in Chapter Three:
Theosony and Scripture.

Hearing, and silence, have been devalued by patriarchy in
Western Christianity and in other disciplines. What is being argued here is the need for liberation of sense perception from
stereotypical categorisation. Humanity needs to hear, humanity
needs to see and it is only through both, and indeed all sensory
perception, that one achieves one's full potential. In the words of
Anthony Storr, sensory expression 'eschews the personal, the
particular, the emotional, the subjective.'[9] Andrew L. Love agrees
that 'the conceptual tradition of Western ontology ... because of
its cognitive emphasis on clear and objective rationality and
"fetishisation of detachment" harbours a bias in favour of masculine models of knowing.'[10]

The omission of auditory religious experience in the primarily
male preserve of Western theology has certain resonances. It is the
claims of Joachim-Ernest Berendt that are briefly presented here.
He suggests that an eye/male, ear/female tendency pervades
Western culture generally and that the fortunes of hearing and listening are in tandem with the rise and fall of patriarchy. He holds

9. Anthony Storr, *Music and the Mind*, NY: The Free Press, 1992, p 38.
10. Andrew L. Love, *Musical Improvisation as the Place where Being Speaks:
Heidegger, Language and Sources of Christian Hope*, PhD thesis submitted to
the University of Hull, 2000, p 148. The quote within this quotation is taken
from Susan Bordo, *The Flight to Objectivity: Essays on Cartesianism and
Culture*, Albany: New York State University Press, 1987, p 7.

that the 'eye is the most expansionist and aggressive, the harshest and most piercing, the most masculine, egocentric, and hungry for power.'[11] For Berendt, earliest history was matri-centred. Women were linguistically and vocally superior to men. Berendt maintains that women make better hearers. Their keener responsiveness to ambient sounds was because women 'were more concerned with processing the information heard and converting it into directives.'[12] To be obeyed, that is listened to keenly, women listened harder, more carefully and precisely, and searched meticulously for the words and the timbre to reflect and convey the fruits of their listening. To the poet, the ear of flesh of every creature in communing with the 'Uncreated' is feminine:

> One song they sang, and it was audible,
> Most audible, then when the fleshly ear,
> O'ercome by humblest prelude of that strain,
> Forgot her functions, and slept undisturbed.[13]

This claim could be trenchantly contested; the eye, for example, has the marvellous capacity to unearth and uncover treasures of gentleness and receptivity in its work of creation and perception. Beauty is in the eye and the ear of the beholder / listener. However, the argument that this work holds is that the auditory religious experience, for whatever and regardless of reason, is a cardinal one in Christianity and has not matured in scholarship or practice. The ear permits human thought about God to sing. In the listening 'ear of the heart', the real thought of God's Word is heard.

Highlighting this omission of the aural sense and its feminine implications in Western theology is not to paint a helpless predicament. It must be acknowledged that theology is now embracing the feminine linguistic expression and voice. Indeed, it could well be argued that feminist hermeneutics, the theory, art and practice of interpretation from a woman's perspective, is contributing to

---

11. Berendt, *The Third Ear*, p 4.
12. Ibid, p 150.
13. William Wordsworth, 'The Prelude, Book Second, 415-418', in William Wordsworth, *The Prelude: A Parallel Text*, ed J. C. Maxwell, Middlesex: Penguin Books, 1971, p 95 / 97.

changing the course of theological reflection.[14] This text does not
attempt a critique of gender interpretations and practices but it
does argue for the reinstatement of one human, sensory medium
to its rightful place in theological speculation.

In short, then, this book is not arguing for any exclusive gender bias around the essentially aural revelation of the triune God.
Male or female concepts of God, and of hearing, simply reinforce
oppression, if not idolatry. God is present for everyone who has
ears to hear.

While it is true that some theologians and commentators have
acknowledged the importance of listening to and hearing the
voice of God, it is argued here that they have failed to explore this
dimension to the full. Most articulation of an aural religious
experience, scriptural, liturgical or personal, has been lip service.
Religious experience, both oral and aural, has for the most part
given way to the visual. Like Thomas, we believe because we
have seen. This book supports the greater blessedness of those
who have not seen. It asks questions such as what each person's
particular experience of hearing the divinity says to that individual; what kind of God is heard in prayer; and what, precisely, is
'the good will'[15] of the hearer and how can it be nurtured?

There is a reluctance in theology to enter into the vulnerable
arena that is experiential and subjective. René Fisichella links the
neglect of silence by theologians with a preoccupation with science. Theologians, he remarks, yearn to become scientists and so
risk distraction from the work at hand.[16] One wonders whether
the scientific theologian regards silence, and indeed all aspects of
listening, as trivial when compared with the sense data of empirical
science. Concurring with Fisichella's observation on the impinge-
ment of scientific methodology on theologians, Winston L. King
finds that the attempt to define religion 'is a natural consequence
of the Western speculative, intellectualistic, and scientific dispos-

14. See the works of Sandra M. Schneiders, Mary Grey, Marina Warner,
Elizabeth Schussler Fiorenza etc.
15. Karl Rahner, *Foundations*, p 26.
16. See article on 'silence' by René Fisichella in *The Dictionary of
Fundamental Theology*, p 1001.

ition.'[17] He further attributes this to 'the Judeo-Christian climate or, more accurately, the theistic inheritance from Judaism, Christianity, and Islam.'[18]

Although it is a contestable claim, perhaps doing theology to date has been more concerned with map-making a route to God than with actually experiencing the contours of that road. Maps are important and helpful in charting directions through the territory. Yet they hardly communicate the lived experience of the terrain; the sensual knowledge which accrues from touching, smelling, tasting, seeing and hearing the reality. This is the reverse of the poetics of experience suggested in *The Dry Salvages* by T. S. Eliot as having the experience but falling short of the meaning: 'We had the experience but missed the meaning.'[19] In short, a diagram of features, although an important initial guide, is experientially unrepresentative of the reality. Reading is in the realm of the cartographer; hearing is the soft, sound-soil of feeling and sensitivity.

17. Winston L. King, 'Religion' in *The Encyclopaedia of Religion*, Vol 12, ed Mircea Eliade, p 282.
18. Ibid, p 282.
19. *The Complete Poems and Plays of T. S. Eliot*, London: Faber and Faber, 1969, p 184.

'Reading between the lines'

The following paradox has been universally recognised: all human linguistic expression of the Divine falls short and trails off at a certain point in our understanding. Karl Rahner holds that 'the word "God" places in question the whole world of language in which reality is present for us ... This reality might be present speaking clearly or obscurely, softly or loud. But it is there at least as a question.'[1] Verbal descriptions of God belong to human thought forms. The word 'God', as well as the Word of God, has sounded out in humankind's historical existence. The very sound of the word 'God' is majestic. It must be acknowledged; it must be faced up to; it must be *obediently* received. Karl Rahner thinks this point significant enough to highlight in italics: 'Rather we *hear and receive the word 'God'* ... the phonetic sound of the word 'God' is always dependent on us ... it creates us because it makes us [sic] men.'[2]

Language is the tantalising, frustrating medium whereby humanity articulates an understanding. It is our only way of giving God a hearing. But as Seán Freyne rightly states, God 'can never be exhausted or fully represented in the words of humans.'[3] Paul Ricoeur, on the other hand, hints at the importance of the aural dimension of language: 'It is always in language that religious experience is articulated, that one *hears* it in a cognitive, practical or emotional sense.'[4]

It is through language that one hears, but what one hears is *more* than language itself can impart. The phrase 'reading be-

1. Rahner, *Foundations of Christian Faith: An Introduction to the Idea of Christianity*, NY: The Crossroad Publishing Company, 1978 (2000), p 50.
2. Ibid, p 50.
3. Sean Freyne, *Texts, Contexts and Cultures*, Dublin: Veritas, 2002, p 95.
4. Paul Ricoeur, *Figuring the Sacred: Religion, Narrative, and Imagination*, Minneapolis: Fortress Press, 1995, p 218. Italics mine.

tween the lines' means to understand or to discover an implicit meaning in addition to the explicit one. We hear more than we see written down. The word 'God' is never silent, even to the profoundly deaf. In aural experience the hidden, mysterious, loving God is intimated between the words. Divine listening is precisely 'hearing between the words'. George Steiner, describing this same phenomenon in articulating the power of music, puts it like this: 'When we try to speak of music, to speak music, language has us, resentfully, by the throat.'[5] In the midst of human linguistic limitation and weakness, God holds us 'by the throat'. One must remain in the presence of a language where, as Fiumara puts it, the 'only thing that counts is to learn to "dwell" in the *saying* of language.'[6]

Karl Rahner concludes that if humanity cannot hear the name God as the ultimate in all speaking, then 'we would be hearing it as a word about something obvious and comprehensible in everyday life, as a word alongside other words. Then we would have heard something which has nothing in common with the true word 'God' but its *phonetic sound*.'[7] There is something hidden in the sound that must be listened out for to be experienced.

Although it is the underlying theme here that all created sounds are the work, the divine kindness of God, it is crucial to make a distinction between hearing and listening: hearing is the mundane biological fact, while listening pertains to the psychological with its highest expression in prayer. So in the context of a theology of sound and listening, hearing refers to mundane aural experiences pertinent to the earth and the universe, while listening refers to heaven and the realm of God. Mundane hearing and mundane sounds speak of the terrestrial as opposed to the celestial world. It is the former, older usage of the word 'mundane' which is relevant. In contemporary linguistics, this word tends to cite what is banal, uninspired, quotidian and lacklustre. Neither does the word 'mundane' deny or dilute the Christian theological

5. George Steiner, *Real Presences*, London: Faber and Faber, 1989, p 197.
6. Gemma Corradi Fiumara, *The Other Side of Language: A philosophy of Listening*, trs C. Lambert, London/New York: Routledge, Chapman and Hall, 1990, p 159. Italics mine.
7. Karl Rahner, *Foundations of Christian Faith*, p 51. Italics mine.

foundational belief in all creation, including its innate silence, being the perennial, active grace of the triune God.

God's self-revelation in phonic Word is proof of the power and possibility of the ordinary words we use. The word is both understanding and doing as the Hebrew *däbär* and the Greek *logos* imply. Scheffczyk puts it this way: 'Thus even if man can only think of God mediately and can only speak of him in a fragmentary way, this possibility exists and is even obligatory through the primal word of God uttered in revelation. By this utterance, God himself has entered human language, and has permanently empowered it to express him.'[8] The force and passion of the Word is accurately suggested in and through the melody, the rhythm and harmony of the word.

---

8. Leo Scheffczyk, 'God' in *Sacramentum Mundi*, Vol 2, p 386.

'Singing from the same hymn sheet'

Ll religions sing in unison in their acknowledgement of the
primacy of word and sound vibrations in their varying
conceptions of an Absolute Other, according to Hazrat
Inayat Khan. 'On this point all the different religions unite'.[1]
Spiritual beliefs are primarily transmitted orally and aurally.

Hindu sacred scriptures, Persian literature, the Qur'an, and
the scriptures of Judaeo-Christianity agree on many levels about
sound, the word, the ear, what is spoken and silence. The early
biographies of Muhammad, from whose prophecies Islam developed, relate how the angel Gabriel revealed to him, over a period
of twenty-two years between 610 and 632 CE, that he was the
Messenger of God. The Qur'an came first as sound. Indeed, the
word itself is said to be derived from the Arabic verb *quara'a*
which means either 'to read' or 'to recite'.[2] On receiving the message, it was clear that Muhammad had to recite and be heard in the
name of the Lord. Hearing and listening in Muslim tradition is responding to heaven and expanding the soul. Khan describes a
personal experience of hearing from out of his own spiritual tradition, Sufiism: 'By hearing I do not mean listening, I mean responding: responding to heaven ... responding to every influence that
helps to unfold the soul.'[3]

Before introducing some sonic factors of the Indian tradition,
one can summarise that East meets West in the simple phrase:
'The origin of the whole creation is sound.'[4] Indian spirituality is

1. Hazrat Inayat Khan, *The Mysticism of Sound and Music*, Vol 2, Geneva:
The International Headquarters of the Sufi Movement, 1960 (1991), p 54.
2. See Charles J. Adams, 'Qur'an' in *The Encyclopaedia of Religion*, Vol 12,
p. 159. However *The Oxford Dictionary of the Jewish Religion* only refers to
'reading'. See 'Qur'an' in *The Oxford Dictionary of the Jewish Religion*, p 566.
3. Khan, *The Mysticism of Sound and Music*, Vol 2, p 267.
4. Ibid, p 17.

the innovator and the summation of attunement to the sound of
the Divine. Some commentators claim that Hinduism is a spiritually superior tradition. To quote just one, David Tame claims,
when it comes to comparing Indian and Western spirituality, that
'weighed on the scales of devotion, India is the First World nation,
and our own might be said to be the land that is backward.'[5]

The sheer beauty of Indian singing has moved me deeply since
I first visited there in 1982. Then and many, many times since, I
have experienced and spoken with Indian singers there of the
power which somehow surrounds these religious songs to transcend the mundane. Secondly, there is a strong musical and linguistic relationship between the spiritual songs of India and the
traditional religious songs of Ireland, particularly women's songs
from both cultures. These subjects are not the main thrust of this
work, however, but a brief mention of Sanskrit 'nada' and 'om' is
pertinent.

The mystical concept of the Sanskrit 'nada' is basically that the
life principle or creative breath of humanity comes from vibrations
which can only be heard from within. This creative sound is God
whose word precedes light. Although outside the scope of this
particular study, one has only to refer briefly to an aural spiritual
tradition based on the sound of the most sacred of Sanskrit sylla-
bles – *om*. This contraction of a three-letter word – a/u/m – is
revered in Hindu tradition for its intrinsic power as sound – oral,
aural and silent. It is the supreme sacred sound of God – the sound
that opens the gateway to God. To chant on *om* is to become the
source and the centre of the universe, which is where the silent
one resides. God is the source of all mundane, (from Latin *mundus*
meaning 'earth') and terrestrial sound. Musician and composer,
Joseph Gelineau makes the same Christian and Hindi connection
through sound. 'The religious significance of the sacrifice of
sound is global ... from the syllable "om" which contains within it
all the acoustic powers, to the vocal expression of a *Kyrie Eleison* or
an *Alleluia*.'[6]

5. David Tame, *The Secret Power of Music*, Northamptonshire: The
Aquarian Press, 1984, (1988), p 184.
6. Joseph Gelineau, ' The Path of Music' in *Music and the Experience of God*,
Edinburgh: T. & T. Clark, 1989, p 137.

In the ancient Indian Vedas, which are much earlier scriptures than the Old Testament, there are two Sanskrit words for sound. One, *ahata*, refers to sounds which can be heard and perceived by everyone through the ear. The second Sanskrit word, *anahata*, however, cannot be heard indiscriminately but can only, according to Tame, be '*experienced*'[7] by the one who contemplates more deeply on the Divine. The concept of *anahata* is akin to the kind of listening out of a Christian perspective that this work promotes; it is an actual 'experience' which a certain kind of listening to God in prayer permits. Moreover, the word *anahata* carries a second meaning: it refers to the most important spiritual centre of the body called the *heart chakra*. It is the *heart chakra* that is most closely aligned with the Divine. The *anahata chakra* is the human realm where the Word of God resounds. The way to God is through a heart-felt experience of word and sound.

In the Hindi tradition, *om* is the human sound that images the Voice of God – a human reflection of that voice. In Indian tradition, as Tame puts it, 'through the use of his vocal cords … man is thought to be a co-creator with God.'[8] Every religion, every language, has its words of great spiritual and sonic wealth. Sanskrit has the three-lettered word *aum*, just as Christianity has the three-character words of 'God' in English, or *Dia* in Irish. These are words of immense sonic grandeur, powerful beyond language in the sounding and in the hearing.

Indian spirituality is keenly aware of an aural relationship with God. This is bound up with its music tradition – 'an inspiration that transcends description except as felt experience.'[9] The *voice*, before any instrument, is the way towards such transcendence. As Menon states, it 'is as a voice that Indian music is heard and not as a sound'.[10] The emotional nature and expression of the voice comes before the sound. Music that is instrumental talks of notes; but it is the work of the voice, which provides free-range,

7. Ibid, p 171.
8. Ibid, p 174.
9. Menon in 'Introduction' to *The Penguin Dictionary of Indian Classical Music*, New Delhi: Penguin Books, 1995, p viii.
10. Ibid, pp vii-xvii.

wholesome nourishment for the soul. Thus the two main musical traditions of India, Carnatic and Hindustani share a vast vocabulary, at once cosmic and transcendent. In one context, a thing, rather than a word, has a very specific meaning; wearing a spiritual cloak, the same word is theosonic. For example, *shruti* in purely musical terms means the microtonal intervals between two notes and the Indian scale has twenty-two such intervals or *shrutis*. On the other hand, for the perfect vocal execution of the *shruti*, it cannot, according to Ustad Fariduddin Dagar, 'exist on paper, however accurately calibrated, for its emotional content is beyond calculation'.[11] (I was blessed to spend an afternoon in the presence of this legendary singer and his brother in 1982 where he spoke at length on the nature of singing, chanting, sounding and silence and its secret structure of divine being. Then he also made this point.)

There are many points of comparison between the Judaeo-Christian tradition and Hinduism. Both religious traditions agree on the concept of sound and silence, although Christian theology has been tacit on the matter. As David Tame puts it, 'one can hardly avoid the conclusion that the OM and the Word of Christianity are one and the same.'[12] *Om* is the synonym of Hindu/Indian race; Jesus Christ, the *logos* of God, is the synonym of the Christian. Both auditory energies are concerned with the coming into being of Creation and each refers to a sonic Divine Energy, which creates and sustains this universe. Both sonic concepts encapsulate a Trinitarian unity. In short, contemporary Western theology could profitably hear and practice wisdom from the East. The Hindu reveres the divine sound and silence of Brahma. 'Om' is the soundless sound. The Christian reveres the revelatory sound and silence of the incarnate Word of God. Jesus Christ is the soundless Word.

---

11. Ibid, p x.
12. David Tame, *The Secret Power of Music*, 1984, Northamptonshire: The Aquarian Press, 1988, p 171.

Introducing and defining 'Theosony'

There are values and energies in the human person – and *per-sonare* means, precisely, a 'sounding' a 'saying through' –which transcend death.[1]

So faith comes from hearing (Rom 10:17)

Theosony refers to any number of factors that are implicated in an aural relationship with God: for instance, listening, hearing, speaking, sonic language, memorisation, reading aloud and silence. The 'Theo' in theosony reflects the fact that all graced experiences (inclusive of the human listening experience) can be interpreted by a Christian sensibility. In other words, this is only the application to a classification of human listening of the traditional, theological principle of grace building on nature.

Theosony describes the *phenomenon* of a listening theology. On the one hand, it attempts to define the fact, occurrences and cir-cumstances in which theosonic moments emerge; on the other, it refers to the sacred aural event as it appears and is constructed by the human experience *per se* as distinguished from the *noumenon*, the objective listening itself.

The lacuna, already lightly touched upon, in theological dis-course around the inclusion of the auditory sense, results from the fact that all aspects of the aural – for example, listening, speaking, conversation, clairaudience and silence – are underdeveloped and underexplored. For instance, the Christian is very aware that no one has ever seen God; the same theological emphasis is not as strong in the aural. Yet the fact is that from Christianity's earliest sources, God has been heard. Abraham, the father of all nations and patriarch of Jewish, Muslim and Christian religions, was to be the first listener to the divine voice. Christ did not see God; but he clearly heard God's message of the kingdom. In short, the word of

1. George Steiner, *Real Presences*, p 226

God will never be tacit or fossilised. In the words of von Balthasar, 'What can escape being destroyed? Nothing – except, for a Christian, the word of God as set down by him.'[2]

'Theosony' is a fusion of two words from Greek and ecclesiastical Latin. In the initial research around this word, the term 'theophony' (Greek *Theos* meaning 'God' and *phone* meaning 'voice / sound') was explored. However, *phone* is limited to vocal sound and I wanted to embrace the widest possible range of sounds created and discernible, capturing all sonic media.

Theos is abbreviated to 'Theo'; *Sonans* to 'sony'. *Sonans* is the present participle of the Latin verb *sonare* meaning 'to sound'. The 'present' tense of verbs describes the action or event occurring at the time of speaking or when the speaker does not wish to make any specific reference to time. The present participle links with the time on hand, it does not refer to past or future but to what is contemporaneous. 'Standing, they prayed' links the participle to the time of the verb. Listening is being in existence at the time when the sound or word is spoken. The notion of being on the alert at the moment of speaking describes an omnipresent feature of our lives. This is the sense of hearing at its most precise. 'I am all ears' means so much more than 'I am listening' or 'I hear you'. Something critically important is about to be heard and its meaning must not go unnoticed. A key sentence that expresses the soul of our being is about to be spoken. We must be constantly at hand, and in the particular moment, to really listen. The eye can revisit its object endlessly; it can look again and again; the ear generally gets one chance to hear. Therefore, the ear has to be much more industrious and active in this mortal coil. The act of conversation, human and divine, is a temporal act of the moment. It is always only now and aural. It is always the sum total of the silent, the visual, the physical and the aural. Yet it is the only real connection between the past and the present; with eyes closed, ears attuned, we say, 'I'm just trying to think back …'

The word 'theosony' is a portmanteau word. 'Portmanteau' has two meanings, one pragmatic and tangible, as a noun, the

2. Hans Urs von Balthasar, *Word and Revelation: Essays in Theology*, Vol 1, p 166 / 167.

other, qualifying and adjectival. Originally, a 'portmanteau' was a large travelling bag designed for riding on horseback. It was hinged at the back so as to open out into two compartments. The second meaning, as a modifier, an adjective, it qualifies or limits a word in the same syntactical construction. It is this second definition that is relevant here; a portmanteau word combines and dovetails two other words, for instance 'brunch' (breakfast and lunch) or 'motel' (motor hotel).

The concept of 'theosony' operates as both noun and adjective: the ear, the sense of hearing, is the noun; insofar as theosony imputes a spiritual characteristic or component to the human aural sense, it is a modifier or adjective. Linguistically speaking, the large indefinite number of meanings around God's self-disclosure which is aural cannot be adequately conveyed through the use of one word only and is more, although never completely, comprehensively understood through the use of two. What cannot be conveyed meaningfully in one word drives us to say it in two, yet under the same cloak or within the one word-bag. A portmanteau word is a 'cut and paste' strategy until a more accurate description is found. The 'portmanteau word' – theosony – is a *sine qua non* in reinstating the aural to its rightful place in theological discourse. The word is absolutely necessary to articulating a universal, *auditory* religious experience of God's self-communication. Finally theosony is divine Esperanto – a concise, allusive, one-for-all word for prayer as the most intimate human expression of the constant conversation between the triune God and humanity. Theosony is the simple language of the praying ear, all about the power to speak to and to understand God. It is an aural language that speaks of sacred and transcendent sounds that are audible and therefore accessible to all human beings in their historical, concrete, existence. Theosony is temporal in every sense of the word; it is concerned with the present life of humanity in its relationship with the triune God, and it is a worldly expression of a timely, rhythmic 'meek stirring of love'.[3]

The discipline of fundamental theology is the home of

3. *The Cloud of Unknowing and Other Treatises*, ed Justin McCann, London: Burns, Oates and Washbourne, 1947, p 5.

theosony. Rahner defines fundamental theology as 'the scientific substantiation of the fact of the revelation of God in Jesus Christ.'[4] Quite simply, fundamental theology interprets religious belief as the quest for ultimate meaning, which is satisfied in divine revelation. It asks such questions as Karl Rahner posed: 'How can man hear the word of God? What is the word of God that man hears? Where does man receive the word of God?'

In musicology, a fundamental note or tone refers to the root of a chord. Likewise, fundamental theology addresses the root of Christian apologetics; it dialogues with and challenges all contemporary ideologies and disciplines. Gerald O'Collins believes that 'even more than other sectors of theology, fundamental theology stands at the frontier in dialogue with a variety of other academic disciplines and modern movements.'[5]

A theology of listening naturally embraces the basic tenets of fundamental theology in four separate, yet inter-related areas: It critically reflects on:
- divine self-revelation
- the religious experience of human *hearers* of the Word of that revelation
- biblical understanding and interpretation
- Interdisciplinary and faith dialogue.

The revelation of God is the basis of all Christian thinking. Christianity is a religion of revelation. 'Fundamental theology itself demonstrates the possibility of a revelation on the part of God.'[6] It is a revelation that is ever old, ever new, in constant obedient flow and operation.

Through the ear, although not exclusively, revelation from God can freely enter and be completed. One important way of being with God is through sound; the auditory is a direct invitation out of oneself towards the Divine. Sensory perception of God's self-communication is vital for humanity and no one sense exists or operates in isolation in the work of this divine communic-

---

4. Rahner, *Hearers of the Word*, p 17.
5. Gerald O' Collins, 'Fundamental theology' in *A New Dictionary of Christian Theology*, eds A. Richardson, J. Bowden, p 224.
6. Rahner, *Hearers of the Word*, p 18.

ation. However, this book aims to prove that the vital role which the functions of the ear, including silence, can play in theology can indeed enhance all other senses and add to their efficiency. Lafont summarises: 'The primordial silence of God liberates speech and calls forth the response, first of all in God himself, and then in every human being and every community on earth.'[7] Hans Urs von Balthasar believes that it is in the very scope of human speech that the echoes of the divine word are heard: 'Human speech ... contains in itself the whole of nature and the whole moral life, the entire history of man; and here its scope extends to the eternal word of the father.'[8] An aural revelation is God's sound-revelation. The ear is already the self-gift and revelation of God. Like the whole of creation, the ear was named and created by God. Isaiah, 'the "greatest listener" among the Bible's great men'[9] strains to hear the invitation to go to God: 'Incline your ear, and come to me' (Is 55:3).

Fundamental theology scrutinises the *hearer*, the *responder* to the divine mystery. How must the human listener listen and respond to the intimate, inner sound of God's own promise? How can a sound that is not made by humanity be heard by human beings of this historical world? Answers to these questions are to be found in the response of fundamental theologians whose task it is 'to prove man's basic reference to his history as the sole realm wherein he can come to his true nature.'[10] Such a response begins with the 'good will' of the hearer.[11] But the rejoin is much more than the happy accident of good will. This good will is the initiation of a longing for the unconditional love that the divine self-gift has already offered through the incarnate Word of Jesus Christ. Rahner regrets that this 'metaphysical anthropology of man as the one who *listens* in his *history* for a possible revelation from God is usually so sadly neglected'.[12]

---

7. G. Lafont, 'Language' in *Dictionary of Fundamental Theology*, p 597.
8. Han Urs von Balthasar, *Word and Revelation: Essays in theology I*, trs Littledale/Dru, NY: Herder and Herder, 1964, p 118.
9. Berendt, *The Third Ear*, p 24.
10. Rahner, *Hearers of the Word*, p 22.
11. Rahner, *Foundations of Christian Faith*, p 26.
12. Rahner, *Hearers of the Word*, p 22. Italics added to 'listens'.

The revelation of God is the primary concern of the fundamental theologian. In the words of Heinrich Fries, fundamental theology 'may be described as a transcendental theology, inasmuch as it considers the nature and event of revelation as such, prior to all special theology or branches of theology.'[13]

Christianity, according to David Tracy, 'does not live by an idea, a principal or an axiom but by an event and a person – the event of Jesus Christ occurring now and grounded in none other than Jesus of Nazareth'.[14] For the Christian, the world is contingent; a future event that is pointing outside itself to God for existence. The Christian reverently bows before God in obedience and patience to discern God's creative will for humanity; in a divine word of beauty and love spoken by God, the world and all within it can remain in that love and become more perfectly alive and human. 'The earth is full of the steadfast love of the Lord' (Ps 33:5b). In the words of von Balthasar: 'A human being means one to whom God has spoken in the word, one who is so made as to be able to hear and respond to that word.'[15] Humanity is destined to find its perfection in the revelation and grace of the eternal word.

Christian doctrine of creation holds 'that we are unities of spirit and matter inhabiting a physical word with which we are intimately bound up ... and that part of what it means to be human is to interact thoroughly with this non-human reality.'[16] This being in the material world is, it is argued here, most powerfully manifested through the graced sense of hearing. Thus a Christian theology of hearing is crucial in this aural revelation between God and humanity. This graced gift, including the miracle which is hearing, is the very sound of 'the river of your delights ... the fountain of life' (Ps 36:8b/9a). Through the sense of the aural and oral which is simply the loving gift of the triune God, every being can develop

13. Heinrich Fries, 'Fundamental Theology' in *Sacramentum Mundi*, Vol 2, p 368.
14. David Tracy, *The Analogical Imagination: Christian Theology and the Culture of Pluralism*, NY: Crossroad, 1981, p 427.
15. Von Balthasar, *Word and Revelation*, p 25.
16. Jeremy Begbie, 'The Gospel, the arts and our culture', in *The Gospel and Contemporary Culture*, ed. Hugh Montefiore, London: Mowbray, 1992, p 70.

as a free person. The self-development promised through being
heard by God is the message of Christianity. As the contemporary
Italian philosopher, Gemma Fiumara suggests: 'It is possible that
evolving humans tend to speak out at their best because they are
listened to – and not vice versa.'[17] It is a salubrious, health-giving
thing to simply listen. Jesus spoke at his best because he was being
heard. For two full days, 'the Saviour of the World' (Jn 4:42) spoke
out to the Samaritans at Sychar. They listened intently and having
heard for themselves, they believed and lived (Jn 4:39-42).

The oral and aural are two juxtaposed elements in the tradition,
the process of handing on Christian belief. Tradition is a living process, which is operative in the living faith of all believers, pastoral
and faithful people alike. Hermann J. Pottmeyer underlines the
auditory factor in tradition: 'Active tradition presupposes *listening* to the word of God and appropriating the previous religious
tradition of the church, implying also a metanoia in thought and
action.'[18]

The revelation that is inaugurated by the Son and Word of God
is a continuity between the old and new covenants. The primeval
establishing connection with the world is through the ear, from
Abraham, through Jesus Christ to humanity. Through the grandeur
of the Word becoming flesh, humanity can through him, obediently listening to that Word, respond to the will of God. The Word
of God is the continuity in history between the two covenants.
God spoke, God has spoken and God speaks. The Word of God is
the alpha and the omega. Humanity is enlightened and placed at
its origin of being when 'in these last days he has spoken to us by a
Son' (Heb 1:1). 'For he sent his Son, the eternal Word who enlight-
ens all men … to tell them about the inner life of God' (*DV* 1:4).[19]
For the Christian, this word-language must make the life and
teachings of Jesus of Nazareth its primary work because 'he

17. Fiumara, *The Other Side of Language*, p 187.
18. Hermann J. Pottmeyer, 'Tradition' in *Dictionary of Fundamental Theology*, p 1125. Italics mine.
19. '*Dei Verbum*, Dogmatic Constitution on Divine Revelation', in *Vatican Council II: The Conciliar and Post Conciliar Documents*, ed Austin Flannery, OP, Dublin: Dominican Publications, 1975, p 751.

whom God has sent speaks the words of God, for he gives the Spirit without measure' (Jn 3:34).

Paul Ricoeur states emphatically that 'there is something specific in the Hebraic and Christian traditions that gives a kind of privilege to the word.'[20] Furthermore, there is something specific in both traditions that honours listening and this takes its origin in the Hebrew imperative word *šema*, and what it stands for. The voice of God was the primary organ of revelation for the Israelites; the ear of the people of Israel is privileged.

'*Hear*, O Israel, the Lord is our God, the Lord alone' (Deut 6:4-9) is referred to in Jewish tradition as the *šema*. This is a Hebrew word meaning 'hear' and although it refers to six verses (4-9), it takes its name, in accord with all ancient literature, from the first word 'hear'. The emphasis is clearly aural from the beginning. This is the central Jewish declaration of faith in one God and one God alone – a declaration that must be heard throughout the land. The *šema* is to be learned off and kept in the heart (Deut 6:6); it is to be recited to children and talked about without ceasing, at home and away (Deut 6:7). Proclaiming one's faith in the one true Lord is effective primarily as something vocal. 'The *recitation* of the *šema*,' Knobel writes, is considered an obligation prescribed by the Bible itself on the basis of the verse: 'and you shall speak of them ... when you lie down and when you rise up' (Deut 6:7).'[21]

Christianity holds and trusts that human creativity is meaningful because of the incarnation, the coming of God to humanity through Jesus Christ. Because of the presence of Jesus Christ, the Word of God now makes complete sense. The Letter to the Hebrews sums up the role of the effective, dynamic, active word to be listened to. Harking back to the invitatory Psalm 95, the unknown author first issues the same warning three times about the act of listening – an act which unites Old and New Testaments. 'Today, if you hear his voice, do not harden your hearts' (Heb 3:7, 8). To harden one's heart is not to listen; to shut out the voice of

20. Paul Ricoeur, *Figuring the Sacred: Religion, Narrative and Imagination*, Minneapolis: Fortress Press, 1995, p 71.
21. Ibid, p 630. Italics mine.

God is to sin. Secondly, the word of God is dangerous; it is 'living and active, sharper than any two-edged sword, piercing until it divides world from spirit' (Heb 4:12). Thirdly, to live with the voice of God resounding in one's ears is to 'enter God's rest ... so that no one may fall through such disobedience' (Heb 4:10, 11).

The fundamental question which theosony poses is: How can one lucidly differentiate God hearing humanity, on the one hand, and humanity hearing God, on the other? Karl Rahner addresses this problem pragmatically. In conversational prayer, God replies. In the actual experience of the praying person 'what God primarily says to us is ourselves in our decreed freedom, in our decree-defying future, in the facticity (that can never be totally analysed and never functionally rationalised) of our past and present.'[22] Through the grace of the Holy Spirit, created beings participate in God's self-communication through the divine word, which they too can participate in through God's address in Christ. This God-talk is beyond interhuman conversation – it is a gifted experience of God's salvific universal will and covenant of love.

The reception of the risen Lord was precisely and uniquely through the sense of hearing for the first witness, Mary of Magdala. Everything comes alive for her at the sound of her name. Although this work singles out the sense of hearing, the work of all the senses – the physical faculties by which humanity perceives the external world – are also faculties by which the resurrection of Jesus is received. As the seventeenth century priest, mystic and physician, Angelus Silesius puts it: 'The senses dwell in spirit as one sense and one use; who sees God savours him, feels, smells and hears him too.'[23] St Paul constantly reminds the first Christians that they are 'the body of Christ' (1 Cor 12:27), the 'image of God' (2 Cor 4:4) and the 'image of the heavenly man' (1 Cor 15:49; cf Rom 8:29). Putting on the body of Christ which is the task of every Christian means imaginatively attending to and fine-tuning all sensory faculties of which the audi-

22. Karl Rahner, *The Practice of Faith: A Handbook of Contemporary Spirituality*, eds Lehmann / Raffelt, London: SCM Press 1983, p 80.
23. Angelus Silesius, *The Cherubinic Wanderer*, trs Maria Shrady, NY: Paulist Press, 1986, p 125

tory sense is one. In summary, Jesus of Nazareth is that persevering, unmistakable Word of God – a word to be listened to, spoken of and spoken to within ear-shot of God, the source of that Word.

'Amazing grace, how sweet the sound ...'

The Christian doctrine of grace is the story of the divine Logos that becomes alive in our world: living, breathing, moving, speaking and listening. 'Listen, so that you may live' (Is 55:3). The human sense which perceives sound is a freely given gift from God before ever it functions. The sensation created in the ear when certain vibrations are caused in the surrounding air is the graced gift of God. Here it is argued that God's self-communication to the human person, which is the essence of the Christian interpretation of grace, is primarily perceived through the aural sense. Therefore, hearing is an important grace of God that prepares the inner ear for the Word of God. The sense of hearing is an act of God's self-love, enabling humanity to listen and hear in such a way as to mould one's moral and religious decisions. For Karl Rahner, such divine grace is 'always the free action of divine love which is only " at the disposal" of man precisely in so far as he is at the disposal of this divine love'.[1]

In other words, God created the human ear and its ingenious ear-work so that the voice of God could be heard and responded to; God brought into being the ear so that humanity could hear that divine calling or invocation. The human ear can hear the Word of God, but it can never speak or become it. Human speech connects humankind and God. The grace of sound and 'sound listening' always surround the human being. There is no escaping from grace or sound. In the end, human re-action, through listening, in response to God's calling, is what ordains one's union with God. Karl Rahner's theology of grace and nature is important to the hypothesis of this work on two levels. Firstly his insistence on the constant, *a priori*, nature of God's grace. Secondly, his insight that nature can be distinguished from, but cannot be divided

1. Rahner, *Theological Investigations*, Vol 4, p 177.

from, the supernatural, given that creation is already the work of
grace. The all-pervasive nature of grace is the legacy that God bestowed on the world through Jesus Christ. God's word exploded
on the earth through the truth which was Christ and who became
human already 'full of grace' (Jn 1:14). The intimate experience of
God, in this case, the listening experience, is, according to Rahner,
'the experience which is given to every person prior ... to religious
activity and decisions, and indeed perhaps in a form and in a con-
ceptuality which seemingly are not religious at all.'[2]

God's entire creation moves and exists in the fullness of the
grace of sounds. Therefore, there is no escaping or bypassing the
stirrings of the ear. Every activity of the ear is an expression of the
glory of God in nature. Humanity, with its mystical ear, is made in
the image of God. 'God saw everything that he had made, and indeed, it was very good' (Gen 1: 31). The multiplicity of aural functions is united in God's unified and triune beauty. The human ear
has an important role in the divine plan that surpasses its human
function and nature. The human ear is from God and is inclined
towards God in special ways. Furthermore, the human word is
the shadow, the whisper of the supreme Word, the Logos, who
became human. The human word is already graced by its very
existence. The gentle word invites gentle listening. The appropriate and proper word for the human being according to Rahner 'in
its true and full reality, is already grace in the word, and the power
of hearing such a word in its true sense is already grace of faith ...
Our actual nature is never "pure" nature. It is a nature installed in
a supernatural order which man can never leave, even as a sinner
and unbeliever.'[3] The theological concept of nature reflects on the
divinisation of the human being in and through the grace of Jesus
Christ. Sharing in the graced glory of Christ is sharing in the mystery of the life of God itself. Christ as a human being listened to
and heard the divine voice; in his image, humanity slowly, obediently and patiently follows suit.

In other words, in Trinitarian theology, nature is undivided and
singular; there is the divine and human nature in Christ that is both

2. Rahner, *Foundations of Christian Faith*, p 132.
3. Rahner, *Theological Investigations*, Vol 4, p 362, 183.

fully human and also the Word of God. Hawkins makes the important distinction here between nature and person terminology. 'Nature
underlines the internal unity of a thing's qualities and powers, while
person underlines a separateness from everything else. In this way
we speak of three divine Persons as three distinct possessors of the
divine nature and of the Person of the Word as also possessing a
human nature without separation from him.'[4] Christ is the spokesperson of the Divine Word of God. The sound of the voice of God is the
very sound of the voice of Christ. John the Baptist was the spokesperson for Christ; John was the voice, Jesus was the Word. The universe
hears the call of God because humanity is beyond nature and therefore has a responsibility to listen to the imaginative sound of that
invocation. The aural sense is a grace in itself – God's self-communication to the human being through Jesus of Nazareth. Therefore, any
theological reflection on the Christian nature and activity of this sense
is concerned with the concepts of grace and person.

The acceptance to listen is in itself a gift of grace. Rahner puts it
in a way that also implies silence: 'Because man's listening must
reckon equally upon God's silence, God's self revelation remains
in every respect incalculable and unmerited grace.'[5] In the courts
of the ear, the realities of the 'word of God' become one in the truth
of God's self disclosure. Theosony refers to the grace of God who
is no longer aloof but clearly revealed. Similarly, for Schneiders,
'the referent of "word of God" is divine revelation, God's accepted
self-gift to human beings.'[6] Attending to such realities in writing,
from a Christian perspective, is the work of this book.

David Tracy's experience of grace is appropriate here on two
counts. Firstly, as a basic definition of what grace means for the
Christian, and secondly, on the permanence and persistence of
Christian grace. 'For myself', he writes, 'the overwhelming reality
disclosed in the originating event of Jesus Christ is none other
than grace itself. From the first glimmers of that graciousness in

---

4. Canon D. J. B. Hawkins, 'On the Nature and Person in Speculative
Theology, in *The Downside Review*, Vol 80, no 258, Jan 1962, p 11.
5. Rahner, *Hearers of the Word*, p 174.
6. Sandra Schneiders, *The Revelatory text: Interpreting the New Testament as
Sacred Scripture*, San Francisco: HarperCollins, p 34.

the uncanny limit-questions of our situation ... in the event of
Jesus Christ, grace prevails for the Christian as the central clue to
the nature of all reality. This grace prevails in spite of all else.'[7]

Rahner defines the theological implications thus: 'If revelation
when heard is to remain truly *God's* word, known as such ... by
falling into the created, finite *a priori* frame of reference, then God
himself, must, in the *grace* of faith ... become a constitutive principle of the hearing of revelation.'[8]

Tracy's outline of grace goes even further, using Rahner's definition as a stepping stone across the river of theosonic language.
Since listening to the sound of God – God's self gift of manifestation – is a choice which humanity can make in human, finite and
historical terms, it still remains, however, a free act from God first
and foremost. In other words, God spoke, listened and heard humanity. Leo Scheffczyk summarises the conversation: 'Fundamentally, man stands under God's call, and his primordial orientation is towards *hearing* God's word.'[9] Humanity is endowed
through the ear with the Trinitarian grace of God. The beginning
of the divine life of grace, its growth, its possible ruin through the
natural tendency to sin, can all be charted aurally.

The personal sound of God is not any particular sound of the
universe; the sound of God is infused in every sound. The marvellous point here is that this easy, obvious listening to the divine in
every sound carries within it the origin of the original sound. This
is the first stage of being; a remembrance of that original murmuring, a memory of the voice of God which, motionless, is still full of
sound. The voice of God echoes in every voice. The sound of the
cosmos is a faint echo of a sonorous God. But there is always more
than meets the human ear in this. Just as no two musical compositions are the same, just as no two performances of any music are
the same, just as no two voices, human or in nature are identical,
just as no two silences contain the same stillness, so too every

7. David Tracy, *The Analogical Imagination*, p 430. Here he is referring to
the overwhelming realisation in his own existence of the original Jesus
event being nothing less than grace itself.
8. Karl Rahner, 'Grace' in *Sacramentum Mundi*, vol 2, p 416.
9. Leo Scheffczyk, 'God' in *Sacramentum Mundi*, vol 2, p 382.

sound, every hearing, every saying, every silence in the dialogue with God is unique. Theosony so defined is reciprocal; the ear is the reciprocal aid to God. Grace is the grain of the originary voice of God, the remembered timbre in the two-way dialogue between God and the Christian. Embroiled in the workings of the auditory sense is a reality about God that all the words in the universe fail to capture. The question of God is answered through a right reading or hearing of divine revelation. A certain kind of right theological hearing is being efficient to hear God's word in scripture in the same way that one can hold a silent piece of musical manuscript and immediately hear the sound of the page. Rahner has the appropriate formulation: 'Because God himself thus produces the readiness to listen as condition of hearing his own word, theology is purely and simply founded upon itself. It is the word of the living God himself.'[10]

Theosony, listening for and to the sound of God, is a graced event, always dependent on the intervention of God. It is about the notion of being favoured by God's gifts. As Love puts it, every man and woman 'must receive from God personally the supernatural capacity for subjective assent to the content of the Christian message.'[11] As theosony is a waiting for the graced sound of God, humanity waits for that voice of God that initiates the conversation between both. The triune God is realised through a listening religious experience: Jesus Christ is the Word; the Holy Spirit is the mouthpiece of this divine/human invitatory sound; God is juxtaposed in the silence between. It is God's Word in silence, through Christ in the Spirit, which turns human beings to attend obediently to God's creative purpose whose full goal is not yet fully revealed.

To sin is to remain stubborn and defiant, numbed and immunised to the sound of the Spirit. In the Old Testament, one of the three Hebrew words for sin is *Hatta* which literally means 'missing the mark'. In theological terms, William May interprets *Hatta* as a word which 'stresses sin as a wilful rejection of the known will

10. Rahner, *Hearers of the Word*, p 174.
11. Love, *Musical Improvisation as the Place where Being Speaks*, p 251.

of God.'[12] Regarding theosony, to sin is freely not to choose to give God a hearing – to block one's inner ear to the *Vox Fortis*. The *Miserere* psalm of pardon and cleansing says it in the inspired words of God's Spirit. Once cleansed and pardoned, 'my tongue will sing aloud of your deliverance ... O Lord, open my lips, and my mouth will declare your praise (Ps 51:14, 15).

All forms of listening should draw one closer to God. Every sound is sacred, it is true. But for whom is it sacred? Every sound is sacred for those who *choose* to hear the breath of God from within. The kernel of the matter and the one question which the term 'theosony' poses is this: how can even a faint echo of this divine breath of God, not created by humankind, be heard even once in a lifetime? There is a paradox here which has a human biological parallel. No human being can reproduce the sound of his or her actual voice; that is, the sound of the voice that is heard in the inner ear and through the resonances of the body can never be replicated. Recorded vocal sounds are very different from the sounds which one can hear in one's own head, as listening to any recording of one's voice proves. Although we hear the sound of the voices of those around, including the animal voices of nature, we can never actually listen to them in total concordance with the speaker. Everyone has a secret sound that can never be accurately reproduced outside of the body. This personal, private sound is akin to the sound of God; the deeper inner voice of God is the primal sound and is heard when the body vibrates and dances to its rhythms. God is the subject of what I am hearing.

---

12. William E. May, 'Sin', *The New Dictionary of Theology*, p 955.

The critical, the obedient, the clairaudient ear and its audience

A critical moment of crisis and shock is the reality of hearing the sound of God. For Christianity is itself a religion of crisis. Golgotha was a crisis-point shrouded in criticism and ending in silence. The words 'crisis' and 'critic' share etymologies. They are both from the Greek word meaning 'to decide or to judge'. From the same source is 'criterion', meaning 'a test'. One must be one's own critic, (from the Greek word 'to judge'), when it comes to being in true relationship and conversation with God. This religious crisis revolves around such oppositions as narration and prophecy, as the philosopher, Iris Murdoch, once defined them: 'In narration, no one seems to be speaking ... the prophetic voice announces itself in the consciousness of being called and sent.'[1]

Theological crisis too is about the shocking and the radical. Steiner talks of 'the shock of correspondence'[2] in the face of the personal experience with *any* work of art. Theosony is a shock of aural correspondence with God. Steiner probes the experience which 'is very difficult to put into words ... it can be muted and nearly indiscernibly gradual – it is one of being possessed by that which one comes to possess.'[3] The sudden and sometimes violent voice of God one possesses and is blessed with, enchants. *Avant-garde* is a term in musicology to describe 'composers who make radical departures from musical tradition.'[4] In an unstinting quest towards inner intimations of musical possibility, the *avant-garde* composer breaks the fetters of convention and expectancy.

---

1. Iris Murdoch, *The Sovereignty of Good*, London: Routledge, 1970, p 225.
2. Steiner, *Real Presences*, p 179.
3. Ibid, p 179.
4. *The New Oxford Companion to Music*, Vol 1, 1.122, 'Avant-garde'.

In one's own desire for partnership with God, radical departures are
often called for. New 'tonalities' emerge, unexpected and un-
planned for 'rests' appear in the silences; all of these are instrumental in the avant-garde relationship between God and humanity. The
praying ear, the strong voice which the Bishop of Hippo, Augustine,
heard in the interior ear, surprises and takes one's breath away and
one must be revolutionary and courageous to discern the organic,
salutary sound. The listening experience is always charismatic in
the Rahnerian sense: 'Essentially new and always surprising ... the
charismatic feature, when it is new, and one might say it is only
charismatic if it is so, has something shocking about it.'[5]

Contemporary musicians have also identified similar crises.
For Pierre Boulez 'the education of the ear is fifty years behind the
education of the eye.' As if to qualify and explain, he adds that
'We are still hostile to sounds that surprise us'.[6] Sometimes we
fear what we might hear. This corollary makes sense in the context
of contemporary music where present-day composers, including
Boulez himself, compose in a surprising avant-garde idiom, sometimes perceived antagonistically as shocking by the listener. Bolts
of sound from the blue constantly astound and jolt the inner ear.

Fiumara confronts a similar crux within western philosophy.
The inability to listen is 'a crisis of a culture tormented by splitting
mechanisms and ... so lacking in methods of reconnecting that the
most disquieting of questions – such as linking branches of
knowledge – are forced into silence since they cannot even be adequately articulated.'[7] Theology, too, is experiencing a crisis of a
God-seeking culture tormented by a rupture, a breach of harmonious relations between theologians and readers, men and
women, clergy and laity, institution and individual. The most con-
troversial and tantalising question for theology is how to facilitate
the work of the Holy Spirit as the instrument of divine action in nature and the human heart. But curiosity is smothered by fear; in the
life-giving salutary search for God, we are afraid to listen and hear.

5. Karl Rahner, *The Spirit in the Church*, London: Burns & Oates, 1979, p 73.
6. Cited without source by Don G. Campbell in a book entitled *Music:
Physician for Times to Come*, Illinois: Quest Books, 1991, p 11.
7. Fiumara, *The Other Side of Language*, p 113.

The second consideration here is about the sound and meaning of four interrelated sonic word images: obedience, clairaudiency, audience and attention. The two words 'obedient' and
'clairaudient' are derived from the Latin *audire*, 'to hear, listen to',
as already pointed out. Hebrew and Greek words for 'to obey' are
also related to the words for 'to hear'. The English auditory word
from the same source is 'audience' which means 'the action of
hearing, the state of hearing or being able to hear'.[8] All three
words, therefore –'obedient', 'clairaudient' and 'audience' – are
about particular definitions or classifications of hearing and listening. 'Obedient' is the combining of the prefix 'ob' to 'audience'.
'Clairaudiency' is, along with theosony, the wedding of the
French *clair* meaning 'clear' with 'audience' and is macaronic, that
is blending of two languages. This is the aural relative or equivalent of clairvoyance; the power of seeing beyond the natural range
of vision. According to *The Oxford Dictionary*, 'clairaudience' was
first coined in 1864 as a 'faculty of mentally perceiving sounds beyond the range of hearing …'[9] In visual terms, 'clairvoyance',
from the French, *clair* and *voyant*, meaning clear seeing, is defined
as 'having the power of seeing objects or actions beyond the natural range of vision'.[10] To be clairvoyant means to have 'keen intuitive understanding'.[11] In aural terminology, therefore, theosony
is a *clairaudient* faculty that tunes into the Sound of God.

To speak of theosony, the Sound of God, is to speak of attentive
aural prayer. Iris Murdoch, echoing Simone Weil, defines prayer
as 'an attention to God which is a form of love.' Søren Kierkegaard
also invokes the aural when it comes to God; the true man of
prayer only attends. The word 'attention' is derived from 'attend'
and one sense of the word 'attend' has to do with the auditory. In
The Britannica World Language Edition of the Oxford Dictionary, the
first category of meanings for the verb 'attend' includes 'to turn
one's ear to, to listen to.'[12] In fact, linking prayer to divine / human

8. See *The Britannica World Language Edition of the Oxford Dictionary*, p 122.
9. Ibid, p 318.
10. *The New American Dictionary*, p 221.
11. *The Collins Dictionary and Thesaurus*, p 175.
12. 'Attend' in *The Britannica World Language Edition*, p 119.

aural encounter and relationship is as old as scripture and as new as contemporary philosophy. For instance, King David cries out vocally for attention to God in his song for salvation from his persecutors: 'Hear a just cause, O Lord; attend to my cry; give ear to my prayer from lips free of deceit' (Ps 17:1).

In summary, four adjectives - critical, obedient, clairaudient, attentive – applied to hearing, take on deeper meanings when employed to narrate the immediate relationship to the mystery of God's self communication. Attending obediently, lending an ear to the Sound beyond all sounds of God is grafting oneself to the triune God so as to become nourished by and united with this Divine. Through such a graft, we are reinvented and transformed. By means of obedient attention, we participate in the very history of the Originator of all Sound. Steiner poses the question: 'How does the graft on to our being *take*? ... The honest answer is that we do not know. Both intuitively and theoretically, Western speculation on the psychology of aesthetic reception ... has been drawn towards intimations of re-cognition ... of *déja-entendu*. We have met before.'[13]

This is an important point theologically and in the contextualisation of an aural theology. Humanity was made for and by God and to God it will return. The human race is born of sound and lives by sound. Humanity evolved and sprang into life at the sound of God's call. God is constantly calling out to every human person. The primal sound out of the primal silence can be intimated. It is a sound that is as familiar as it is distant. It is an auditory originary identity, which the act of listening hears. That forgotten sound is like the forgotten nursery rhymes of childhood. Through the word of Jesus, the Holy Spirit fleshes out the sound of God in our bones. Our dry bones have been fleshed out as once the dry bones of the whole house of Israel were: 'O dry bones, *hear* the word of the Lord. Thus *says* the Lord God to these bones' (Ex 37:4, 5). The incarnate Speaker awakens for mortality, the Divine Word, which, like the sense of hearing, never sleeps.

God calls and humanity turns its ear towards the Divine.

13.Steiner, *Real Presences*, p 180.

Jonathan Sachs wrote about a 'new act of listening'[14] to which he
believes God is calling creation back. God in Jesus Christ and
through the Holy Spirit earths that invocation to the human ear.
As that invocation makes the connection, response is inevitable.
For Joseph Gelineau, that response is theosonic: 'To the one whose
voice has created or called us ... the response must be to make the
sacred offering of sound.'[15]

14. Jonathan Sachs, *The Dignity of Difference: How to Avoid the Clash of
Civilisations*, London / NY: Continuum, 2002, p 19.
15.Gelineau, 'The Path of Music', in *Music and the Experience of God*,
Edinburgh: T & T Clark Ltd, 1989, pp 136, 137.

Summary

This first chapter introduced the concept of theosony, situating it in its theological and interdisciplinary settings. A sound is the sensation produced by the organ of hearing when certain vibrations are caused in the silence of the surrounding air. In the words of T. S. Eliot, 'by the delicate, invisible web you wove / The inexplicable mystery of sound.'[1]

The neologism 'theosony' is necessary and useful as a phenomenology of theological listening for two reasons. Firstly, it has begun, and will continue, to define the fact of the aural nature of Christianity. In doing so, the specificity of Christian theosony will paint the canvas of neglect around this aural sense. Secondly, theosony will attempt to be specific about some novel, different, fresh approaches towards a forgotten aural theology. In some senses, this is a new word about an old thing: the phenomenon of listening is ever old, ever new. What theosony does suggest is a lively, vibrant, innovative, perhaps unfamiliar and unusual way of experiencing the loving revelation of the triune God. Absurdly, (a powerful little word from Latin *surdus* which means 'indistinct', 'voiceless' or 'deaf') God is an inaudible reality transcending the range of human hearing. The court of last appeal is the inner ear – *in aurem interiorem* – of the praying one. God is the permanent inhabitant of every human ear. Every cosmic resident retains its sound and voice like a fossil that is still alive. A deeper understanding of God and participating in such theosonic listening unlocks the door of personal alienation and restlessness. Tracy puts it thus: 'Every human understanding of God is at the same time an understanding of oneself – and vice versa.'[2] When God chooses to speak to human beings and when they choose to

---

1. T. S. Eliot, 'To Walter de la Mare', *The Complete Poems and Plays of T.S. Eliot*, London: Faber and Faber, 1969, p 205.
2. Tracy, *The Analogical Imagination*, p 429.

listen, it is humanity becoming more fully human, living and free. 'O that today you would listen to his voice! Do not harden your hearts' (Ps 95: 7, 8).

Avant-garde composer, John Cage's play on words is relevant here: Theosony becomes an aural question when 'personal ability to respond becomes in turn personal responsibility'.[3] Cardinal John Henry Newman summarises such responsibility that befits the curious vocal Christian: 'In religious enquiry each one of us can speak only for himself, and for himself he has a right to speak. His own experiences are enough for himself…'[4] A development of this rather radical thought is heard through another theologian and a philosopher: Dom Sebastian Moore claims that 'Theology has to be autographical', writing in *The Downside Review* in April 1993; similarly, philosopher Nicholas Berdyaev concurs about philosophical knowledge which 'cannot have its source in books or schools … The only true philosopher is he who has an intuition of being, whose philosophy has its source in life. Genuine philosophy has immediate connection with being.'[5]

Divine self-communication is when God communicates to the human ear in all infinite reality; the created listener shares, participates in the sound of God's Being and becomes fully alive. It is precisely because God is beyond sound that God is also behind and within every sound. Theosony – sounding God and the sound of God – is about striking the tuning fork and with 'good will', listening to the powerful note of wisdom which is God's abundant grace of the Holy Spirit.

> … and what happens next
> Is a music that you never would have known
> To listen for …
> You are like a rich man entering heaven

3. John Cage, *Silence: Lectures and Writings*, London: Marion Boyars, 1987, p 10.
4. John Henry Newman, *A Grammar of Ascent*, NY: Doubleday, 1955, p 300.
5. Nicholas Berdyaev, *The Meaning of the Creative Act*, (1916) London: Victor Gollancz, 1995, p 52-53.

Through the ear of a raindrop.
Listen now again.[6]

.

6. Seamus Heaney, *The Spirit Level*, London: Faber & Faber, 1996, p 1.

CHAPTER TWO

The Human Ear

Hearing is a physiological phenomenon: listening is a psychological act. – *Roland Barthes*[1]

2. Roland Barthes, *The Responsibility of Forms: Critcial Essays on Music, Art
and Representation*, trs Richard Howard, Oxford: Basil Blackwell, 1995, p
245. It would appear to be Barthes who first made this important distinction between 'hearing' and 'listening' which has later been adapted by
Maudelle, Tomatis and is highly pertinent as a distinction in this book.

Biological and Acoustic Facts

Having defined the parameters of the concept 'theosony', the primary task now is to acquaint the reader with the biology of the human ear and to reflect on its functions with the intention of discovering its theological expediency. There are six biological facts which are integral and helpful to the overall argument here.

First, the ear is, scientifically, the most sophisticated and sensitive sense in interpreting and understanding the outer physical world. The human ear has a miraculous ability to receive information from the world without, and within the body itself, above and beyond any other physical sense. From an attention to the biological detail of the human ear, we can then attend to the religious dimension present in all human hearing.

Secondly, serious attention to this sense has been neglected. This is not only in theological scholarship but in many other disciplines as well. Although some theologians have alluded to the aural religious experience, no one, in my opinion, has adequately explored the experience or managed to describe it accurately.

The third reason for examining the aural sense as a biological apparatus, is to apprehend the *listening process* itself, which, according to audiologists and scientists alike, defies full verbal, understanding. Audiologist and scientist, J. R. Pierce, concedes: 'A great deal is known about the structure of the ear and about the neural pathways from the ear to the brain, but our sense of hearing is understood *only in part*.'[1] This resonates

---

1. John R. Pierce, *The Science of Musical Sounds*, NY: Scientific American Books, 1983, p 96. Italics mine.

theologically: like human understanding of the mystery of God, the aural process defies human knowledge.

The fourth reason for understanding the physical ear is that herein resides the seat of emotion. Religion is an emotional relationship with God. Religious emotion that is excited by the contemplation of God is called 'Theopathy' and also defines a particular innate, inner sensitivity and response to St Augustine's *vox fortis in aurem interiorem* (a strong voice in the inner ear), so beautifully described in his *Confessions*.

Fifth, the ear generates and provides sensory *energy* essential to the brain. The brain is dependent upon three main sources of energy: food, air and 'sensory energy'.[2] The aural sense provides most of this third source of energy to the brain. The ear never sleeps. It is constantly providing and supplying energy. According to the French physician, Dr Alfred Tomatis, 'The ear provides the nervous system with almost 90 per cent of its overall sensory energy.'[3]

Finally, one's sense of *balance* resides in the ear. Although not the primary focus of this book, we will do well to keep this aural function in focus. Again, Tomatis is to the fore here and the ear as the locus of balance is fundamental to his auditory theories. Balance is essential to the state of rest which is equilibrium. Holding oneself in equilibrium is vital to the attainment of inner peace.

Five acoustic facts, although less salient are nonetheless relevant:

Firstly, the speed of sound is slow compared with the speed of light. Hearing has to be patient and has to wait. The speed of light travels at up to 300, 000 kilometres per second. The speed of sound is 330 metres per second. It takes eight or nine minutes for the light of the sun to reach the earth. On the other hand, a sound emanating from the sun would not reach earth for some 5,400 days and its arrival would depend upon con-

2. Madaule, *When listening comes alive*, p 59.
3. Alfred Tomatis, *The Conscious Ear*, Barrytown / NY: Station Hill Press, 1991, p 186.

stant temperature in space, which is an impossibility. Sound travelling from the sun would be a physical impossibility since sound, as opposed to light, depends upon a medium for its transmission. Furthermore, there are three ways of comparing sight and sound frequencies: the frequency range of hearing is ten times greater than that of sight. The highest visible frequency is approximately ten times the lowest visual frequency. The highest audible frequency is one thousand times the lowest audible frequency. Therefore, the ear is vastly more efficient in terms of frequency rates. The ear has, it could be argued, a greater range of sensitivity.

Secondly, in the light spectrum, that is the band of colours, there is a series of seven colours usually described as red, orange, yellow, green, blue, indigo and violet. These are produced when white light, such as sunlight, is passed through a prism which decomposes into rays of different colour and wavelength. For instance, the rays of longest wavelength produce the colour red, the shortest produce violet. Although these seven colours can be perceived in varying degrees of colour between the primary colours themselves, they can only be looked at in one frequency, as it were. The point is more readily understood when compared with a sound analogy. For example, in Western Classical music, there are seven notes in the musical scale. However, these notes can be heard in higher and lower frequencies. Take, for instance, the note known as 'middle C' at the centre of the piano keyboard. This note can be heard at higher and lower frequencies depending on the amount of octaves on that particular keyboard. Colours cannot be seen in different frequencies. There is only one octave of colour perception.

The third point is that the human body through sound vibrations can discern sounds beyond the audible. The body is, in this sense, an extension of the ear. The first attachment and connection to the world is through the ear of the womb. The eye is not a comparable extension or as attuned to the reception of the world around. Neither can the eye behold the external world in darkness; on the other hand, the ear hears in both light and darkness. Endorsing this from another standpoint, Paul Newham states that 'people who are mugged or attacked late at night are left only with the sound of the persecutor's voice.'[4] Darkness, on another note, is the symbol of creativity and imagination. One hears differently in the dark; to listen deeply and thoughtfully is enhanced when one closes one's eyes. Because, as Bachelard puts it, the ear 'knows then that the eyes are closed, it knows that it is responsible for the being who is thinking … Relaxation will come when the eyes are reopened.'[5]

The fourth point is amazing. Because there is a direct line from the throat to the inner ear which, in turn, runs on to the mind / brain, bodily sounds do not have to leave the body to be heard. In other words, feedback takes place from the brain to the inner ear; a part of the sound returns from the brain to the cochlea. Every spoken sound is heard in the ear. The larynx cannot keep secrets from the ear. The voice and the ear are one; they are simply two sides of the one coin. Each individual voice only contains sounds that each individual ear can hear. The aural precedes the oral. The aural dictates the parameters of the oral. There is no personal orality without the aural. No other person can hear precisely these head sounds; once the sound of the human voice leaves the body to communicate to the world around, the sound changes. (It is as if God is the only one who can hear every human being in its own voice.)

Fifthly, advancements in the area of the aural lag behind the visual. In medicine, there have been considerable advances in relation to the doctoring of the eye. The cornea of the eye can be reshaped and adjusted by laser treatment to enhance sight. The failing ear has still to resort to the mechanical, digital hearing aids. The blind have access to the world through animals. The blind person can be guided by a guide dog. No such aid has been developed for the deaf person.

The two eyes have been carefully protected for decades by sunglasses that filter the damaging glare of the sun. However, the two ears are totally and constantly exposed to damaging

4. Newham, *The Singing Cure*, p 213.
5. Bachelard, *The Poetics of Space*, p 181.

decibels of noise, but noise pollution is a relatively new concern. In short, sunglasses are commonplace; earmuffs are rare.

Finally, in *capturing* sound and sight, the visual wins out:
photography can capture a close up with the aid of a zoom
lens; in sound recording, the microphone is much more difficult to work with and must be close by to pick up the sound.
Yet in the transmitting of sound and sight, the aural and oral
telephone and radio preceded television.

Biological hearing in such a context raises the question of biological deafness and dumbness: Is the person deprived of hearing
also deprived of religious experience? Of course not. No human
being is deaf to the sound of God. Many people with perfect hearing and perfect pitch choose not to listen. St. Augustine describes
the moment in his own conversion when such spiritual deafness
was dispelled. *'Ad haec tu dicis mihi, quoniam tu es deus meus et dicis
voce forti in aure interiore servo tuo perrumpens meam surditatem.'*
'You answered me, for you are my God and your voice can speak
aloud in the voice of my spirit, piercing your servant's deafness.'[8]
Restored sacred hearing is to live in a different reality, to understand the new language of sound. God remains the same; sounds
remain the same. What is different is the calling, the evocation, the
perception of the sound. Theosony refers to a revolution in experiencing God's self-communication and love.

The whole of humanity has the capacity to be in the image of the
deaf inarticulate man from the land of the Decapolis who encountered the articulate, incarnate Word of God (Mk 7:31-37). By dint of
belief in the divine power of Jesus to heal, his ears are opened and
his voice is restored. Here, in the shortest and almost certainly the
earliest gospel of Jesus, the message is loud and clear. Jesus embodies the sound of God, which he whispers symbolically through his
fingers into the ear and through his spittle on the tongue of all believers. 'Then looking up to heaven, he sighed and said to him,
"Ephphata," that is, "Be opened" (Mk 7:34). The actual sound of
that healing is in the one tri-syllabic Aramaic word *Ephphata*. This

6. Saint Augustine, *The Confessions of Augustine*, eds Gibb and
Montgomery, Cambridge: CUP, 1908, Bk XIII: XXIX, p 442.

Greek transliteration is a passive imperative of the verb 'to open'. Emily Cheney writes about this word: 'Hellenistic miracles often contained unusual words which conveyed extraordinary power. If the gospel of Mark was written primarily for people who understood Greek, then the Aramaic command may have sounded magical.'[7] The image is powerful and once heard cannot be forgotten. It suggests the phenomenon of modelling; the ear and spittle are modelled to praise the Lord in the summertime air. The divine/human saliva merges into the soil of deafness to create the nest of the auditory. The sound of it was definitely and clearly heard, but it was well hidden to the rest of the world. *Ephphata* is the tonic-note of baptism.

God can be reached on every human level; it is *belief* that is the ultimate criterion. The mystery of God's revelatory promise and love is manifested beyond all human sensory horizons. God's self revelation is too important to be confined to human sensory impulses. The Voice of God is softer and louder than the softest and the loudest human voice. On the other hand, any human opening can be access to the divine. The relevant sensory medium argued for here is the sense of hearing.

7. Emily Cheney, 'Ephphata' in *Eerdmans Dictionary of the Bible*, p 416.

The Human Ear: A miraculous little apparatus

Hearing – 'a physiological phenomenon'

The human ear has three functions: it experiences and correlates *sound*; it maintains physical *balance*; it can be a transcendental medium. The ear has three regions: the external, or outer, middle and inner regions. The purpose of the outer ear is to catch, collect, pick up or gather the sound vibrations travelling through the air and direct them into the external auditory *meatus* that is the ear canal. This outer ear, composed of cartilage covered with skin, visually resembles an embryo; inside, the resonating ear canal is funnel-shaped. Remaining with this visual analogy of the visible ear-lobe or *pinna* as embryonic, it is as if this outer ear is the midwife – the *maieutria* – of the physical ear inviting the sound to travel into the birth canal towards listening. This visually embryonic, funnel-shaped external ear is the aural 'magpie' collecting what appeals to it sound-wise. The work of the *pinna* is to protect the middle and inner ear sound-boost entering the ear canal and to localise the source of the sound.

Once captured, the sound vibrations are channelled along the ear canal, which is approximately 2.5 cm long (1 inch), inside the head. At the end of the ear canal is the eardrum or 'tympanic membrane'. Also called the tympanum, (which immediately conjures up, for the musically orientated, orchestral drum sounds) it is a quarter of an inch in diameter, three hundredth of an inch thick, smaller than the head of a thumb tack. Skin covers all of the ear canal and the eardrum. The outer third is cartilage and the inner two thirds are bone. Hairs in the outer part of the ear canal produce secretions that, along with the shedding skin, form wax. This wax ensures that the eardrum does not dry out and it prevents small foreign bodies from entering. Sound now reaches the middle ear which is the realm of the eardrum.

The eardrum is a grey translucent membrane that sits at an

angle in the ear canal. There are some fibres in the upper part of the eardrum and a greater number in the lower section, which are important in the passage of sound. Located directly behind the eardrum are the three small bones of the inner ear, the tiniest bones in the body: the *incus*, the *malleus* and the *stapes* aptly named purely because they vaguely look like a hammer, an anvil and a stirrup. These tool-bones form a bone-chain to transmit sound to the cochlea of the inner ear. The handle of the *malleus* (hammer) rests on the eardrum and covers more than half of it; the foot-hold of the *stapes* (stirrup) rests against the wall of the middle ear chamber and the *incus* (anvil) 'holds hands' with both to form the acoustic bridge.

Because we are never silent and never out of earshot of bodily or physical sound, these bones are constantly awake and in motion. From before birth to death, and even as we sleep, these ear-bones are on constant alert. At birth, they are fully mature and from then on do not grow in size. In the process of ageing, as this bone-trio grows rigid, hearing deteriorates.

Advancing sound in the relay race of hearing reaches the eardrum and buckles. The *malleus* is displaced and moves its interconnected bone neighbours, converting low pressure sound waves to high pressure small ranging sounds. Through the foot-stand of the *stapes*, sound enters the inner ear through the oval window. Two muscles – one the *tensor tympani*, the other the *stapedius* – attached to this tripartite bone group are on constant alert to sounds. Their work is to temper, to tone down loud noise – they must protect the delicate inner ear. If loud sounds enter the middle ear, then the action of both these muscles affects the chain of minute ossicles to weaken their efficiency in transmitting sounds. This mechanism does not operate immediately, there-fore, damage to the ear can be caused by sudden, loud sounds, such as gunfire.

The inner ear is connected to the middle ear by a membrane that covers an opening which is known from its appearance as the oval window. This oval window separates the middle ear, full of air, from the inner ear which is full of fluid. Half the sound energy absorbed by the eardrum of the middle ear is actually transferred into the inner ear. In the inner ear, sound vibrations are converted into electric impulses. Furthermore, for this transmission from the middle to the inner ear to take place, the air in the middle ear should be at normal atmospheric pressure. The normal pressure is maintained by the eustachian tube. This auditory canal extends from the middle ear to the nasopharynx, a tube that connects with the mouth and nose. When the eustachian tube opens and closes, it fulfils this function of pressure equalisation.

The inner ear is part of an enclosed fluid system contained within the cochlea. It is a complex of interconnected fluid-filled canals called the osseous labyrinth, which contains three semi-circular canals controlling balance. These are not involved in hearing. Receptors of balance are regulated and angular velocity measured. This canal is never redundant, constantly informing the body about space relationship, poise and equilibrium. Body movements are carefully monitored in the vestibular labyrinthine organ of the inner ear.

The cochlea is shaped like a snail shell, doing two and a half turns around a middle core of bone and comprises three divisions: a cochlear, a vestibular, and a tympanic canal. Membranes separate them and on the membrane between the cochlear and the tympanic canals is the organ of Corti. 'The organ of Corti, the most important element in our hearing, is developed directly from the embryo's skin.'[1] Through receptor cells, this organ, 33 cm in length, plays its vital role in the hearing process.

When sound reaches the oval window, it makes it move inwards, displacing the fluid called the perilymph fluid. From now on sound is bathed in fluid. The waves of disruption reach the organ of Corti and other membranes. Thus begins the charting of the map from the inner ear to the brain. At this point, the transition from hearing to listening takes place.

As many as 30,000 nerve fibres connect the inner ear to the brainstem, three times as many as the nerve connections between the eye and the brain.[2]

1. Berendt, quoting without reference, S. S. Stevens, an ear physiologist, in *The Third Ear*, p 37.
2. Alfred Tomatis, *The Third Ear*, p 16.

Sounds are partially coded in the first part of the journey along the auditory canal. The temporal lobe of the brain must unscramble pitch, intensity, speech production and language understanding. Feedback from the brain to the cochlea presumably allows every sound to return to sender, to return to the ear of the hearer.

Listening – 'a psychological act'

For Barthes this hearing is 'essentially linked to evaluation of
the spatio-temporal situation (to which humanity adds
sight, animals smell).'[1] Biologically speaking, Barthes outlines the function of the listening ear as follows: 'Morphologically
... the ear ... is motionless, fixed poised like that of an animal on
the alert; like a funnel leading to the interior, it receives the greatest
possible number of impressions and channels them toward a su-
pervisory centre of selection and decision; the folds and detours of
its shell seem eager to multiply the individual's contact with the
world yet to reduce this very multiplicity by submitting it to a filt-
ering trajectory; for it is essential – and this is the role of such initial
listening – that what was confused and undifferentiated becomes
distinct and pertinent.'[2] It is against 'the domiciliary symphony'[3]
of the familiar environment that hearing begins its selective process. Domiciliary hearing is *cosmic*, earthed, and mundane.

Barthes explains that 'this second listening is religious: it *ligatures*
the listening subject to the hidden world of the gods, who, as
everyone knows, speak a language of which only a few enigmatic
fragments reach men, though it is vital – cruelly enough – for them
to understand this language'.[4] Barthes' third act of listening is
where unconscious messages from a client to a listening analyst
transfer. The analogy here between psychoanalytical listening
and theological listening has led to interesting debates. In both
disciplines, this listening has been referred to as 'listening with
the third ear'.[5] Indeed this was the title of a book, published in

1. Barthes, *The Responsibility of Forms*, p 246.
2. Ibid, p 248.
3. Ibid, p 247.
4. Ibid, p 249.
5. See Theodor Reik, *Listening with the Third Ear*, NY: Farrar, Straus, 1949
and 'Listening for God with the Third Ear' by Frederic A. Alling, in
Journal of Religion and Health, Vol 39, No 4, Winter 2000, pp 305-317.

1949, on the listening role of the analyst receiving the spoken words of the analysand. In the words of Reik: 'The voice that speaks to him[the analyst], speaks low, but he who listens with a third ear hears also what is expressed noiselessly … It can hear voices from within the self that are otherwise not audible.'[6] The voice that the analyst listens for is the unconscious mental reality which is 'not just a theoretical concept, but a vitally important part of our mental apparatus which communicates clearly.'[7] Alling, in his article entitled 'Listening for God with the Third Ear', (and indeed more indirectly, Barthes), rightly calls for more dialogue between the theologian and the psychoanalyst. The psychologist's focus, beyond the physiology of the ear, dwells in the inner realm of the ear-labyrinth. Victor Zuckerkandl speaks about the threshold existence between the outer and inner worlds of perception: 'The outer world is the world of bodies … it is the world we meet in our sense perceptions. The inner world is the world of the mind … the world of thoughts, feelings, imaginings … an immaterial world.'[8]

Even the most basic audiological research shows a lacuna between the physiological and psychological acts of the ear. At a certain biological point, the road becomes nebulous. Pierce agrees: 'A great deal is known about the structure of the ear and about the neural pathways from the ear to the brain, but our sense of hearing is understood only in part.'[9] Its mysterious physical functions and effects have inspired awe throughout the ages. During the course of my own research consulting with biologists, scientists and audiologists, all reluctantly concur that at some point in the time and space continuum of sound's penetration of our being, the radar device ceases to determine the presence and precise location of the sound biologically. The musicologist, Victor Zuckerkandl, disavows the many attempts to describe

6. Reik, *Listening with the Third Ear*, p 146.
7. Alling, 'Listening for God with the Third Ear', p 316.
8. Victor Zuckerkandl, *Sound and Symbol: Music and the External World*, Princeton, NJ:Princeton University Press, 1969 (1973), p 55.
9. John R. Pierce, *The Science of Musical Sound*, NY: Scientific American Books, 1983, p 97.

these adequately: 'Far from accounting for the efficiency of our organ of hearing, [they] make it appear all the more miraculous.'[10] Music educationist David Elliott marvels at how the listening process 'proceeds with an ease and an accuracy that are nothing less than miraculous.'[11] More than that, the ear is coextensive with our being: 'The entire surface of the skin serves as an extension of the ear.'[12] And Berendt goes even further by suggesting that to hear is to be.[13] This exploration argues that to hear is also to pray; theosony is a theology of being as listening. Sound can be traced to the threshold of the brain but from there on enter the mysterious, the spiritual and the silent.

10. Zuckerkandl, *Man the Musician: Sound and Symbol*, Vol 2, trs Norbert Guterman, Bollingen Series XLIV. 2, Princeton NJ: Princeton University Press, 1973, p 85.
11. David J. Elliott, *Music Matters: A New Philosophy of Music Education*, NY/Oxford: Oxford University Press, 1995, p 81.
12. Therese Schroeder-Sheker, *Transitus: A Blessed Death in the Modern World*, Missoula: St Dunstan's Press, 2001, p 58.
13. Berendt, *The Third Ear*, p 48.

Brain/Mind considerations

B
efore proceeding beyond the body to the mind or brain, it
might be helpful to clarify what the terms 'brain' and
'mind' mean. Neuroscientists and linguists agree that the
terms 'mind' and 'brain' are simply two different ways of looking
at the same thing in human functioning. Naom Chomsky in his
seminal work on the understanding of basic human nature,
Language and Problems of Knowledge, draws on the dual term
'mind/brain' consistently.[1] According to two neurotheologists
who straddle the disciplines of biology, theology and medicine to
bolster their arguments, Andrew Newberg and Eugene d'Aquili,
'the mind and brain are intimately intertwined in human behaviour and thought.'[2] Again Eastern spirituality and thought
knows this well. There is a wonderful koan from the Zen tradition
about two young monks discussing the nature of a flag swaying in
the wind. One monk believes that it is the flag that moves, the other
holds that it is the wind that is the nub of the matter. A master overhears and summarises: it is neither the flag nor the wind, it is your
mind that moves. This wisdom has much to teach about hearing,
the physiological phenomenon too; all true, realistic listening with
the ear of the heart is nurtured by the mind. As Peter Kivy suggests
'what we expect has a great deal to do with what we "hear".'[3]

The brain and the mind are co-dependent: two performers in
the same human performance. 'One might argue that there can be
no brain without mind and no mind without brain,'[4] Newberg

1. Naom Chomsky, *Language and Problems of Knowledge*, MA: The MIT
Press, 1988, pp 15-17.
2. Andrew Newberg/Eugene d'Aquili, *The Mystical Mind: Probing the
Biology of Religious Experience*, Minneapolis: Fortress Press, 1999, p 22.
3. Peter Kivy, *Music Alone: Philosophical Reflections on the Purely Musical
Experience*, Ithaca/London: Cornell University Press, 1990, p 7.
4. Ibid, p 50.

and d'Aquili suggest. The brain / mind functions as a system within other systems. 'The mind is the name for the intangible realities that the brain produces. Therefore, thinking, logic, art, emotions, and intentions all fall into the realm of the mind.'[5] Of the five human functionings mentioned here, one omission is spirituality.

How does the brain turn raw auditory impulses, i.e. energy, into meaningful verbal expressions? Enter the twin hemispheres. The cerebral hemispheres are the two halves of the upper front brain. The right hemisphere excels in the intuitive, creative, receptive and insightful; the left brain processes the rational, the logical. Andrew Cyprian Love holds 'that human speech functions are found in the left cerebral hemisphere, while musical information is processed mainly in the right.[6] He supports the widely held theory of music's right-hemispheric association. 'This hemisphere now seems, in sum, to be responsible for: emotion, music, narrative and improvisation.'[7] Impulses from primary hearing centres of the ear reach the brain's main language centre, the left hemisphere. Processed through this left half of the cerebrum, the brain hears, for example, the sound 'soul', which sounds exactly the same as 'sole', 'sole' (fish) and 'Seoul'. It is at this mysterious stage that 'this auditory input is converted into intelligible words and sentences and understood logically, in the context of grammar and syntax.'[8] Left-hemisphere dominance for language dates back to 1885 when Pierre Broca published his famous pronouncement: *Nous parlons avec l'hémisphere gauche* (We speak with the left hemisphere)[9]

However, it is the right side which discerns emotional tones and verbal inflections, all the qualities according to Newberg and d'Aquili which 'give spoken language its subtle shades of meaning.'[10] Discerning the grain of the voice is the concern of the right

5. Ibid, p 47.
6. Ibid, p 140.
7. Ibid, p 171.
8. d'Aquili / Newberg, *The Mystical Mind*, p 22.
9. Christine Temple, *The Brain: An Introduction to the Psychology of the Human Brain and Behaviour*, London: Penguin, 1993, p 48.
10. Andrew Newberg / Eugene d'Aquili, *Why God Won't Go Away*, NY: Ballantine Books, 2001, p 22.

hemisphere. It is not what is being said particularly, but how it is heard and how the emotion of the speaker communicates with the listener.

Hemispheric traits, some research has shown, seem to be gender determined. Summarising this research, Bumbar notes that 'women react intuitively and make judgements on the basis of feelings. They show a right hemisphere dominance. Men ... analyse and make judgements on the basis of conclusions. They display a left hemisphere dominance.'[11]

11. Paul E. Bumbar, 'Notes on Wholeness' in *Aesthetic Dimensions of Religious Education*, eds Gloria Durka / Joan Marie Smith, NY: Paulist Press, 1979, p 52

Neurotheology

N eurotheology is a neologism or new word coined by
James Ashbrook in an article published in *Zygon* titled
'Neurotheology: The Working Brain and the Work of
Theology'. It defines a science that presents the physiological arguments for religion and is a neuropsychological approach to religious phenomenology. Along with psychotheology, it is a contemporary scientific discipline that tries to articulate a concrete,
biological / psychological / theological synthesis, although not
necessarily restricted to the aural sense. The particular school of
thought that is presented here is that of Andrew Newburg and
Eugene d'Aquili.[1] The following examination of this school is for
its own sake rather than being in parallel to the argument of this
book. Their biology of belief is 'a hypothesis that suggests that
spiritual experience, at its very root, is intimately interwoven with
human biology. Biology, in some way, compels the spiritual
urge.'[2] This is of course a fascinating commentary on the Roman
Catholic idea of grace building on nature. It is in the elusive, intangible realm of the mind that such transcendental experiences are
monitored. In Newburg's and d'Aquili's terminology, 'it is always

---

1. Newberg and d'Aquili used scanning techniques to map the brains of
Tibetan Buddhist and Franciscan nuns. The scans photographed blood
flow – indicating levels of neural activity – in each subject's brain at the
moment of intense spiritual experience. They found that in a chunk of the
brain's *left* parietal lobe – the orientation association – (this is the area responsible for drawing the line between the physical self and the rest of
existence) – requires a constant stream of neural information flowing in
from the senses. When the blood flow was dramatically reduced – deaf-
ferentation – the brain was deprived of information needed to draw line
between the self and the world, the subject would experience a sense of
limitless awareness of merging into infinite space.
2. Newberg / d'Aquili, *Why God Won't Go Away*, p 8.

the mind that moves, regardless of whether it is experiencing our usual baseline reality or whether it is experiencing God.'[3] There are areas of the brain associated with the five senses, which are set in motion by motor behaviours; in other words, the brain can permit God's radical free self-communication. Christianity believes that God created and sustains humanity – God created the brain. But everyone must also be open to the notion that the brain quite naturally and efficiently could develop, in light of God's plan of salvation, the mechanisms for religious experience.[4]

Are there any links between the workings of the brain and God? This question has implications for theosony. One way or another, according to some neurosurgeons, humanity yearns for a relationship with God. Given and accepted, then, my argument is that the ear is a powerful medium for the bringing to fruition of that relationship. Attention to the biological workings of the ear is the holistic, organic way to relating to God.

The parameters of the arguments of one particular school of neurotheological thought are outlined to support a physiological component to religious experience. This harks back to the ear's natural ability to measure and differentiate the sounds heard, already stated above. To reiterate, information from an ear event is more reliable than from visual input. The eye's capacity to inform is ten times more restricted than the ear's. The proof of this hypothesis is presented scientifically by Berendt[5] who claims that the 'ear thus registers ten octaves and the eye just one.'[6] As stated above, the eye perceives seven primary colours; the ear can hear infinite nuances of sound according to the frequency received through the outer, middle and inner ear.

This is important and relevant to theosony; after all, the work

3. Newberg / d'Aquili, *The Mystical Mind*, p 120.
4. In February 2001, the Vice President of the Pontifical Academy for Life, the Vatican's leading expert on bioethical and medical issues, Bishop Elio Sgreccia, responds: 'You can't say it's the brain that causes prayer. That would be confusing the effect with the cause. As for the idea that the feeling of being in God's presence might simply be the result of the brain's activity indicates a mistaken, materialistic view of human actions.'
5. See Berendt, *The Third Ear*, pp 16 / 17.
6. Berendt, *The Third Ear*, p 17.

of theosony is to prove that the ear, efficiently attuned to God in prayer, prompted and guided by the Holy Spirit, is a highly efficient midwife and operator. But as Newburg and d'Aquili rightly assert 'tracing spiritual experience to neurological behaviour does not disprove its realness. You would need auditory processing to hear his voice ... and cognitive processing to make sense of his message.'[7] They suggest that 'as far as we can determine, all human experience enters human awareness via the function of the brain. It certainly seems reasonable to reach the conclusion that the brain is the structure that gives all of us our thoughts, feelings and experiences.'[8]

If there is a God, our experience of what we mean by God must pass, via the senses, through the mind/brain. Speaking in non-psychological, non-physiological terms, religion, Herbert Farmer believes, is 'a great reinforcement ... a necessary function of human personality in its life task ... a feeling of confidence and optimism, a stimulus to the will to go forth confidently to conquer its world, a reinforcement of the hold upon the mind of moral ideals'.[9] The theological argument rests, Farmer states, 'on the assertion that religion is beneficial in its effects, not temporarily and incidentally, but in a very profound, creative and indispensable way.'[10] The discovery of spiritual truth 'provides believers with a powerful sense of control over the otherwise uncontrollable whims of fate ... that goodness rules the world, and even that death can be ultimately conquered ... If God is not real, neither is our most powerful source of hope and redemption ... it is a matter of existential survival.'[11]

To summarise: the sign is the secret. In theosonic listening, God is the secret which, hidden in reality, can reach the deepest human consciousness. It is the unravelling of that secret code, enciphering and deciphering God that is crucial here. Barthes lines

7. Newberg/d'Aquili, *The Mystical Mind*, p 44.
8. Herbert H. Farmer, *Towards Belief in God*, London: SCM, 1942, p 169.
10. Ibid, p 175.
11. Newberg/d'Aquili, *Why God Won't Go Away*, p 164.

up the aural and visual codes on equal terms: 'Here ... begins the
human: I listen the way I read, i.e. according to certain codes.'[12]

This book argues for the presence and restoration of the sense
of hearing as a prime mover in the revelation of God to humanity.
What do we hear that is new is the question that theosony poses.
The answer is everything and nothing; because theosony refers,
for the Christian, to the song of the triune God alone, it is not
manipulable but manipulates. God controls and influences what
is heard in the divine name cleverly and skillfully. In describing
the religious effect of Wolfgang Amadeus Mozart's music, Karl
Barth so well defines the precise experience which theosony
embraces in all its human, limited capacity: 'Mozart ... does not
reveal in his music any doctrine and certainly not himself ...
Mozart does not wish to say anything: he just sings and sounds.
Thus he does not force anything on the listener, does not demand
that he make any decisions or take any positions ...'[13] Through the
receptive, open ear, God does not whisper any particular dogma
nor is there any trace of the grain of God's own voice; God does
not announce anything that is distinctively human. The Godhead
freely sounds in the hollow of the ears of anyone who chooses, un-
conditionally, to hear.

In hemispheric concepts, theosony, listening for God in the
universe, argues for a right-hemisphere approach to God. The
right cerebral hemisphere is also the seat of emotion, imagination,
music and artistic creativity. Music and religion are closely related.
The Irish traditional musician Seán O Boyle is quoted as saying: 'I
have always thought that, for me, the glory of good music is the
final proof of the existence of God.' In fact, Joachim Braun tells us,
the Bible was 'considered the main source for the study of music
in ancient Israel.'[14]

Applying these theories of right/emotional, left/rational processes to Western Christian theology leads to the claim that it is
left hemisphere routes which have become dominant to the point

12. Barthes, *The Responsibility of Forms*, p 245.
13. Karl Barth, *Wolfgang Amadeus Mozart*, Grand Rapids: Eerdmans,
1986, p 38.
14. Joachim Braun, 'Music' in *Eerdmans Dictionary of the Bible*, p 927.

of being overwhelming. Ultimately, however, polarisation of right and left hemisphere function is unhelpful. In terms of theology, there is no part of the human body or psyche that is deaf to, or bereft of, God's revelatory self-disclosure. It is important, indeed necessary, to compartmentalise; humanity likes to categorise. However, there is a danger of rigid dualism, which is ironic when discussing the ear, part of whose function is to provide balance.

Alfred Tomatis discovered that 'there was a marked difference between voice quality when controlled with the right versus the left ear, the right ensuring much better quality ... the right ear is the leading ear.'[15] The right ear is connected with the left side of the brain, the left ear with the right-hand side. Sounds, heard through the right ear in the right-handed person, tend to be processed rationally by the left hemisphere, whereas sounds received to the right temporal lobe are understood and interpreted emotionally as environmental sounds. This is in synchronicity with right/left hand function and perception.

Hemispheric theories have symbolic implications for praying through the body. The sound of God is listened for and through an alignment of both ears where there is a democracy of hemispheres. A government of the hemispheres is in conversation with a government of the senses in the work of theosony, which is the business of God's self-presentment to humanity. It is the symbolic image of the 'third ear' which is the leading ear attuned to the Word of God. In making sense of divine Revelation, the circle is tripartite: firstly there are the impulses of the third ear which, in turn, orally and aurally energise the inner brain and mind where the love and salvation of God resides, which finally returns to rest in human response and obedience. Musicologist Zuckerkandl says: 'No matter how you look at it, there is no way out of the circle of the audible.'[16]

So humanity listens to God, then starts at the beginning: listening is an inherently human activity; it affects our biological, emotional, cognitive and spiritual responses. How and what we listen to is, was and always will be, crucial. 'At the magical stage [of

---

15. Madaule, *When Listening Comes Alive*, p 35.
16. Zuckerkandl, *Man the Musician*, p 84.

early man's relation to the world] the crucial organ was the ear, the crucial sense the sense of hearing.'[17] This primitive primacy of the aural still remains unchanged yet unchallenged; memories, after all, are profoundly elusive but they are full of sounds. The ear powerfully governs the emotions in relationship. Anthony Storr attributes this to a depth inherent in the functions of the ear. 'At an emotional level, there is something "deeper" about hearing than seeing; and something about hearing other people which fosters human relationships even more than seeing them.'[18] The elusive profundity of listening nurtures and enhances the relationship, which is fulfilled in the ultimate truth of Christianity: God's self-disclosure.

17. Ibid, p 73.
18. Storr, *Music and the Mind*, p 26.

'The grain of the voice'

This delicate little Aeolian harp that nature has set at the entrance to our breathing is really a sixth sense, which fol-
lowed and surpassed the others. It quivers at the merest
movement of metaphor; it permits human thought to sing.[1]

This section will consider the human voice, the unique timbre, the grain of the voice, the eroticism of the voice, which
is 'really a sixth sense'.[2] Vocal sounds are perceived by the
ear of both the maker of the sounds and the listener. In other
words, hearing and the voice are totally related in the self and
one's encounter with the external world of things and people. The
voice is all sounds, particularly articulate sound, uttered through
the mouth of sentient beings. In human beings, these sounds, naturally emitted in speech, shouting and singing, are often characteristic of the utterer. The timbre of the voice is always dynamic
and in flux.

Only the sounds which the human brain can imagine, create
and make sense of, can be physically birthed through the auricul-
atory system that is the voice. The brain controls all sounds made
by the human voice. The brain is the voice. It is also the human
brain that controls the production and understanding of the or-
ganised sounds, which is language. 'The singer or player cannot
help hearing what he sings or plays: the circle must be closed.'[3]

The organ of the voice is the larynx. It is a cavity at the upper
end of the windpipe containing the vocal cords. It forms part of
the air passage to the lungs. The two pairs of membranous folds in
the larynx are called vocal cords. The upper pair, called false vocal
cords, is redundant in the production of vocal sound; it is the

---

1. Bachelard, *The Poetics of Space*, p 197.
2. Ibid, p 197.
3. Zuckerkandl, *Man the Musician*, p 12.

lower pair, called the true vocal cords, which is activated to produce sound when air from the lungs passes through them. The
edges of these true vocal cords are drawn tense as the breath from
the lungs makes them vibrate, producing vocal sound. Sounds
from the larynx then proceed to the organ on the floor of the
mouth, the tongue. The ear has three functions, the voice has two:
that of taste and, in God-created humanity, of speech.

In girls between ten and fourteen years old, the vocal cords increase from about fifteen millimetres to seventeen millimetres.
This lowers the range of the voice. Vocal timbre changes for
women also during menstruation, pregnancy and menopause.
The larynx increases, which allows access to lower sounds. The
vocal cords of a boy increase up to twenty-three millimetres. His
larynx not only increases but also drops in position and the resonating cavities in the chest and pharynx enlarge. To summarise
the biology of the voice, therefore, is to say that for the voice to live
and speak, another miraculous coalition is evoked: the lungs create
the breath which glides through the vocal cords in the larynx;
sound lands on the tongue which moulds the sounds into verbal
sculpture.

Roland Barthes, addressing the timbre, which he calls the
'grain', highlights the power of the voice in terms of desire, emotion and eroticism. Stirred and given sound by the life-giving
breath, which never rests in life, the voice bursts forth out of the
silence and arrests both the voiced and the listener. The timbre is
always in flux; register changes in the voice are directly in the control of everyone and can be manipulated according to the chosen
shape of the voice's resonators in the chest, the larynx, the mouth,
the nasal cavities and the skull. Just as a cathedral space or a concert hall has a fundamental timbre, so too, every voice possesses
its own unique vocal resonators. This timbre is the grain of the
voice. According to Barthes, 'the grain of the voice is not indescribable (nothing is indescribable), but I don't think that it can be
defined scientifically, because it implies a certain erotic relationship between the voice and the listener. One can therefore describe the grain of a voice, but only through metaphors.'[4]

4. Barthes, *The Grain of the Voice*, p 184.

When the voice ceases to affect in a profound way, it is imaged by Barthes to be white and cold without fulfilling its innate capacity for love and eroticism. Every human voice is connected to desire; every act of the voice is an act of the erotic. 'There is no human voice which is not an object of desire ... there is no neutral voice – and if sometimes that neutrality, that whiteness of the voice occurs, it terrifies us, as if we were to discover a frozen world, one in which desire was dead.'[5] The word 'erotic' is understood in contemporary linguistics as pertaining to the arousal of sexual love or marked by strong sexual desire. 'Erotic' derives its meaning from the world of the gods. Eros is the Greek god of love. For the Romans, Eros was identified as Cupid. Love is the business of the god who is the harbinger of peace. *The Encyclopedia of Mythology* defines Eros as the one 'who "brings harmony to chaos", and permits life to develop ... He was armed with a bow and arrows whose prick stirred the fires of passion in all hearts.'[6]

What does the concept of voice mean in scripture? *Cruden's Concordance* answers: 'By this word is not only understood the voice of a man or beast, but all other sorts of sounds, noises, or cries. And even thunder is also called the voice of God.'[7] In ancient culture, according to Thomas Allen Seel, the Greek word *phone,* meaning both sound and voice, 'could be made by animals, nature, humankind, and by the Godhead.'[8] In other words, this one word for voice could mean a cosmic voice, a human voice or the voice of God. In the Book of Revelation, for instance, *phone* can represent 'both vocally and non-vocally produced sound. It can be literally translated to mean "a sound" or "a voice"...'[9]

5. Barthes, *The Responsibility of Forms*, pp 279, 280.
6. *The Larousse Encyclopedia of Mythology*, p 132.
7. *Cruden's Complete Concordance to the Old and New Testaments*, p 724.
8. Thomas Allen Seel, *A Theology of Music for Worship derived from the Book of Revelation*, Metuchen, NJ & London: The Scarecrow Press, 1995, p 95.
9. Ibid, p 93.

Three theosonic conversion stories

So far in this chapter, our themes have centred on the biology, the physiology of the ear and the voice, some considerations about the overlap between science, biology and theology and some methods of listening. All findings, scientific and biological, although not exhaustive, favoured the sense of hearing as more all-embracing, consistent, reliable in receiving information; furthermore, this aural sense is underdeveloped and underused in human life experience. The most appropriate preparatory transition to the third part of the book which centres on scripture is through the audio-centric theology of two remarkable saints of hearing; Paul and Augustine. St Patrick's story, in its resonances with both saints, is relevant too.

Paul of Tarsus (d.c. 67)

For Paul, graces are all the favours of God freely bestowed by the Holy Spirit. The listening experience is always a graced charism in the Rahnerian sense of the word: it is always new, surprising and shocking. Rahner holds that 'these special charismata need not necessarily always concern extraordinary mystical things. The simplest help, the most commonplace service can be a charisma of the Spirit.'[1] 'For we are what he has made us, created in Christ Jesus for good works, which God prepared beforehand to be our way of life' (Eph 2:9).

St Paul's theology is both audio-centric and spirit-filled. 'My speech and proclamation were … with a demonstration of the Spirit' (1 Cor 2:4). Paul, an ardent lover and reciter of the oral Talmud from his Jewish heritage, is now unashamedly committed to the incarnate Word of God, the second person of the Trinity with God the Father and the Holy Spirit. The Spirit functions to

---

1. Karl Rahner, *The Spirit in the Church*, p 47.

teach St Paul to speak the truth. Then on speaking this truth, the listener holds it in the lobe of the ear. The Spirit of God, who reveals God, now turns to the receiver of the teaching 'interpreting spiritual things to those who are spiritual' (1 Cor 2:13). Paul's teaching is brought to perfection in God's people, the people who love him, through that Spirit from God. He calls the members of the churches of Galatia foolish and asks them five angry, rhetorical questions. The first and the fifth clearly state that God's own Spirit is received not by doing but by hearing, by 'believing what you heard' (Gal 3:2, 5). It is the Spirit, therefore, that acts and gives life and freedom. The gifts of the Spirit of God are freely given through the ear (1 Cor 12:8).

There are two germane points about the Pauline corpus. Firstly, these letters themselves are essentially oral/aural preaching and teaching. The saint of an aural, theosonic conversion wrote letters *faute de mieux* in the impossibility of being physically present to address the first Christians who came to listen.

Secondly, Paul's letters, unlike the four gospels, did not have a story line to captivate the listeners. Paul wrote down his own story of God. As James Dunn puts it, 'by their very nature, Paul's letters are highly personal communications, not dispassionate treatises.'[2] To effect this communication, he relied on the power of the vocal sounds to arrest and carry meaning. To interest the listener, Paul drives home his theology by repeating words and ideas over and over again. These forms or techniques of repetition, Achtemeier calls 'clues to organisation so the listener would not simply be lost in the forest of verbiage'.[3] As Dundes put it, Paul 'recognised the importance, the power, of both the oral word and the written epistle in his efforts to proselytise prospective Christians.'[4] 'So then, brothers and sisters, stand firm and hold fast to the traditions that you were taught by us, either by word of mouth or by letter' (2 Thess 2:15).

---

2. James D. G. Dunn, *The Theology of Paul the Apostle*, Edinburgh, T & T Clark, 1998, p 8.
3. Achtemeier, 'Omne Verbum Sonat', p 22.
4. Alan Dundes, *Holy Writ as Oral Lit: The Bible as Folklore*, NY/Oxford: Rowman & Littlefield, 1999, p 16.

Paul believed that the Gospel was pronounced in advance by the prophets in scripture (Rom 1:1-2). Kelber maintains that the Gospel for Paul 'is constitutionally and operationally defined in oral terms. Not by association with writing...'[5] The important point here is that Paul believed in a fundamental auditory power inherent in the Gospel. The message is through the upshot it has on its hearers, speakers, and readers. 'The "word of life" ... is less a message about life than the power of life transmitted by the word ... By endowing the gospel with power, the apostle has assigned to it the very quality which is consistent with its oral operation.'[6]

This very passage from the apostle Paul was to be the culmination of an aural experience of the Holy Spirit of another saintly aural conversion, that which St Patrick underwent. Patrick describes an aural mystical encounter with the Spirit. On one occasion, on being drawn into himself, he not only observed a Spirit-presence praying within him, but the Spirit clearly spoke. 'He *spoke* ... saying that he was the Spirit. In this way, [aurally], I learned by experience ...'[7] At that moment, the words of St Paul to the Romans above flooded his memory. Once again, the supreme example of which is to come is the experience of Mary of Magdala, the eye fails to recognise; the ear hears the voice instantly, obeys and believes. Paul is not content to rely on the written word. The medium he chooses very deliberately to convince the original listener and the contemporary reader/listener is the sense of hearing. Kelber has the final word: 'It is fair to say that in Pauline theology the ear triumphs over the eye.'[8]

Paul's theology, therefore, is a theology of the ear. First, Paul's own conversion was, as were those of Augustine and Patrick after him, based on a call – a call 'through [God's] grace (Gal 1:15). God's call is God's power to heal, to give life and to call into existence by name all of creation. It is this personal, as opposed to dog-

5. Werner H. Kelber, *The Oral and the Written Gospel: The hermeneutics of Speaking and Writing in the Synoptic Tradition, Mark, Paul, and Q*, Philadelphia: Fortress Press, 1983, p 144.

6. Ibid, p 145.

7. Joseph Duffy, *Patrick in His Own Words*, Dublin: Veritas, 2000, p 18. Italics mine.

8. Kelber, *The Oral and Written*, p 143.

matic, experience that makes Pauline writings still so captivating. Paul clearly enunciates that it is the Holy Spirit who intervenes from above and below in this salvific process: from below this Spirit intervenes on our behalf to God, from above, that same Spirit communicates our needs to God and in turn reveals the theosonic response from God. The Spirit 'helps us in our weakness ... intercedes with sighs too deep for words (Rom 8:26), and God 'knows what is the mind of the Spirit (Rom 8:27).

Augustine of Hippo (354-430)

The theology of Augustine is already well introduced with the quotation cited twice before : *Vox Fortis in aure, in vocem interiorem*: 'For God does not speak with man through the medium of matter, with vibrations of air causing his voice to be heard by the ears of the body ... But he speaks by means of the truth itself, and to all who can hear with the mind rather than with the body.'[9] Gibb and Montgomery are in agreement about the *Confessiones*: this spiritual autobiography is 'in an unchallenged position, as a religious classic, as a classic of theology and ... of psychology.'[10] Augustinian scholar, Frederick Van Fleteren attests to its continuing popularity and importance: 'It is a literary, theological, and philosophical masterpiece. The most studied of all Augustine's works in the twentieth century, it continues to attract the attention of historians, theologians, philosophers, philologists, and psychologists.'[11]

Augustine's autobiography – the *Confessiones* – is also a theology of the human, physical senses and specifically of the auditory sense. Augustine knew the business of the ear, physiologically, psychologically and theologically. The underlying message of the thirteen books is one of desire for right listening. Every human being impregnated with *desiderium*, desire to fulfil this pure holy yearning, is according to John Burnaby 'the constant theme of

---

9. Saint Augustine, *The City of God*, Bk XI, Ch 2, trs Walsh / Mohan, Washington DC: Catholic University Press, 1952, p 188, 189.
10. *The Confessions of Augustine*, eds Gibb and Montgomery, p xi.
11. Frederick Van Fleteren, 'Confessiones' in *Augustine Through the Ages: An Encyclopedia*, ed Allan D. Fitzgerald OSA, Grand Rapids: Eerdmans, 1999, p 227.

Augustine's teaching'.[12] Until the moment of Augustine's conversion, he blocked his ears to the sound of God.

Augustine did not, unlike Paul or Patrick, prioritise one particular sense. For him, all the God-created senses were equal. Like the entire creation, the body with its five 'bodily senses' replies to Augustine's vital questioning: 'Are you of this world'? 'No', the 'whole fabric of the world' – the earth and all within it – answered 'I am not he but he has made me' (*Confessions* 10:9). For 'the founder of the Western Spirit', as Karen Armstrong calls him,[13] all five physical senses are pathways to the Creator / God. 'The outer man … is divided into five parts: sight, hearing, smell, taste, and touch. But … it is hardly necessary to question these five senses … for what one of them informs us also applies to the rest' (*De trin.* 11:1).[14] But the information supplied by the bodily senses in the pursuit of the love of God is inadequate. True theological love is embraced in a 'certain' sense which is a 'certain voice … where he utters words that time does not speed away' (*Confessions* 10:6:8). It is all about the soul's pilgrimage of longing and love of God, whether through ear or eye.

The Word of the Master is the true voice that teaches. 'In the eternal Truth … there, O Lord, I hear your voice speaking to me, since he who teaches us speaks to us' (*Confessions* 11:8:10). Learning to listen in truth and faith to that voice demands rigorous discipline and training: 'Therefore, he gave them the words, as he said, which the Father gave him; but when they received those [words] spiritually, not outwardly in their ears, but inwardly in their hearts, they have received in truth because they have known in truth.'[15]

Listening to the Word made flesh is bypassing the biological ear in favour of the heart. Six words define Augustine's aural

12. See John Burnaby, *Amor Dei – A Study of the Religion of St Augustine*, (1938), Norwich: Canterbury Press, 1991, p 97.
13. Karen Armstrong, *A History of God: The 4,000-Year Quest of Judaism, Christianity and Islam*, NY: Ballantine, 1993, p 119.
14. Saint Augustine, *The Trinity*, trs S. McKenna, p 316.
15. *The Fathers of the Church, St Augustine Tractates on the Gospel of John*, Vol 90, trs John W. Rettig, Washington DC: Catholic University of America Press, 1996, tr 106.6, p 272.

theosony: heart, truth, faith, voice, listening and learning. 'Everyone who belongs to the truth listens to my voice' (Jn 18:37). In his
commentary on this verse only three things matter: listening,
obeying and believing. 'He listens, of course, with the inner ears,
that is, *he listens to* my voice, and this would mean just the same as
if he were to say, "believe me".'[16]

The ear of the heart is obediently tuned to the heart of heaven;
it has a direct line to the joyful, soundful festivities of 'the house of
God' Augustine promises, provided cosmic noise does not
drown it out. 'A certain sweet and melodious strain strikes on the
ears of the heart, provided only the world do not drown the
sounds' (*En in Ps* 42).[17] We must pursue the sound field and walk
therein even though the ultimate prognosis is bleak as we hear the
sounds of the groaning of human frailty. However, if we walk 'for
a brief while … within reach of that sound … we may catch something from that house of God' (*En in Ps* 42).[18] Conversion is precisely through 'the sweetness of that inward spiritual sound to
feel contempt for all outward things' (*En in Ps* 42).[19]

One cannot but conclude that Augustine was aware of the
biology of the ear as well as its innate possibility for conversation
with the divine. He was also sensitive to maternal bonding. In *De
Trinitate*, he makes a claim for the sense of sight of a mother, given
that she gazes on anything with love and passion, 'Whatever they
gaze upon with great delight' (*De Trin* 11:2:5), will directly affect
the fruit of her womb. Examples of this phenomenon, the bishop
continues, are commonplace but the most trustworthy tale of this
visual power of will is found in Genesis (30:37-41). 'In order that
the sheep and she-goats might give birth to speckled offspring,
Jacob had rods of various colours placed before them in the wa-
tering-troughs, to look at as they drank, during the period when
they had conceived' (*De Trin* 11:2:5). Since the visual sense is just a
model of other senses for Augustine, could we infer that an

16. Ibid, Tr 115.4, p 24.
17. *Exposition on the Book of Psalms by S. Augustine, Bishop of Hippo*,
Oxford: John Henry Parker, 1847, Vol 2, p 189.
18. Rettig, p 189, 190.
19. Ibid, p 190.

expectant mother who bathes herself in the sound of God in prayer would also surround her embryonic child with those same sounds? The aural message, the messenger and the receiver are united momentarily in that sound field. The sound that is heard is 'what is proper to the soul alone ... the will' (*De Trin* 11: 2:5).

The second point to be made about Augustine is that he was an orator *par excellence*. The art of rhetoric, which is learning to speak eloquently and to recognise the sound of one's own voice ringing in one's ear, he mastered at the age of eighteen. The spoken word was wisdom and its intention was to affect the thought and conduct of its hearers. It was not necessarily a question of what was being said but how it was vocalised and sounded. Describing the influence of the 'sweetness of discourse' of St Ambrose, his baptiser, Augustine admits that he 'was not anxious to learn what he said, but merely to hear how he said it.'[20] So the *sound* of the spoken word takes precedence over the meaning of what is being said. The heart is opened wide by the honeyed sound. In that awakening, truth is revealed. '[A]nd when I opened up my heart to receive the eloquence with which he spoke, there likewise entered ... the truths that he spoke.'[21]

Thirdly, the *Confessions* are *stories*, told and retold. Augustine kept many a friend in thrall telling tales of his exploits in his insightful descriptions of characters and events. He felt obliged eventually to submit such tales to writing – either by himself or again through the ear of a scribe. But the stories, as in the case of scripture, came first. The oral / aural gave way to the silent visual. Augustine's autobiographical *Confessions*, the greatest theological autobiography ever written according to Sebastian Moore,[22] were in origin verbal before being written, his admission of the truth of his life was heard long before it was read. As Gibb and Montgomery put it, 'Augustine wrote at the request of friends who begged him to commit to writing those recollections of his former life to which he often referred in private conversation.'[23]

---

20. Ryan, *Confessions*, p 130. Italics mine.
21. Ibid, p 131.
22. See 'Four Steps Towards Making Sense of Theology', *The Downside Review*, Vol III, No 383, April 1993, p 82.
23. Gibb and Montgomery, p ix.

Fourthly, the *Confessiones* are in the form of a conversation. The reader, from the outset, is the 'fly-on-the-wall' in the conversation-space between Augustine and his God and Lord whose power and wisdom knows no boundaries or limitations, '*non est numerus.*'[24] But yet, the reader is forcefully drawn into the monologue cheering Augustine on. Here he so eloquently and perfectly articulates, on humanity's behalf, the sum total of all Christian theology, namely that '*fecisti nos ad te et inquietum est cor nostrum, donec requiescat in te*' 'you have made us for yourself, and our heart is restless until it rests in you' (*Conf* 1:1:1). The reader of this classic is left in no doubt that it is God who hears this longing prayer. 'It is true that the sense of God as the supreme listener is never absent.'[25] Furthermore, the eavesdropper in Augustine's speech to and with God comes away convinced that God is responding in the real ear of the mind. Were Augustine never to have alluded to the inner ear at all in the *Confessions*, there are signs everywhere that point to the aural: this is a conversation – human words, divinely inspired, in praise of God.

The fifth point revolves around two foundation stones of Augustinian theology. Wisdom is, firstly, understanding of God, which is love of God, who is creator of the world and all that it encompasses. Humanity who walks in that world comes to hear God not through the physical senses but through empirical faith. However, the senses can be taught to discern this faith in truth and love; a discernment, by name the Holy Spirit. 'When God the Holy Spirit … has been given to man … He inflames him with the love of God … For man does not have whence to love God, except from God' (*De trin* 15:17:31). Making sense of all of this means acknowledging that each and every God-created sense is pure gift. The concluding book of what Rowan Williams calls 'one of Augustine's supreme theological achievements',[26] *De Trinitate*, Book 15, is a clarification of the role of the Holy Spirit in enabling a Trinitarian relationship with God. Augustine's theology of the

24. *Confessions*, Bk 1:1.
25. Gibb and Montgomery, p xv.
26. Rowan Williams, 'Trinitate, De', in *Augustine Through the Ages, An Encyclopedia*, p 850.

Holy Spirit is relevant to this work because its conclusions are closely connected to Trinitarian theology. The Holy Spirit is the *ostinato*, (an Italian musical term which literally means persistent or obstinate and refers to any melodic or rhythmic figure that constantly persists) of love in the Trinity. Secondly, wisdom is of the divine (*De trin* 14.1.3). 'Ultimately, there is very little that wisdom is not. It embraces all the Christian values, intellectual as well as moral, and it implies a state of perfection in which the soul is anchored in love, enjoying interior peace and habitual joy in God.'[27]

Augustinian thinking on listening, therefore, charts a path through the theosonic labyrinth, which leads to conversion. The voice is to be listened to; whether it is the analogical voice of Augustine's personal conversion, or the voice of the incarnate Word of God. *In aurem interiorem* – the inner ear literally takes that voice to heart. It is, to quote Reik, 'to be very aware of what is said inside himself, *"écoutes aux voix interieures"'*.[28] The heart is the haven of truth and faith and therein God lies in waiting. The process is complete. 'These words of yours ... the outer ear reported to the understanding mind, whose interior ear was placed close to your eternal Word' (*Conf* 11:6:8). Up to the shock of conversion, God was waiting in the inner ear while Augustine hovered around the outer ear. Hearing the command of God to read and enunciate was the experience of hearing his own voice as the graced voice of the peace of God coming alive.

The relationship, the conversation is consummated. The *Vox Fortis* of God is the object, the message one awaits; the hearing of it – *in aurem interiorem* – is the sense that makes sense out of it. The manner and degree of attention of mind and soul on that same grain of the voice is the power to convert, to become, to change radically, to turn towards. The convert of Milan tells us that 'now is the time for turning unto God' (*En in Ps* 6).[29] Augustine's powerful description of an aural theology, discerning that strong Voice

27. K. Conkey, 'Wisdom' in *The New Catholic Encyclopedia*, p 785.
28. *Listening With the Third Ear*, p 147.
29. *Exposition on the Book of Psalms by St Augustine, Bishop of Hippo*, Oxford: John Henry Parker, 1847, Vol 1, p 38.

of God, is a balance of natural knowledge of the physical sense of
hearing and the metaphysical possibilities of that sense.

One final point that is highly relevant here is that Augustine's
conversion in the midst of psychological turmoil was auditory.
God called him one day in late summer or early autumn of 386 in a
Milanese garden, in a voice which he could only describe analogi-
cally. 'A voice like that of a boy or a girl, I know not which.'[30] This
incessant mantra – *tolle lege, tolle lege*,[31] take read, take read – 'he
certainly regarded … as the vehicle of God's message.'[32] All reading in antiquity was simultaneously spoken out loud, as we will
see below. Thus, from the moment Augustine read *aloud*, the true
story of God's incarnate word became the story of Augustine's
true self. As the sound of the Word of the Lord Jesus Christ res-
onated through him, the ego is silenced and *metanoia* vibrates.
'Hitherto God had spoken to him by his Word, or by the words of
others. Now, as Augustine believed, he received a direct call.'[33]

Patrick of Ireland (d.c. 461)
On this detail of aural conversion, St Patrick's memory speaks.
There are strong resonances between Patrick and Augustine. Both
were bishops: one a North African Bishop of Hippo, the other declared himself Bishop in a tri-lingual – Latin, Irish and English –
letter to the soldiers of Coroticus.[34] Both lived at roughly the same
period in history and were founders of the early Christian
Church. Both were spiritually transformed by the sound of God.

Conversion, however, was far less dramatic for the British
missionary and bishop, who also wrote about it in his own words
in Late or Vulgar Latin, which he also called his *Confessio*. What is
certain, however, is that his conversion and relationship with God
were also clearly aural. Messages from the divine Voice crowded
his dreams. Once, in these dreams, when he was tempted by

30. *The Confessions of Saint Augustine*, trs John K. Ryan, NY: Doubleday,
1960, p 202.
31. *The Confessions of Augustine*, eds Gibb and Montgomery, viii, 29, p 230.
32. Ibid, p.lvi, fn.
33. Gibb and Montgomery, p lvi.
34. See Appendix Two in Joseph Duffy, *Patrick in His Own Words*, p 130.

Satan, he shouted out frantically the name of God, *Helia*; the veils
of deep depression lifted and he writes: 'I believe I was sustained
by Christ my Lord and that his Spirit was even then *calling out*
(*clamabat*) on my behalf.'[35] This is a powerful sonic statement and
event; from the depths of his loud cry, the triune God, in turn resounded and saved. Joseph Duffy summarises Patrician aural and
oral prayer thus – a mental prayer wherein practice makes perfect:
'As the years passed, his prayer grew in intensity. He learned to
listen carefully to the promptings of his mind and to see them as
coming from God…'[36]

All three conversion stories, that of Paul, Augustine and
Patrick, are about aural midwifery. As Karen Armstrong puts it:
Augustine's 'final conversion was an affair of *Sturm und Drang*, a
violent wrench from his past life and a painful rebirth, which has
been characteristic of Western religious experience.'[37]

I will pursue this intellectual metaphor of midwifery now by
briefly intorducing the 5th century BC Athenian philosopher,
Socrates.

35. Ibid, p 17.
36. Ibid, p 63.
37. Armstrong, *A History of God*, p 119 / 120.

Socrates: midwifery and the daimonion

S ocrates worked on two very audio-centric levels. He worked orally and aurally to act as rational midwife and to birth an intellectual conversion in his hearers. Secondly, his inner voice, the personal power or discernment with which he was graced to bring about this, he could only vaguely describe as the *daimonion*, an inner, elusive figure which prompted him constantly aurally.

Midwifery is the practice and art of assisting women at childbirth. *Maieutics* is an intellectual philosophical discipline that refers to a method of instruction of this Athenian philosopher immortalised by Plato. Socrates preached an aural/oral/listening method that assisted the birth of ideas.

Socrates (469?-399 BC) was apparently the son of a midwife. Immortalised in Plato's dialogue, *Theaetetus*, Socrates asks the intelligent, although confused, young man Theaetetus, if he has not heard that he, Socrates, is the son of 'a very famous and solid midwife, Phaenarete.'[1] Socrates poses this question by way of introducing himself as a midwife in certain aspects of that metaphorical role.

But Socrates' 'art of midwifery' is very selective and distinct from the common art of midwifery on two counts: firstly, it attends only to men and secondly, it is concerned only with the delivery of the soul. Its relevance here is that his philosophy was audiocentric. In other words, what is important and relevant to us is that this process or technique of Socratic midwifery was essentially *aural*. Socrates asked questions. He is the *maieutria* – the midwife – of true conversation. Two other central Platonic points about mid-

1. *The Theaetetus of Plato*, trs Benjamin Hall Kennedy, Cambridge: CUP, 1881, p 111.

wifery are interesting for this discussion of religious experience
and sound: only women at that time who were mothers themselves were allowed to act as midwives, 'because human nature is
too weak to acquire an act of which it has no experience.'[2]
Secondly, a midwife hastened or delayed the birthing process 'by
chanting incantations.'[3]

Midwifery in the Bible is a metaphor for God 'creating the cosmos, birthing the first humans, beginning each day, and deliver-
ing the eschaton.'[4] God assisted creation into existence through the
sound of the wind on the face of the waters. From out of silence, the
sound of God's own voice called the cosmos into being (Gen 1).
The first chapter of the Book of Exodus suggests that there were
women named apart to play the role of midwife. There are two
named here – Shiphrah and Puah, both displaying great invent-
iveness in the face of Pharoah's plot for the infanticide of Hebrew
baby boys (Exod 1:15-21).

The Old Testament confirms that early Israelite mothers had
midwives by their sides. Indeed they had important roles in the
birthing process: their role was not only to console the woman
giving birth but also, on occasion, to suggest the name of the fruit
of the womb, according to the manner in which the baby appeared. Tamar's assisting nurse at birthing is responsible for naming. The resourceful Tamar, one of the four women mentioned in
Matthew's account of the ancestors of Jesus (Mt 1:3), is described
as birthing twin sons of Judah. In the original 'breach' birth, the
midwife errs in assuming that the first little hand to appear out of
the womb is that of the first born. She tags the first-seen hand with
crimson thread. But the brightly-tagged hand withdraws again
into the womb and provides the breach or gap for the second son
to emerge first. The son with unthreaded hands is named Perez,
which means 'breach'. His name will always recall and refer to the
midwife's exclamation at first sight. 'What a breach you have
made for yourself!' (Gen 38:28).

Alongside the imagery of midwifery, Socrates talked through

2. *Theaetetus*, p 111.
3. Ibid, p 112.
4. See 'nurse' entry in *Eerdmans Dictionary of the Bible*, p 976.

another metaphor which has audiocentric connotations; the *dai-monion*. This was a gnome/spirit-like voice that dwelled in the lobe of his ear prompting him into action. The *daimonion* was 'his household spirit, living with him in close companionship – that kept off everything that need keeping off ... and advised him of all that he needed to know in advance.'[5]

The prophetic voice whispers itself into the consciousness of being. In the following quote, in pre-Christian thought, and related through Zenophon, Socrates outlines a taxonomy of voices somewhat akin to the three theosonies to be outlined later in this book:

> As for introducing 'new divinites' how could I be guilty of that merely in asserting that a voice of god is manifest to me indicating my duty? Will any one dispute either that thunder utters its 'voice', or that it is an omen of the greatest moment? ... But more than that, in regard to god's foreknowledge of the future and his forewarning to whomsoever he will, these are the same terms, I assert, that all men use, and this is their belief. The only difference between them and me is that whereas they call the sources ... 'birds,' 'utterances,' 'chance meetings,' 'prophets,' I call mine a 'divine' thing. ... I have revealed to many of my friends the counsels which god has given me, and in no instance has the event shown that I was mistaken.'[6]

5. Apuleius, *De Deo Socratis*, XVII, 157, trs A. H. Armstrong. Cited in Micheline Sauvage, *Socrates and the Conscience of Man*, NY: Harper, Men of Wisdom Books, 1962, p 126.
6. Quoted from 'Zenophon on Socrates' Defence to the Jury', *Philosophers Speak for Themselves: From Thales to Plato*, ed. T.V. Smith, Chicago: Chicago Press, 1934, p 107.

Socrates and Jesus Christ: Men of the Word

hristian writers from the early centuries have compared
Socrates and Jesus Christ. Both were men of the word;
both profoundly moved their listeners even to recording
the words they spoke; both were guided by an inner, transcendental voice; and both sought to influence the lives of their
pupils / disciples for the good. Socrates considered himself the
maieutria, the midwife of self-knowledge, *par excellence*; Jesus is
also *maieutria* to a new birth in the kingdom of God through the
sound or voice of the Spirit (Jn 3:8). The Spirit binds us through
sound to Christ and we come to share in the present transfigured
moment where the glory of the past is not lost but carried forward
towards the future of *Basiliea Tou Theou* (the Kingdom of God).
Present, past and future are continuous and uninterrupted in the
new feat of divine listening. The covenant is now between the
heard and listened for Word of God. The one dissimilarity between Christ and Socrates is, as Kelber puts it, that 'unlike
Socrates, Jesus did not have a single literary heir to collect and in-
terpret his message.'[1] Jesus of Nazareth, on the other hand, had
four heirs and hearers. The ultimate similarity is that both men
died for the message they proclaimed.

What Jesus pinpointed forcefully as aural, the Holy Spirit (Jn
3:8), Socrates called the *daimonion* – the animate inner voice sitting
in his ear lobe. God lives in his ear – the divine *Daimonion* – whom,
as Jesus promises, can be heard and learnt about through him (Jn
6:45). This divine *Daimonion* resides in the *Holy Spirit* who crowns
the revelation of Jesus Christ. As Francesco Lambiasi writes: 'All
revelation ... is a love story that comes *a Patre per Filium in Spiritu
Sancto ad Patrem.*'(from Father, through Son in the Holy Spirit to

1. Kelber, *The Oral and the Written Gospel*, p 21.
2. Francesco Lambiasi, 'Holy Spirit' in the *Dictionary of Fundamental
Theology*, p 456.

the Father)[2] The Holy Spirit will teach the apostles to listen and recall the sound of the incarnate word of God (Jn 14:26). The Holy Spirit of truth will enlighten and guide, following the message of what the Spirit hears. 'For he will not speak on his own, but will speak whatever he hears' (Jn 16:13). Kelber too is convinced of the work of the Spirit in an aural understanding of the Word of God: 'If we are to understand gospel in terms of the efficacy of the sounded word, the agency of the Spirit cannot be neglected.'[3]

Angelus Silesius allegorically describes the role of the Holy Spirit in aural and musical terms: 'God is the organist, we are his instrument, his Spirit sounds each pipe and gives the tone its strength.'[4] It is in the presence, the *locus*, of the Holy Spirit that divine and human nature speaks; the Spirit is the interpreter for both. The *pneuma* translates what is said and what is to be listened for by both. This Greek word *pneuma* means 'wind', 'spirit' and 'breath'.

Jesus as God's anointed *Christos* is the ultimate bearer of the Spirit of God. Through baptism of the Sound-Spirit, also claimed by Paul for himself and other Christians, humanity forevermore is anointed by God through the reception of the Holy Spirit (2 Cor 1:21-22). 'The same Holy Spirit who shaped Christ's body and humanity ... used the sacred writings of Israel to shape Christ's religious vision, his way of looking at things and events, of speaking to God and men.'[5]

To summarise: the ear is the highly qualified midwife not just to sounds of the world around, but to the presence of God through those sounds. The one midwifery technique in the birthing of this presence is obedience; complying with the preaching of the Obedient Son of God is allowing the ever-new, ever-old message to be heard and then to act upon it. 'But be doers of the word, and not merely hearers (Jas 1:22). Humanity's openness to the womb of divine sound, the conversational interplay between the Creator and the created is both the oneness and twoness of true prayer.

From its inception, this theology of listening has had to be mid-

---

3. Kelber, *The Oral and the Written Gospel*, p 145.
4. Angelus Silesius, *The Cherubinic Wanderer*, p 125.
5. Guillet, *A God Who Speaks*, p 68.

wife even to the birthing of a new word to embody its implications. 'Theosony' is listening *in a certain way* to the message deep
down in the voice of God. This certain way demands a listening
which is receptive and responsive: in the listening and silent space
God and self are intertwined in the communication. In the womb
of God's self-revelation that carries the Christian, all other sounds
are set free to make room for the sound of the divine. In human
terms, it is enough, in fact plenty, for the little resident in the
womb to just listen to every foetal tone; determining the precise
pitch or meaning of the foetal symphony is irrelevant.
Experiencing the mature soundscape of God, which is Silent
Theosony, is deeply embedded in the dual archetypal elements
that have traditionally and unfortunately been categorised as either masculine or feminine. In terms of human communication,
Kelber defines this three-way encounter as interaction: 'As words are
carried from persons to persons, an interaction develops between
speakers, hearers and message. The process of communication is
contingent on the nature of this interaction.'[6] Such reciprocal human
action calls forth a further step in the journey towards, and conversation with, the Divine. Ricoeur claims that true religious listening calls for 'a second letting go, the abandoning of a more subtle and more tenacious pretension than that of onto-theological
knowledge. It requires giving up (*dessaissement*) the human self in
its will to mastery, sufficiency, and autonomy … It is here where
God has been named.'[7]

6. Kelber, *The Oral and Written Gospel*, p 23.
7. Ricoeur, *Figuring the Sacred*, p 224.

CHAPTER THREE

Theosony and Scripture

Integral transformative interpretation [of the biblical text] is an interaction between a self-aware reader open to the truth claims of the text and the text in its integrity, that is, an interaction that adequately takes into account the complex nature and multiple dimensions of the text and the reader.[1]

---

1. Schneiders, *The Revelatory Text*, p 3.

The Reader and the Voices of the Pages

Reading and hearing scripture is very different from reading and hearing any other tome; it is to live in the revelation of God's self love through the reading/sounding/hearing. The act of reading and simultaneously listening is the very medium of divine Revelation. 'So faith comes from what is heard, and what is heard comes through the word of Christ' (Rom. 10:17). Here is St. Paul echoing the mighty promise of the Johannine Messiah (Jn.5: 24).

Clearly, as the biological appraisal of the ear demonstrates, the functions of the human ear extend beyond the skills and reliability of the other senses. Surely, since the ear offers such effective encounter mechanisms with the physical external world, such encounter efficiency can be applied to the relationship with God. Theosony is the missing, undiscovered category of revelatory theology and the contribution that an aural theology has to offer is considerable.

In the words of Vatican II's *Dogmatic Constitution on Divine Revelation*: 'Sacred scripture is the speech of God as it is put down in writing under the breath of the Holy Spirit' (*DV* Ch II:9).[1] Reading scripture, therefore, is a conversation between the speech of the Prime Author, the human scribe and the reader that takes place in the concrete here-and-now. Reading, listening and responding are all going on simultaneously. In modern biblical studies, this approach is known as synchronic exegesis. The word 'synchronic' is an adjective made up of two Greek words: *syn* meaning 'together and *chronos* meaning 'time'. Literary criticism turns from the author to the manuscript itself, embracing and im-

---

1. *Vatican Council II: The Conciliar and Post Conciliar Documents*, ed Austin Flannery, Dublin: Dominican Publications, 1975, p 755.

plicating the reader/listener. Here is a hermeneutics that begins with words and ends up as meaningful literature; after all, according to Schneiders, 'Scriptures are ... literature.'[2] Scripture is both a classic and a work of art.

David Tracy defines a classic as a 'disclosure of a reality we cannot but name truth ... which surprises, provokes, challenges, shocks and eventually transforms us.'[3] According to this description, scripture is a religious classic. Therefore, it must be submitted to the criteria of the classic for understanding. A work of art becomes a classic for the reader, Tracy believes, 'if the reader is willing to allow that present horizon to be vexed, provoked, challenged by the claim to attention of the text itself.'[4] Every book of the Old and New Testament is a full musical score waiting to be heard in the reading; the tune is familiar; it is already off by heart. That is the God-given grace of scripture, and listening for the theme song of each book is the essence of the theory of theosony.

A dynamic conversation between text and reader is the process that takes place. Embarking on a dialogue with scripture is to oscillate between the mysterious and the revealed. Tracy describes this conversation with the real meaning of the text thus: 'For conversation will demand that movement back and forth between discovery and concealment, respectful awe and critical freedom, suspicion and recovery that characterises the dialectic of authentically critical understanding.'[5]

A conversation, as we have stated again and again here, is all to do with listening. By entering into a dialogical relationship with the written word, the word communicates powerfully through an obedient listening. The reader is given a share, a part in the thoughts and the hopes of the Bible, and is in the very sharing, being prepared to impart that knowledge received. To quote Paul Ricoeur, 'a text is first a link in a communicative chain.'[6] To use the

2. Sandra M. Schneiders, 'History and Symbolism in the Fourth Gospel,' in Marinus de Jonge, ed, *L'Evangile de Jean: Sources, Redaction, Theologie*, BETL 44, Louvain: Louvain University Press, 1977, p 371.
3. Tracy, *The Analogical Imagination*, p 108.
4. Ibid, p 105.
5. Ibid, pp 105/106.
6. Ricoeur, *Figuring the Sacred*, p 219.

analogy of conversation as interpretation and understanding of any text, indeed any classic, be it event, image, symbol, person, is to ignite audible images and the auditory imagination. As opposed to more traditional approaches to biblical literary criticism which, according to Schneiders: 'refers to the exploration of such historical issues as author, time and place of composition, nature and provenance of sources, and socio-religious implications of literary forms,'[7] one method conforms with the experiential approach to theology under scrutiny here.

Reader-response criticism holds that the heart of the matter in reading scripture is the actual human experience, not the abstract information, either didactic or historical. Understanding the Bible depends largely on the reader's capacity to receive the depiction of human experience portrayed in the overall story about God. The real question is what can be seen in sacred scripture through the optic transference to the ear which is the essence of theosony; what can be seen through being heard which has not been heard before?

Schneiders believes that, 'the primary meaning of the text does not lie behind it in history but in it as text ... This is why the reader returns again and again to it, entering more deeply in successive encounters with it into the mystery of conversion ...'[8] Every reading is dynamic, yet evanescent, which means that the deepest transformation is barely perceptible. Every single reading is, in the phrase of George Steiner, 'perpetual re-invention.'[9] This act of devising something new, in literary terms, is the exercise of imaginative or creative powers on the text; responding to the sacred texts of scripture allows one's imagination and creativity to respond to the voice of the God who cries out (Is 40:3) – 'A voice cries out ...' – and who says to cry out (Is 40:6) – 'A voice says "cry out!".'

There is a process involved here, which Steiner describes as humane literacy. 'In that great discourse with the living dead which we call reading, our role is not a passive one ... reading is a mode of action. We engage the presence, the voice of the book. We

---

7. Schneiders, 'Hermeneutics', *The New Jerome Biblical Commentary*, p 1158.
8. Schneiders, 'Born Anew', p 194.
9. Steiner, *Real Presences*, p 126.

allow it entry, though not unguarded, into our inmost.'[10] The reader
is the word. Theosony is concerned with a heuristic approach to the
actual *experience of reading*. It is an experience of reviving and
restoring the order of the sound of things.

Pitting a particular literary passage against the backdrop of
one's own truth experience of human life is only the measure of
one's own experience within that life and is thus limited and finite.
On the other hand, bowing before the possibility of the fulfilment
or completion of the words in our own life invites, welcomes, indeed expects, the exalted company of the Holy Spirit in its relational role between God the Father and God the Son. It is the reader's response to the response of God through scripture. God is the
authority[11] behind the author. Biblical studies to date have been
'more pragmatic (reader-centred)'[12] rather than reader-respon-
sive.[13] 'It is ultimately the *readers* of a text who must determine
what it means.' Mark Patrick Hederman puts it: 'The important
books in life are not the ones which we read: they are the ones
which read us.'[14]

Biblical reader-response criticism goes three steps further. For
Sandra Schneiders, 'to engage the meaning of the text at this level
is to court conversion.'[15] It has to do with a balance of power.
Referring to the prologue of the gospel of St John, Thomas L.
Brodie writes: 'when the prologue is read aloud ... it has unity and
power.'[16] 'We have lost this unity, we whose religion should be
the most incarnate of any. We must rediscover it.'[17] Of all reli-

---

10. George Steiner, *Language and Silence*, p 28
11. The etymology of the word 'author' implicates 'authority'. See Skeat,
p 43
12. Mark, Allen, Powell, *What is Narrative Criticism? A New Approach to
the Bible*, London:SPCK, 1990, p 16
13. Ibid, p 16.
14. Mark Patrick Hederman, *Tarot: Talisman or Taboo? Reading the World
as Symbol*, Currach Press, Dublin, 2003, covernote.
15. Schneiders, *The Revelatory Text*, p 17.
16. Thomas L. Brodie, *The Gospel According to John: A Literary and
Theological Commentary*, NY / Oxford: OUP, 1993, p 136.
17. Simone Weil, *Intimations of Christianity among the Ancient Greeks*, trs
Elisabeth Chase Geissbuhler, London: Routledge Keegan and Paul,
1957, p 137.

gions, Christianity knows the sound of the word; knowing the
sound is through the flip side of language which is listening.

The New Testament shares with all other creative literature its
original impact, which according to Beardslee, is a 'deformation'
of language, a stretching of language to a new metaphorical
meaning which shocked the hearer into a new insight'.[18] 'Every
work of art is a dynamic structure whose purpose is to create its
viewer/reader/hearer.'[19] This, Schneiders calls 'Aesthetic Surrender'.[20] The reader must surrender, give way to the message, must
obey the call inherent in the message. For Steiner, the word, read
or spoken, is there to awaken to the resonance of 'its entire previous history ... To read fully is to restore all that one can of the im-
mediacies of value and intent in which speech actually occurs.'[21]
How one scrutinises words and sentences is the measure of how
one hears and listens to them.

The temporal and the spatial merge through the eye and the
ear. Times past are alive in the present space for the reader. The
future lies in the power of the listening to convert the reader. The
reader *is* in the text. 'We must imagine ourselves in it and moving
with it.'[22]

Reader-response criticism is a shared experience that resides
not in a past historical age and social culture. The reader sounds
the depths of the fertile space between the written word and the
eye. This sounding listens for the voice behind and within the
words. It listens for the wider event from out of which the language, the vocabulary on the page, was conceived. 'Indeed the
words of God, expressed in the words of men, are in every way
like human language, just as the Word of the eternal Father, when
he took on himself the flesh of human weakness, became like men'
(*DV* 3).[23] Reader responsive listening 'means that from the vast,

18. Beardslee, *Literary Criticism of the New Testament*, p 11.
19. Schneiders, *The Revelatory Text*, p 172-173.
20. Ibid, p 172.
21. Steiner, *After Babel*, p 24.
22. Morton T. Kelsey, *The Other Side of Silence: A Guide to Christian
Meditation*, London: SPCK, 1976, p 210.
23. *Vatican Council II*, ed Austin Flannery, p 758.

entangled legacy of the past, criticism will bring to light and sustain that which speaks to the present with particular directness or exaction … that which enters into dialogue with the living.'[24]

Because scripture is no textbook or manual, its court of last appeal is in the realm of imagining. Through the powerful storehouse of memory, God is suggested and known above and beyond what is actually present in sight and sound. Imagining oneself through oral discourse with God in prayer finally yields to the ultimate silent theosony. It is no illusion or false mental image or conception. The coda of all codas is entered most frequently through the protective veil of silence. If, in the depths and layers of that silence, all is mute and overwhelming, if that silence is dumb and impenetrable, then theosony fills the void and dispels the doubt. The experience of the mystic is a huge treasure trove of theosony here.

'Writing, in its turn, is restored to living speech by means of the various acts of discourse that reactualise the text.'[25] Ricoeur clarifies: 'Reading and preaching are such actualisations of writing into speech.'[26] In this sense, a hermeneutics of scripture is an event, a performance, where the reader is actively participating in the silent drama of the text rather than being a passive interpreter of inherited doctrines. The experience embraced in *listening* is the crucial occurrence that leaves the impression. The scriptural word event is a movement from the page to the inner ear of the reader. It must be an interaction which is living, active and transformative which invites and allows the Holy Spirit to mix and match the written word, the sound of the word, and the resonance which amplifies that sound in the human body. It is the written word become incarnate in memory, and later 'by heart'.

Reader-response criticism is, as is deconstructionism, an offshoot of literary criticism. Deconstructionism seeks to 'understand the meaning conveyed by a text *to those who read it* rather than the

24. George Steiner, *Language and Silence: Essays 1958-1966,* London: Faber and Faber, 1967, p 26.
25. Paul Ricoeur, *Figuring the Sacred,* p 219.
26. Ibid, p 219.

meaning which the original author intended to convey.'[27] Past
concedes to the present – the future can only be determined
through the reader's ability to walk the verbal labyrinth, which is
the text. The reader/hearer receives the text in the present, not in
the past of the ancient writer. In contemporary post-modern,
post-structuralist literary circles, Steiner tells us 'it is the reader
who produces the text ... It is in the reader's free experience and
ontologically irresponsible response that worthwhile games can
be played with meaning.'[28] In other words, it is not what the actual
texts precisely say or from what context and reference point they
emanated. What is important in literary/linguistic criticism is
how the text is actually heard and made meaningful to the present
individual engaged with the text. According to Begbie, it is simply
that texts no longer 'point to authors or things or events'.[29]

Texts point to, and at, the reader, not the author. This is not to
reduce the text to the subjectivity of the reader, or indeed the
author, and all of his or her deafnesses and limitations. The
majesty of a classic text is the mystery of its own achieved autonomy in the very event of its form. But the reader is brought in on the
story. The text has the final say in divine revelation. In the words
of Schneiders: 'revelation ... lies not in the deeds of the earthly
Jesus in their historical facticity but in our encounter with him
through the written account of those deeds.'[30] This encounter is
more than the reading, the listening and the silence; the Holy
Spirit permits the answer to two-way, dialogical prayer which is
the important and sobering principle of God's love: 'I will wait for
the God of my salvation; my God will hear me' (Mic 7:7).

A methodology of theosonic biblical criticism is one of aural
recognition of scripture: divine revelation eventuates in listening
to the word as something previously heard in the mind as true; a
true realisation of the spoken, sounded and listened for Word of
God's self-announcement. The reader must be 'all ears' and alert

27. Jeremy Begbie, 'The Gospel, the arts and our culture,' in *The Gospel and
Contemporary Culture*, ed Hugh Montefiore, London: Mowbray, 1992, p 67.
28. Steiner, *Real Presences*, p 126.
29. Begbie, 'The Gospel, the arts and our culture,' p 67.
30. Sandra M. Schneiders, 'Born Anew', *Theology Today*, 44, 1987/88, p 195.

to the sonic communication that is ingrained in the voices of the pages. In the act of recognition, divine revelation is realised where the imaginative world of unheard divine sound federates the mundane world of human word of mouth, which has been inscribed in the Book of Books. Beardslee, the pioneer of such literary criticism, has this to say on the reader/text conversation which is critical of previous theologians: 'The reader's participation ... as an intrinsic part of entry into the imaginative world of the work ... is toward inclusiveness, toward the understanding or appreciation of a variety of visions, rather than toward exclusiveness, as is the tendency of so much theology.'[31]

To summarise on a listening-response criticism inherent in the concept of theosony is to build on the endorsements presented above and to suggest another listening model which concretises the aural in approaching sacred scripture. The real question is what can we hear in scripture that we have not heard before? The secondary challenge is how to hear a new arrangement of an old familiar theme. The eye and the ear work closely here in tandem. The eye hands on the object to the ear in the relay race of God's self-revelation. It is the ear that brings the object to the winning post. These are potent actualities: a full score in music is the silent, visual reality of the sound. To the composer of the piece and to the skilled 'reader', every written dot, separate or combined, can be heard instantly in the silence of the inner ear. The ear takes over the sound bite; the meaning is carried and discovered through the sound.

The discipline which theosony endeavours to purport is how to listen, to give attention in order to hear and understand the meaning of that delicate eternal reverberation. There is no silent reading. Even when we read silently, the words are reverberating unconsciously in the inner ear. Understanding is reached by the sounds which the words of scripture make when sounded, never by the pattern which appears before our eyes on the silent page; written words are almost meaningless until, like the stemmed dots and mystifying rests that adorn the musical stave, they happen in sound.

31. William A. Beardslee, *Literary Criticism of the New Testament*, Philadelphia, PA: Fortress Press, 1970, p 13.

On a very personal note, I experienced this reality. In 2009 I wrote an aural autobiography – *Listen with the Ear of the Heart*. The response to the daunting undertaking was beautiful. So many people, strangers and friends alike, responded, and continue to do so. But the persistent, recurring theme – the *ostinato* – from the people who knew me personally was that they could hear the sound of my own voice as they read.

Yet in our sacred Judaeo-Christian scriptures, we are dealing with the written word that has endured for three thousand years; the fact is that the optic can co-operate with the aural to further enhance the power, the understanding of the message. Effective reading depends on effective hearing. This also involves the idea of understanding. After the language confusion at Babel, human beings could no longer 'hear', that is, 'understand' one another (Gen 11:7).

The oral/aural nature of scripture

Reciting and listening to Jewish scripture are the foundation stones upon which Christianity was built. A renowned theological scholar has this to say: 'An oral tradition was both current and influential in the first century of Christianity's existence.'[1] 'Influential' is the important, relevant word here; what influences, is that which has the power to sway and transform, to inspire and encourage by means of its orality and total sound. In and through the spoken word of mouth, the power of the Christian message is effected in the most powerful manner. The key that unlatches the door into the written word is the secret theosonic key of orality and aurality. Put another way, there is a secret theosonic door into the world behind the text. It is the door that opens out from the eye, giving access through the halls of the ear to the inner sanctum of the praying heart. Here again is an anthropology which embraces body, mind and spirit. Silent reading is so familiar that this fact can be muted. The spoken word, not to mention the phenomenon of sound, has survived for at least twenty thousand years; only for the last four thousand years has writing been around. If the life-span of humanity were measured in terms of an hour, writing arrived some twenty minutes ago; sounding, listening, hearing and silence, along with the God who created the world and all that is within it, were there at cosmic conception and birth.

Oral and aural experience was nothing new in the history of biblical revelation. Hans Urs von Balthasar says: 'Revelation never falls directly from heaven to make supra-mundane mysteries known to men. God speaks to man from within the world, taking man's own experiences as a starting point, entering so intimately

1. Harry Y. Gamble, *Books and Readers in the Early Church: A History of Early Christian Texts*, New Haven/London: Yale University Press, 1995, p 32.

into his creature that the divine *kenosis*, to be fulfilled later in the incarnation, already has its beginning in the word of the Old Testament.'[2] The task of this section of the book is to explore the reality of the oral and aural implications of the linguistic term 'word of God' as applied to the Christian scriptures. Firstly, it is necessary to reiterate the basic distinctions and similarities that the two words – oral and aural – embrace.

Oral

Oral is what is uttered by the voice and spoken through the mouth, the sound produced by air passing over the vocal cords. The word is formed from the stem of the Latin word '*os/oris*' meaning 'mouth'. Add to this the suffix '*al*' again from the Latin '*alis*'. 'Al' in this context and in the context of 'aur-*al*' means 'of or pertaining to,' 'connected with,' 'of the nature of,' 'like,' 'befitting,' etc.'[3] The word 'oral' has theological implications, being etymologically connected to *orare*, not meaning 'to mouth' but 'to pray'. The word 'adore' meaning to worship comes from the Latin *adorare* literally 'to pray to'. There is a vital distinction to be made here: oral and verbal are not synonymous in this work. What is oral is uttered, spoken and *heard*; verbal 'applies to the words, spoken or written, in which thought or feeling is conveyed: a *verbal picture*.[4]

Reading aloud is dialogue between voice and ear. The voice *enhances* the aural experience. The written word comes alive to the world through the sound vibrations it creates in the external world. Storr makes the point that the very act of reading one's own writings as if hearing them aloud actually enhances the final text. 'Writers who "hear" their sentences as if read aloud tend to write better prose than those who merely see them.'[5]

How many people had access to reading in antiquity? Harry Gamble proposes some statistics around literacy in the early church: 'The extent of literacy in the ancient church was limited.

---

2. Von Balthasar, *Word and Revelation*, p 102.

3. *The New American Dictionary*, p 28.

4. Ibid, p 851.

5. Storr, *Music and the Mind*, p 41.

Only a small minority of Christians were able to read, surely no more than an average of 10-15 percent of the larger society and probably fewer.'[6] The early Christians were almost totally dependent on the spoken word. What are the implications of this for the few writers of the time? The answer is obvious: 'Knowing this, ancient authors wrote their texts as much for the ear as for the eye.'[7] It was the ear that governed and perhaps still governs most understanding. 'Sound has a pervasive quality: it permeates one's whole physical existence.'[8]

Aural

Aural means that which is received by the organ of the ear. 'So faith comes from what is heard' (Rom 10:17). Again, the word 'aural' is coined from the Latin *auris* meaning 'ear' and the same suffix *al*, meaning 'of or connected with'. Therefore, the aural is ear-work to be heard and listened to. Words isolated or in the context of other words, are physical sounds emitted, sent forth from the vocal chords. Scriptures in early Christianity were almost exclusively auricular. The tongue of the preacher was the teacher. To listen was to learn. 'What is heard must first be preached.'[9] In the very act of listening to that tongue, energy and faith are restored. 'The Lord God has given me the tongue of a teacher, that I may know how to sustain the weary with a word' (Is 50:4). The listening experience of this scripture servant is in theosonic realms.

The aural has to do with community and culture. Inherent in every culture is a familiar linguistic communication. 'A kind of natural rhetoric occurs in all societies and some kind of formal pattern is necessary for communication of any kind.'[10] There is interplay between the teacher, the storyteller and the listener. That speaker/listener relationship and the formulation of a discourse

6. Gamble, *Books and Readers in the Early Church*, p 10.
7. Ibid, p 30.
8. Werner H. Kelber, *The Oral and the Written Gospel: The Hermeneutics of Speaking and Writing in the Synoptic Tradition, Mark, Paul and Q*, Philadelphia: Fortress Press, 1983, p 146.
9. Ibid, p 146.
10. Achtemeier, 'Omne Verbum Sonat', p 20.

on the actual *experience* of that relationship are at the heart of
theosony. The major question implicated in the aural is how the
sound of Jewish scripture can be heard and imagined through the
murmurs of translation, which is another resonance entirely. A
theosonic theory would address this problematic question by
evoking the phenomenon of transposition in musical practice.
Music transposition is when the notation or performance of music
in its original pitch is altered to answer more agreeably the needs
of a given situation or person. The same musical intervals assume
a new sight and sound. Translation is transposition; the rendering
of scripture into the familiar language of the reader just reorders
the code of the original message so that it can be deciphered and
heard more easily. The transposition is made through the wisdom
of the triune God who knows the perfect pitch for each one which
will be an evocation from the pitch of the world to the pitch of the
divine. All languages have sacred, mysterious words that are revealed through the phonetics. Soundless, such words are only
half-heard.

To conclude, the aural relates to the sense of hearing. The aural
is about what is perceptible to the ear. A listener attends to cosmic
sound, to the voice of another, or to the voice of the page, before
reading merges into listening. All keen listening is metamorphos-
ing and transmutations. Listening with the ear of the heart –
Ausculta as the Prologue to the Rule of St Benedict advises – is to be
completely changed in character and in form. From the act of
choosing to listen in the first place, the change takes place through
various kinds of listening until the ultimate change is achieved
that is complete conversion and oneness in the triune God. The
rapid transformation, the metamorphosis, from the chrysalis to
the butterfly is aural. It is the *how,* not the *what,* that is the birthing
process to what is really heard, understood and ultimately communicated. The artist Bridget Riley counsels the observer face-to-
face: 'You will have to learn to listen, because it is through a special sort of listening, a sort of "listening-in", that one learns how to
speak.'[11]

11. Bridget Riley, *The Eye's Mind: Collected Writings 1965-1999,* London:
Thames & Hudson, 1999, p 211.

Prayer is the little implement
Through which Men reach
Where Presence – is denied them.
They fling their speech
By means of it – in God's Ear –
If then He hear –
This sums the Apparatus
Comprised in Prayer –[12]

There are four important aspects to a tradition that is both oral and aural, which are relevant and desire to be brought to the table of this phenomenology of theosony.

Firstly, any consideration of scripture must begin with the recognition of the *integral role* that the oral and aural Old Testament played in the fulfilment of the New Testament event. Christianity emanated from Judaism and was moulded, orally and aurally, by Jewish culture. St Augustine summarises: 'Christ teaches, his inspiration teaches. Where his inspiration and his anointing are not, words from outside make useless sounds.'[13] Theosony suggests that the actual experience of the oral and aural component of God's loving message of God's self-dissemination to humanity is crucial in the overall religious experience.

Secondly, the concept of the tradition of committing Hebrew scriptures to memory aurally, rather than through writing, is important. Hebrew scriptures, described by George Steiner as 'archetypal foundational language-acts in our civilisation,'[14] were learned 'off by heart' and retained there by every Jew. When some truth is deposited in the inner ear, 'by heart', the remembrance of it is in the recognition of knowing it before. At the heart of a theory of theosony is the concept of recognition, realising and respecting the God of sound.

The third ramification has to do with the *folkloric, storytelling* nature of scripture. Basically, the story of the Bible is a 'once upon

12. Emily Dickinson, *The Complete Poems*, London / Boston: Faber and Faber, 1970, p 210.
13. Rettig, *St Augustine*, p 172.
14. George Steiner, *No Passion Spent: Essays 1978-1996*, London / Boston: Faber and Faber, 1996, p [x].

a time, there was the word' story with a happy ending: God is saviour and redeemer of all humanity. The power of storytelling is in the telling, the sounding and the listening. Suspense is heightened; tension is resolved in the cadences, the momentary ends of the word sounds. Questions are asked and answered in the sonic forum. Theosonic methodology puts forward the central importance of the spoken story as religious act. Speaker and listener are related in the act, quite apart from the content and information imparted. The meaning and the power of sacred language surfaces from the actual sounding of the story by the living. This has pragmatic implications for liturgical practice, which will only be touched on here.

The final point is that, in ancient times, reading was a *trilogy*, a three-part alliance of contemporaneous reading, speaking and listening. The spoken in antiquity accompanied both reading and writing. A word read or written was a word spoken aloud. This tradition offers imaginative levels of religious experience; to write a passage of scripture or a psalm while speaking it, is birthing the sacred sound to the world in sight and sound. Before getting to the heart of these four matters, there are two observations to be made. Firstly, in contemporary Western theology, the first premise above, the interrelationship between the Old and the New Testament, is widely accepted. The remaining three, memorisation, the spoken narration of a chain of events which is story-telling, and the audio-centric nature of reading and writing, are largely ignored. Secondly, within the context of Western theology, it appears that when the term 'oral' is used, either in firsthand or in borrowed quotations, it is intended, unless specifically implied, to include the 'aural' also. In fact, the term 'aural' does not figure at all, to the best of my knowledge. It is significant that the oral phenomenon dominates the aural, particularly in theology, almost to the exclusion of the latter. The importance of the aural experience of God, the thrust of this study, is largely ignored in biblical scholarship in favour of orality. Jewish theological reflection does refer to 'the mouth-to-ear tradition' however.[15]

15. See Hayim Goren Perelmuter, 'Conversation Two: A Response to Clemens Thoma' in *Reinterpreting Revelation and Tradition: Jews and Christians in Conversation*, Wisconsin: Sheed & Ward, 2000, p 64.

Contingency and continuity

The Old and New Testaments are related in a definite and creative manner. One cannot be understood without reference to the other. They are both parts of the same historical conversation between God and creation that is the mystery of salvation. The common denominator is the truth of the word of God that hovers over the waters of scriptural aqueducts. This entire tapestry of both Testaments is embroidered primarily with a sonic thread. In short, the inherent power of the Bible is lost in a context that excludes the heard, the spoken word.

In the history of the Judaeo-Christian scriptures, as Domeris states, 'biblical revelation is essentially an oral experience. Accounts of theophany are full of *sound*.'[1] The hearing sense is the prime figure of speech in the Bible. References to hearing, listening to the Word and to silence are all employed as metaphors and similes, where they are used out of their ordinary or literal locutions or expressions. Leland Ryken summarises: 'It is hard to find a page of the Bible that does not contain figurative language.'[2] The metaphorical 'speech of God as it is put down in writing under the breath of the Holy Spirit' (*DV* 9) thunders forth, illuminating not just what one can hear but what one ought to and should listen to. The act of listening is fundamental to God's self-disclosure to the universe; it is partly, as Jonathan Sachs suggests, through 'going back to the sources of our faith and *hearing* in them something we missed before.'[3]

The Old Testament relies on the *word* of a God who historically saves and directs 'his people, Israel'. It is well documented in bib-

1. William R. Domeris 'Voice' in *Dictionary of the Bible*, ed D.N. Freedman, Cambridge, UK: William B. Eerdmans, 2000, p 1360. Italics mine.
2. Leland Ryken, 'Literature, The Bible as,' in *The Oxford Companion to the Bible*, p 462.
3. Jonathan Sachs, *The Dignity of Difference*, p 19. Italics mine.

lical scholarship that the Hebrew scriptures were first heard and
listened to long before they were read. Kelber sums it up: 'The
Hebrew scriptures were a highly oral and aural reality in ancient
Jewish and Christian communities ... the visual experience of the
text was secondary to its oral presentation.'[4] The Hebrew word
haga, appearing particularly in the Book of Psalms and the Book of
Isaiah, means to learn the oral precepts of the Torah while pronouncing them in a low, murmuring tone. Achtemeier suggests
that *haga* refers to both reading aloud and vocalised writing.[5] It is
the learning by the mouth through to the heart. It is the mouth that
teaches and utters wisdom. *Os justi meditabitur sapientiam* (Ps
36:30). The same word refers to the praying psalmist crying to
God for help: 'Give heed to my groaning' (Ps 5:1). Ancient vedantic scriptures, Tame states, 'never were primarily intended to be
read and quietly studied, but were sacred hymns which were intoned and sung.'[6]

The Jewish practice of vocalising sacred scriptures is in response to the command of the Lord in Deuteronomy: 'Surely this
commandment ... is not too far away ... the word is very near to
you; it is in your mouth and in your heart' (Deut 30:11, 14). The
commandment of the Lord is a knowing in full heart and soul
through the mouth, orally, into *the heart*, aurally. It is a manage-
able, understandable knowledge freely available to everyone
who chooses to listen obediently. In the words of Joseph
Blenkinsopp on this particular passage, 'The law is not esoteric
knowledge requiring that a chosen intermediary like Enoch as-
cend to heaven in order to communicate it. It is recited ... and God
has now put the disposition to obey it in the heart.'[7] In the act of
prayer, scripture was half-read and half-heard.

There is a danger here of oversimplification and subjectivism
which must temper any discussion on interpreting scripture as
God speaking directly to humanity. Karl Rahner poses the rele-

4. Kelber in *Teaching Oral Traditions*, p 330.
5. Achtemeier, Omne Verbum Sonat, p 15, fn 85.
6. Tame, *The Secret Power of Music*, p 174.
7. Joseph Blenkinsopp, 'Deuteronomy' in *The New Jerome Biblical Commentary*, p 107.

vant question: 'How can the content of a human consciousness, which in consciousness has become a part of man's subjectivity and suffers from all its limitations, and is ultimately to be interpreted as the effect of this human causality, be heard and understood as the word of God?'[8] The impetus *behind* the engagement is one of remembrance of God's everlasting and abiding salvation covenant. The impetus *towards* the engagement is the promise of all future conversations to come. Within the general phenomenology of sound, the criteria which distinguish the sound of the Word of God have to do with remembrance, memory, recognition and naming. Humanity overhears the unheard-of whisperings of divine hope through human consciousness, which is heightened and highlighted through memory and promise.

In the New Testament, the message of salvation history and God's incarnate Word is a direct invitation to share in the life of the Trinity. Scripture resounds with the audible profusion of life which is the Father, with the reality of truth that is Jesus Christ, and the exuberance of love that is the Holy Spirit. Life, truth and love are the trilogy of voices of the book of Christ which Angelus Silesius recommends as the bestseller of life: 'Too many books cause stress; who reads one thoroughly/(I mean the book of Christ) gets well eternally.'[9]

Faith in scripture is the *conversation* between the text and the living of what it is and what it says. The three-way conversation between scripture, reader/listener and God reveals the glory of God abundantly in the voice of Jesus Christ. The interpreter at work both below on the part of humanity and above from God, is the Holy Spirit.

The relationship between both testaments, von Balthasar writes, 'for the biblical personages, for Christ himself and for the fathers of the church was always considered the fundamental, inexhaustible proof of the truth of God's word.'[10] The entire corpus of scripture is what God is and does for humanity from the beginning until the end of the world.

8. Rahner, *The Practice of Faith*, p 78.
9. Angelus Silesius, *The Cherubinic Wanderer*, p 109.
10. Von Balthasar, *Word and Revelation*, p 98.

The New Testament sings the same song of God through the uniqueness of Jesus Christ. In the words of Pawlikowski, 'The uniqueness of the Christ event arises from the complete identity of the work of Jesus, as well as his words … with the work of God.'[11] What Jesus heard from God is the message of Christianity; Jesus talked and walked in the recognition of the sounding message from his Father. The truth of this epoch-making fact is *au fond* of theosony. The incarnate Word of God is the main character of the scriptural drama. It is '… the evolutionary character of all sacred history, the conception of the church as a growing body and this body being the total Christ.'[12] 'The New Testament perfects the Old; but the Old began the New.'[13] The Old Testament shares in the work of the New. It is one and the same story of the revelation and the question of God that is inherited by humankind.

Christ is the fulfilment of the religion of his ancestors. He adhered to the tenets of faith of the earliest biblical character known to him in Abraham, and through the leader of the Israelites in their Exodus, Moses. Jesus Christ is within, and of, the faith of Horeb, the mountain of God. The important point here in this familiar fact is that Jesus was keenly aware and conscious of the power of the spoken, living, sounding, heard word and this is the clear message of the evangelist Matthew. 'But blessed are … your ears, for they hear. Truly, I say to you, many prophets and righteous men longed to … hear what you hear and did not hear it (Mt 13:16, 17). The unknown Jewish-Christian writer of the Letter to the Hebrews is acutely aware of the inherited power inherent in the incarnate word of Christ. The Letter begins firmly rooted in an aural reference to the diversity of God's speech to the ancestors and the prophets: 'Long ago God spoke to our ancestors in many and various ways … but in these last days he has spoken to us by a Son … he sustains all things by his powerful word' (Heb 1:1, 2, 3). Humanity is reminded of the primacy of the spoken Word.

11. John T. Pawlikowski, 'Conversation One: The Search for a New Paradigm for the Christian-Jewish Relationship: A Response to Michael Signer' in *Reinterpreting Revelation and Tradition*, p 38.
12. Jean Leclercq OSB, *The Love of Learning and the Desire for God: A Study of Monastic Culture*, trs Catharine Misrahi, London: SPCK, 1974, p 101.
13. Ibid, p 101.

Sound preceded sight in antiquity. Writing was the privilege of the few; the ability to read, likewise. Early writers, therefore, were keenly aware of this and knew that what they were writing down was meant to be heard, spoken and listened to. Achtemeier puts it: '[O]rganisation of written materials will depend on sound rather than sight for its effectiveness.'[14] This is the most important piece of knowledge and the most pertinent point of this theory of theological listening. The written word is a poor reflection of the listened to word. Every word transmitted to manuscript was heard in the mind as 'events in sound'[15] first and foremost. Every author of antiquity wrote first for the ear. Add to this the point that every written word in ancient history was spoken simultaneously. The spoken word could exist on its own; the written word, never. All writing was an *anamnesis* (Gk, 'a recalling to mind, a recollection, a remembrance'): The written word was a recalling of past words spoken and heard. Achtemeier holds that 'writing itself in the earliest Greek period served simply as a reminder of oral pronouncements …'[16] In the distant past of Christianity, the oral and the aural continued and survived long after the word was written down. Kelber summarises: 'The oral medium was tenacious and literacy by itself slow in undermining the world of oral values.'[17]

Just as these scriptures have survived through many copyists, these copyists in turn reflect the enigmas and imaginations of oral tradition. 'Although the gospels are written, the tradition behind them was orally proclaimed and the marks of orality are still strong in the written accounts,' is how Raymond Brown explains it.[18] Alan Dundes concurs: '… one goal of which was to reconstruct the oral state that immediately preceded the written Bible.'[19]

14. Achtemeier, Omne Verbum Sonat, p 19.
15. Kelber, *The Oral and the Written* p 15.
16. Achtemeier, Omne Verbum Sonat, p 9.
17. Kelber, *The Oral and the Written*, p 17.
18. Raymond E. Brown, *An Introduction to the New Testament*, NY: Doubleday, 1997, p 28.
19. Alan Dundes, *Holy Writ as Oral Lit: The Bible as Folklore*, NY / Oxford: Rowman & Littlefield Publishers, 1999, p 13.

The gospel, according to the letters of Paul, is a faith that is born of sound and hearing. To hear is to be saved through faith. God's call, the sound of God, 'gives life to the dead and *calls* into existence the things that do not exist' (Rom 4:17). Paul immediately 'transports us into a particular sensory field, that of sound, speaking and hearing.'[20] This ambassador of the gospel to the gentiles, according to Kelber, 'leaves no doubt that the gospel, when it came alive, was spoken aloud and, if it is to bring life again, must be sounded afresh.'[21] The gospels are historical proofs of how people listened to and heard about the death and resurrection of the Messiah of God. Welner Kelber condenses the point: 'Death … is overcome by the very medium of life, the sounding of God's call.'[22]

In short, the people of the gospels were an aural / oral people; to hear the word of God was the essential, obedient religious experience. This first point is well acknowledged and researched in the field of Christian theology. By simply declaring it here and repeating the point, I intend to argue for a recovery of the particularly powerful, transformative, sensory field of *sound, speaking and hearing*.

20. Kelber, *The Oral and the Written*, p 143.
21. Ibid, p 144.
22. Ibid, p 144.

'Off by heart'

Speaking, thinking, committing to memory and acting upon the heart-work is a powerful quartet of human experience. It is a hierarchical process: speech or sound is first heard, once taken in through the ear it proceeds to the heart wherein it resides from then on, constantly alert to be reconvoked and acted upon. The learning 'off by heart' of the sound of the sacred word was essential to being. It is a very mature practice in the age-old pursuit of wisdom and spiritual advancement. However, Philippe Borgeaud suggests that: 'In the Christian tradition, the role of memorisation seems to be much less important …'[1] What a shame! What is commited to the memory – *anamnesis* – is never forgotten and never gone back on. It will never break your word or your promise. John Cassian, Abbot of Marseilles and St Benedict's acknowledged mentor on monasticism, pragmatically refers to this naturally in his treatise on how to grow in virtue: 'Each one does the task laid on him, such as memorising a psalm or some passage of scripture …'[2] Although this treatise was addressed to male monks in the fifth century, it has much to contribute in any and all of our spiritual quests for divine wisdom and discernment. Some good senses never change.

What does learning 'by heart', memorisation, signify in terms of techniques and effectiveness? The basic technique of retaining or storing an idea in the memory can become a reality through two sensory media: visual images facilitate recall through association of sight and sound and secondly, audial sound-patterns embody meaning and emotions too which make them unforgettable. In the overall epistemology of theosony, that is, the knowledge of God,

1. Philippe Borgeaud, *The Encyclopedia of Religion*, vol 9, p 369.
2. John Cassian, The Monastic Institutes, Chapter 15, in *The Monastic Institutes: On the Training of a Monk and The Eight Deadly Sins*, trs Jerome Bertram, London: The Saint Austin Press, 1999, p 25.

which is to be acquired through the ear, memorisation is an important prayer method. But it is a lost art in contemporary society. Steiner regrets the danger to heart knowledge: 'There is no doubt that patterns of articulate speech, reading habits ... are under pressure ... we know less *by heart*.'[3]

In terms of the theological memorisation, visual images of parables and narratives arise naturally and easily from the heard word. On the other hand, catch phrases, pithy prayers become automatic and constant through sound patterns. For example, the Greek exclamation, *Kyrie Eleison* or the Hebrew *Hallelujah* do not necessarily call up visual imagery although their mysterious resonances continue to put us under a divine spell. It is the hidden aural sensation which Ted Hughes depicts as 'almost as a physical momentum of inevitability, a current of syntactical force purposefully directed like the flight of an arrow in the dark.'[4] Jacques Guillet expresses the voice of God in a way that implicates human memory and attention: 'Hearing God speak in scripture is both a human operation, involving intelligence and attention and a spiritual one, involving adhesion to God.'[5] The human operation, the human work is committing this scriptural voice to memory. In short, it is to fuse the human and the divine work through memorisation.

Lectio Divina/Audio Divina

Such power of remembered language is particularly religious and taps into the ancient practice transmitted by a fourth century monk, John Cassian and now known as *lectio divina*. The Irish theologian, Una Agnew, describes this daily monastic activity: 'Each day the monk took a passage of scripture, his "sacred page", read it slowly [aloud], paying attention to each word and its various shades of meaning, and as the Holy Spirit illumined the page with insight, the monk was counselled to stay where he found

3. George Steiner, *After Babel: Aspects of Language and Translation*, London: OUP, 1975, p 467.
4. Ted Hughes, *By Heart: 101 Poems to Remember*, London: Faber & Faber, 1997, p xv.
5. Jacques Guillet, *A God Who Speaks*, trs Edmond Bonin, Dublin: Gill and Macmillan, 1979, p 68.

nourishment, to ruminate, repeat it continuously until he had learned it by heart. Passages thus learned belonged to the memory of the heart and led the monk to prayer.'[6] In other words, the power of the spoken word committed to heart and memory in the work of the self-revelation of the triune God is not confined to the monk alone but is the privilege and grace of all humanity. One living proof of this prayer method in action was the Monaghan poet, Patrick Kavanagh. Agnew proposes that Kavanagh discovered the power of such a method of attuning himself to the Holy Spirit and maintained this as an exercise into later life.[7]

Such monastic practices have much to share outside of the cloister structure. What we are suggesting here is a form of this ritual – an *Audio Divina* – *sacred hearing* counterpart: A spoken word, a cosmic sound – the sound of a blackbird – is heard; it reflects or considers a thought through the very listening; and it remains in the ear of the heart to foster and nurture a secret room in the house of the heart where the word resonates in the inner ear to bring the soul to God.

Jean Leclercq suggests the connection between memorisation and contemplation in his description of *meditari*, which is a verb meaning 'to think over, contemplate, reflect: to practice, study.' The term *meditari*, implies '… thinking of a thing with the intent to do it … to prepare oneself for it, to prefigure it in the mind, to desire it, in a way, to do it in advance, briefly, to practise it.'[9] The important thing is to pronounce the words in order to commit them to memory. 'To speak, to think, to remember, are the three necessary phases of the same activity.'[10] I would wish to add 'to listen' to this list.

Learning by heart is the fullest expression of one's whole body and being – *Audio Divina* – I listen today with an open heart and I hear the Divine. Learning 'by heart' is the process by which 'the

6. Una Agnew SSL, *The Mystical Imagination of Patrick Kavanagh: 'A Buttonhole in Heaven?'*, Dublin: Columba Press, 1998, p 98.
7. Agnew, *The Mystical Imagination of Patrick Kavanagh*, p 98.
8. See *Collins Latin Dictionary*, p 132.
9. Leclercq OSB, *The Love of Learning and the Desire for God*, p 20.
10. Ibid, p 21.

mouth pronounces it ... the memory ... fixes it ... the intelligence
... understands its meaning and ... the will ... desires [it] to be put
into practice.'[11] Learning by heart is what the ear first hears, understands and then acts upon. Leclerq says it is all about practice:
'To practise a thing by thinking on it, is to fix it in the memory, to
learn it.'[12]

A distinction should be made here between learning by heart
and learning by rote (interestingly pronounced 'wrote'). The latter
is to commit to memory in a mechanical way without any
thought, understanding or empathy with the meaning. This per-
functory, unconscious memorising by rote, the poet Ted Hughes
holds, is 'for most people the least effective'[13] remembering technique. Such emotionless, spiritless learning is anathema in a theological context where meaning and understanding are based on
love and spirit-filled emotion for God. In stark contrast, Hughes
goes as far to say that rote work 'creates an aversion to learning.'[14]

------

11. Ibid, p 22.
12. Ibid, p 20.
13. Hughes, *By Heart*, p ix.
14. Ibid, p ix.

Simone Weil on memorisation

Two experiences of hearing for Simone Weil are exemplary of the power of the theosonic religious experience of memorisation by heart. The first revelatory experience was in the act of listening. The second, in the act of memorisation, precisely through an aural and oral encounter with a religious poem, came to her as an experience the 'virtue of prayer'. Weil was born in Paris into a secularised Jewish family. On a visit to the Benedictine monastery of Solesmes in 1938, she first wrote that, on simply *listening* to the Gregorian chant, 'each sound hurt me like a blow … in the unimaginable beauty of the chanting and the words … the Passion of Christ entered into my being for once and for all.'[1]

The second she described as 'a real contact, person to person, here below, between a human being and God.'[2] But the heart of the matter is that reciting a particular prayer-poem by heart engendered this intimate relationship. The genesis of this second moment of theosony was also during her sojourn at Solesmes. She met a young English Catholic man. 'Chance – for I always prefer saying chance rather than Providence – made of him a messenger to me.'[3] This young man introduced her to the metaphysical English poets of the twelfth century and she particularly warmed to a poem of George Herbert, 'Love bade me welcome':

> Love bade me welcome, yet my soul drew back,
> Guilty of dust and sin.
> But quick-ey'd Love, observing me grow slack
> From my first entrance in,
> Drew nearer to me, sweetly questioning
> If I lack'd anything.

1. Simone Weil, *Waiting on God*, London: Routledge and Keegan Paul, 1951, p 20.
2. Ibid, p 21.
3. Ibid, p 21.

'A guest,' I answer'd, 'worthy to be here:'
Love said, 'You shall be he.'
'I, the unkind, the ungrateful? Ah, my dear,
I cannot look on Thee.'
Love took my hand and smiling did reply,
'Who made the eyes but I?'

'Truth, Lord, but I have marr'd them; let my shame
Go where it doth deserve.'
'And know you not,' says Love, 'who bore the blame?'
'My dear, then I will serve.'
'You must sit down,' says Love, 'and taste my meat.'
So I did sit and eat.

The recitation of this prayer 'learnt ... by heart'[4] was the transformation of body and spirit prayer to God. It had to do with the
actual experience of reciting the prayer, becoming the prayer in
sound and story. She describes the theosonic religious experience
thus: 'I used to think I was merely reciting it as a beautiful poem,
but without my knowing it the recitation had the virtue of a
prayer. It was during one of these recitations that ... Christ himself came down and took possession of me.'[5] Expressing in similar
terms this aural, verbal experience, Joseph Gelineau puts it: 'The
strange divine power of the voice derives from the fact that this
message ... enters into me by the sense of hearing and invades me
completely without my awareness of its arrival and its source ... it
is pre-logical communication, preceding the words as articulated
language.'[6]

Simone Weil's experience of the presence of God does not end
with an off-by-heart experience of George Herbert. The Greek
words of the 'Our Father' also moved her deeply 'by the infinite
sweetness of this Greek text.'[7] The essence of this profound mem-
orisational experience, one not reliant on the visual text but upon
the effect of the actual verbal sounds on the body, is the exploration of this work. This deeply spiritual visionary who waited on

4. Ibid, p 21.
5. Ibid, p 21.
6. Gelineau, 'The Path of Music', p 136.
7. Weil, *Waiting on God*, p 25.

God in obedient, listening patience describes an experience which goes far beneath the superficial, the external and the obvious: 'The effect of this practice is extraordinary and surprises me every time for, although I experience it each day, it exceeds my expectation at each repetition. This is the fruit of practice that animated my soul.'[8]

Simone Weil rejected her secular Jewish identity and through repeated mystical experiences – two to do with memorisation already recalled – came close to Christianity. She never became a Christian and was never baptised. Her visits to Solesmes were not indifferent to the sound of the Gregorian chant of the Benedictine community there. Kingsley Widmer concludes that this poor tormented soul who choose to end her short, brilliant life at thirty-four was 'if not a saint without God and church, a poignant witness to the possible social-religious transcendence of unmerited human suffering.'[9]

In the Judaism that Weil rejected, learning by heart is the way to God. Learning sacred texts by heart was not a new idea for her. 'In ancient Judaism … scribes and rabbinic scriptural experts routinely committed the entire text of scripture to memory.'[10] Learning the Torah off by heart, committing it to memory, is the first stage of encounter; meaning, interpretation and understanding follow. The process is described by Kelber: 'Time and again words were recited by teachers, repeated by students, individually and in chorus, in turn corrected by the teachers, until the students knew them by heart.'[11]

The relevance of the theosonic depths of Simone Weil's religious experience is twofold: in her openness to receive ambient, cosmic sound, in the certain kind of listening which she paid to the monastic chant around her, beauty resounded and was in the ear of the listener at that moment and continued to reside there from then on. Secondly, an aural theosonic experience does not go

---

8. Ibid, p 24.
9. Kingsley Widmer in 'Weil, Simone (Adolphine)' in *Thinkers of the Twentieth Century*, eds Devine / Held / Vinson / Walsh, London: Macmillan Publishers, 1983, p 609.
10. Jaffee in *Teaching Oral Traditions*, p 327.
11. Kelber, *The Oral and the Written Gospel*, p 10.

away. There is a permanence which one kind of listening promises. That constancy of Christ entering her being for once and for all, it is suggested, through the illustration of her story, is transcribed in her soul through a listening and a memorisation. To forget is a natural phenomenon; to remember everything is absurd. God's love and its presence in one's life is never forgotten.

Folklore, poetry, storytelling and literacy

Alan Dundes, advocator of the Bible as masterpiece of folklore, maintains that 'the Bible consists of orally transmitted tradition written down. Certainly there were collations, "literary" emendations and editorial tampering, but the folkloristic component of the Bible remains in plain sight'.[1] He blames biblical scholars for not acknowledging this element in biblical criticism because these 'blind scholars have failed to recognise it.'[2]

Multiple versions of major biblical events 'attest to the folkloricity of the Bible.'[3] The implications of interpretation as folklore 'may represent a new paradigm with which to appreciate and better understand the Bible.'[4] But the crucial question remains: why is the oral more important than the written and what is the full implication of this pre-literal stage? It has first of all to do with the source material, which is the greatest story ever told beyond all human stories. Spoken aloud, memorised or simply read, the Bible is divine storytelling: the story of God's healing salvation. A storyteller is not simply entertaining: a storyteller is converting his or her listeners through the sound of the story. Words comes first, the imaginative powers of the listener come next. In the space created by synergised imagination, the story is carried and convincing.

The Irish are a people of a strong ancient aural culture, and the Christian religion of the Irish is primarily a religion of the ear. The God of the Irish, and the Jewish people, is aural and oral. This must be taken into account in any research which attempts to reappropriate Irish Christianity. Writing and literacy were late acquisitions of the Irish; the ear held court in the early days. Robin

---

1. Dundes, *Holy Writ as Oral Lit*, p 20.
2. Ibid, p 20.
3. Ibid, p 118.
4. Ibid, p 115.

Flower, in his influential study in 1947, goes as far as to suggest
that: 'there was ... no written tradition in ancient Ireland.[5] The advent and growth of literacy in Ireland is almost exclusively linked
to ecclesiastical scribes. It 'centred in the monasteries and all the
evidence goes to show that, whatever parts the poets played in the
oral preservation of the tradition, its written record was the work
of the church.'[6] Literacy is linked to the advent of Christianity in
Ireland: 'No evidence has ever been produced to prove the existence of writing ... in Ireland before the coming of Christianity.'[7]

The storytelling, folkloric aspect of traditional Irish spirituality
is present in traditional religious song, a major source of Irish spirituality.[8] Celtic scholar Eleanor Knott emphasises this aurality in
poetry: 'There is one essential fact about Irish poetry which must
never be forgotten ... it is ... composed for the ear ... we must accept the fact that aural enjoyment was ... an integral part of every
poem.'[9] The same holds true of the traditional religious prayer-
poem. These centre on the aural experience of the listener to a certain type of poetic metre: 'The "strict" or *dán díreach* metres ... for
more than nine centuries were to delight the ears and feed the
imagination of Irish listeners.'[10] Knott merges the act of listening
and the imaginative possibilities, which are alerted and enabled
through such listening. To be a poet, religious or secular, in early
and medieval Ireland, was to be an expert on the sound of every
word of one's poem; a poem lived through the sound of the speaking voice. Robin Flower witnessed one particular moment when
time stood still through the sound of a voice. On the Aran Islands,
presumably in the 1930s, he, quite by chance, stumbled on an island potato digger in a field. This island octogenarian, as Flower
puts it, 'fell to reciting Ossianic lays.'[11] (These are ancient poems

5. Robin Flower, *The Irish Tradition*, Oxford: OUP, 1947, (1979), p 6.
6. Ibid, p 73.
7. Ibid, p 73.
8. See Nóirín Ní Riain MA thesis, The 'Nature and Classification of
Traditional Religious Song in Irish', University College Cork, 1980, p 131.
9. Eleanor Knott, *Irish Classical Poetry: Filíocht na Sgol*, Cork: Mercier Press,
(1957), 1978, p 17/18.
10. Ibid, p 11.
11. Flower, *The Irish Tradition*, p 105.

and prose in Irish relating stories of Fionn and his friends in his adventures in Ireland and around the world. This particular blend of *chanted* prose and poetry recalled a mythological visit to Greece, and the marvellous events that unfolded there. The late professor of Celtic Literature at University College, Dublin, Gerard Murphy, claimed that the chanting of Irish Ossianic balladry resembles Plain chant.[12] The old man is possessed by the telling and the sound, the power of every vibration surrendered to the air around them. 'At times the voice would alter and quicken, the eyes would brighten, as with a speed which you would have thought beyond the compass of human breath he delivered those ... passages ... full of strange words and alliterating rhetorical phrases ... I listened spellbound ... a real and vivid experience.'[13]

Adding a layer of sung sound to the text intensified Irish eighteenth and nineteenth century poetry. Tadhg Gaelach Ó Súilleabháin (1715-1795), following his conversion around 1775, was inspired to write a poem entitled *Duain Chroí Íosa*. He requested this poem should be sung to the secular air of *San Mhainistir Lá*.[14] To this day, both religious poem and secular tune are still conjoined.

In the field of storytelling too, Murphy, confirms: 'Old and Middle Irish storytelling had an oral origin ... we may be certain that all Irish tales and ballads ... were intended primarily to be told or chanted rather than to be read.'[15] All Irish prayers, sounded and sung were oral and aural; all categories of earliest religious song[16] depended on and still depend on oral and aural transmission for survival. More importantly, the inherent religious experi-

12. Gerard Murphy, *Ossianic Lore: Fiannaíocht agus Rómánsaíocht*, Cork: Mercier Press, (1955), 1971, p 59.
13. Flower, *The Irish Tradition*, p 105.
14. This was published in *The Pious Miscellany and Other Poems* by Tadhg Gaelach or Timothy O' Sullivan, ed John O Daly, Dublin, 1868, p 60.
15. Murphy, *Ossianic Lore*, pp 59/61.
16. According to my research, these three categories of authentic traditional religious song are the *Amhrán* type (for example the Tadhg Gaelach song referred to above), the Numerical Carol (a song-type employed by the Franciscans as a mnemonic aid when they came to Ireland in 1226) and the Religious Ballad (which is akin to Ossianic lore referred to also above). See MA thesis, pp 130-135.

ence is totally dependent on the sounding and the hearing. This
aurality contrasts with the Greek optic. The German theologian,
Karl Dann, puts this primacy of the eye in Greek religion in a
wider context: 'Greek religion, like that of antiquity in general,
was a religion of seeing.'[17] Victor Zuckerkandl says of Grecian
music: 'To the Greeks, the art of sound and that of words were intimately related: there was no music without words, and poetry
was not spoken, but sung and chanted.'[18]

Irish church-going people, up to the advent and application of
the Second Vatican Council's doctrines, were a people of the ear.
On Sunday, everyone went to 'hear' Mass. One could ponder well
on that 'hearing'. This was a kind of hearing which was far removed from the rational understanding of the actual meaning of
each word, which was in Latin. No simultaneous translation appeared on sheets; presuming the priest knew the meaning of the
Latin words spoken, he alone placed meaning on his utterances
other than the pure effect of sound. Such sounds fed the imagination and formed images beyond the senses of God's presence and
proximity. Such is the Irish theosonic tradition. Although one
could argue that much of this going to 'hear' Mass was passive on
the part of the congregation, this work suggests the opposite: re-
moving the aural in favour of the rational and literate was, and
still is, detrimental to the emotive, rousing stirrings of the Holy
Spirit.

17. Karl Dann, 'See, Vision, Eye' in *The New Dictionary of the New
Testament*, Vol 3, p 513.
18. Zuckerkandl, *Man the Musician*, p 1.

To write is to hear – To read is to hear

Every writing event in antiquity was a word event. Presented another way, the word being transcribed was spoken aloud simultaneously. Whether this word was one's own or the creation of another, the work of transcribing was, at one and the same time, seen and heard. Transcription or dictation was a sound event. Be it the author, the amanuensis or secretary, words were written through the channel of hearing.

This wedding of sound and sight, writing and word is the healing moment for Zechariah, the father of John the Baptist. The moment he wrote 'His name is John' (Lk 1:63), his gift of speech is reinstated. Luke, the evangelist, is anxious to outline the restoration of speech: not only is his mouth opened immediately, but also his tongue is loosened and he spoke the fulfilment of Gabriel's announcement (Lk 1:64, 20). Through the very sound of this song, the echo of universal peace and salvation is heard. Walter Bruegemann aptly calls this the 'answering song of Zechariah: 'It is a song of new possibilities given late, but not too late, possibilities of salvation/forgiveness/mercy/light/peace … The song releases energy … The transformation is unmistakable. Tongues long dumb in hopelessness could sing again.'[1] Achtemeier connects the miracle to the writing event: 'Luke's Greek (1:63), demonstrates that it is the act of *writing* that proved his speech had been restored!'[2] All writing had to be sounded and the powerful ritual inherent in this dual act restored sound and speech to this old man, now filled with the Holy Spirit, which in turn would allow him to speak prophetically (Lk 1:67).

Reading was accompanied by spontaneous oral and aural response. As Michael Coogan puts it: 'In Hebrew as in other lan-

---

1. Walter Bruegemann, *The Prophetic Imagination*, Philadelphia: Fortress Press, 1978, (1982), p 99.
2. Achtemeier, Omne Verbum Sonat, p 15.

guages, the verb meaning 'to read' ... literally means 'to say aloud.'[3] There was no reading or writing done which was silent or solitary.

An oral theology focuses on listening, not proposition, on the sound, not the system. To verbalise the sacred texts is to hear what the eye sees. To turn one's ear to the sound of the Word is to receive and usher in the life-giving force of that Word. This is the existential effect which theosony makes available. The Word of God becomes inscribed in the body and in the soul. The senses merge to become a total body prayer. This is the existential effect. Referring to the practice and tradition of St Augustine, Gibb and Montgomery write: 'Throughout the Greek period and far into the days of the Roman Empire – to the third and fourth century of our era – the custom survived of reading both in prose and verse, not silently but aloud and in company.'[4] To communicate, to win influence and relationship was to entice others through the grain of the voice. Kelber is convinced that in antiquity, 'composing in a hearer-friendly manner and reading aloud were prerequisites for gaining a hearing.'[5]

In his *Confessiones*, St Augustine laments being deprived of the aural and oral wisdom and company of the contemporary bishop, St Ambrose.[6] Augustine almost curses the 'throngs of busy men who cut me off from his ear and mouth, (ab eius aure atque ore) men to whose weaknesses he ministered.'[7]

The Benedictine, Jean Leclercq, eloquently describes such a reading aloud as listening to the 'voices of the pages'. Our ancestors apprehended the meaning of the written word in such a manner: 'They read ... with the lips, pronouncing what they saw, and with the ears, listening to the words pronounced, hearing ... the "voices of the pages".'[8] 'It is a real acoustical reading: *legere* means at the

---

3. Michael D. Coogan, 'Literacy in Ancient Israel', in *The Oxford Companion to the Bible*, p 437.

4. See *The Confessions of Augustine*, ed John Gibb and William Montgomery, p 141.

5. Kelber in *Teaching Oral Traditions*, p 331.

6. St Augustine, *Confessions*, trs Vernon J. Bourke, Bk VI, Ch III, p 193.

7. Ibid, p 193.

8. Leclercq OSB, *The Love of Learning and the Desire for God*, p 19.

same time *audire*; one understands only what one hears …'[9] Gamble concurs: 'In antiquity virtually all reading, public or private, was reading aloud: texts were routinely converted into the oral mode.'[10] *Legere, audire* and indeed *lectio* are genuinely integrated body and soul prayers calling for full corporeal and spiritual response. In the sounding, the echoing, the silent reality, the meaning is grasped and comprehended.

The author of the book of Revelation makes an emphatic point about saying the words of the page out loud. The written revelation of the risen Christ to John on Patmos is to be read out aloud and all who do read aloud are blessed. 'Blessed is the one who reads aloud the words of the prophecy, and blessed are those who hear … it' (Rev 1:3). The reader can hear the same call to *'tolle, lege'*. It is an *audientia divina* – a hearing, a listening and a silence with God in the courtroom of the heart.

In *reciting* scripture, there are four factors which theosony suggests might coax conversion. There is the sacred word itself, which is to be read as God's action in the here and now of the present, addressing the reader through the score. There is the overall context. Then there is the pronouncing or resounding of that syntax. Finally, there is the presence of God inherent in that oral/aural (through the mouth and/or ear) event.

The term 'oral' has negative connotations in Western civilisation that may have spilled over into Western theological expression. Western education is literacy based; nobody is taught how to listen. Western classical music is always read before sounded. The concentration is on one's ability to read, that is, the mental powers acquired to read. This ability to read holds the ability to hear in disdain. Andrew Love articulates this as follows: 'Written from within, and into, the horizon of Western literateness, the word "literate" possesses a primary resonance of approbation, while "oral" possesses a primary resonance of denigration.'[11]

There is the well-known anecdote told in traditional music circles in Ireland. Two traditional musicians are in conversation

9. Ibid, p 19.
10. Gamble, *Books and Readers in the Early Church*, p 30.
11. Love, 'Musical Improvisation as the Place where Being Speaks', p 92.

and one asks the other: 'Do you read music or are you gifted?'
There is truth in this pithy aphorism when considered in a theological light: having a natural ability or aptitude for a relationship
with God, which is what being gifted means, requiring no other
capacity than the one of listening and hearing. Love tentatively
suggests about notated polyphony of the late Middle Ages that its
validation was 'by the look of the page, rather than solely the *effect*
of the sound.'[12]

In theological discussion, likewise, the thrust has been to regard words as a record of events rather than as 'events in sound'[13]
themselves. Indeed, as Love points out generally, in the 'present-
day West, orality is perceived as the marginalised "other" of literacy.'[14] Kelber believes that theologians generally think in terms of
the written. 'Literacy is so deeply implanted in every twentieth-
century biblical scholar that it is difficult to avoid thinking of it as
the normal means of communication and the sole measure of
language.'[15] For Alan Dundes, 'Oral tradition is deemed untrust-
worthy and must be confirmed by written documents ('Get it in
writing'), and this is also true in the case of the New Testament.'[16]
'Thinking about NT writings as both produced and used orally,'
writes Achtemeier, 'is something scholars are not accustomed to
doing.'[17] Although theologians have acknowledged the oral
background of scripture, it is the actual power of the oral performance of these words, which has been undervalued if not passed
over. What is labelled the 'auditory field',[18] is the nearest that
theologians have come to defining the essential theosonic experience, and even this term is undeveloped and ill defined.

12. Ibid, p 103. Italics mine.
13. Kelber, *The Oral and the Written Gospel*, p 15. For example, see Rudolf
Bultmann, *The History of the Synoptic Tradition*, trs John Marsh, NY:
Harper & Row, 1963, and Birger Gerhardsson, *Memory and Manuscript:
Oral Tradition and Written Transmission in Rabbinic Judaism and Early
Christianity*, ASNU 22, Copenhagen:Ejnar Munksgaard, 1961 as repre-
sentatives of this school of thought.
14. Love, 'Musical Improvisation as the Place where Being Speaks', p 91.
15. Kelber, *The Oral and the Written Gospel*, p 32.
16. Dundes, *Holy Writ as Oral Lit*, p 17/18.
17. Achtemeier, Omne Verbum Sonat, p 25.
18. Kelber, *The Oral and the Written Gospel*, p 150.

What is heard is open to the process of change – what is committed to paper can resist change and dynamism. A classic in literature or visual art can embrace conversions of change, which are held deep within the form itself. Knowledge imparted through the ear, on the other hand, easily adapts and reflects itself to embody the time, the culture, and the religion of the hearer, ancient or contemporary. Catherine Bell defines the negative forces which literacy can engender: 'In comparison to oral societies … change in literate societies is much more apt to be deliberate, debated, ridden with factions, explosive, and concerned with fundamentals. In other words, in literate societies change can be very untidy.'[19]

Recognition of the crucial role which the ear, not the eye, played in all reading in late antiquity carries wider-ranging implications; for instance, textual inconsistencies and references to other texts, to name but two. Participation in this auditory field is the purpose of this work which defends 'the epistemological principle of orality' which is that to know something means actually 'to participate in it.'[20] In this sense, theosony is heuristic; in serving to further investigation on the theology of listening, it is a methodology which encourages the praying one to find out, given the various oral and literacy traditions, what is meaningful and potent in one's own spiritual development. The ear is a ready partner in unfurling God's saving plan for the listener and ultimately humanity. In the act of finding out the sound of God, patience is the key that releases the dual prayer world from the cosmic praying one to the depths of the divine spirit. *Festina lente* – make haste slowly – is the sacred auricular threshold to a new way of being with God. Humanity is born to listen; the first task in the growth towards maturity is to hear the original murmuring.

Meaning in religious discourse, therefore, is born in the space between hearing and listening. The difference between these two modes of aural attention is simply that hearing is biological, listening is psychological and spiritual. The drift of the theosonic message is in living to hear the silent sound of the Triune God.

---

19. Catherine Bell, *Ritual: Perspectives and Dimensions*, NY / Oxford: OUP, 1997, p 204.
20. Kelber, *The Oral and the Written Gospel*, p 150.

This space is an aural ladder between heaven and earth; the graded stages forming the ascent and descent represent the varying stages of the aural. In this structural metaphor of theosony, the ladder of success to God rises to eminence in Jesus Christ, through the work of the Spirit. Finally, in the reading relationship, theosony is best understood in the opposition between text and reader, between sight and sound. Here ends the reading.

Through this progress of thought, the present theme should be a variation of some of the oncoming themes in the development and eventually with the overall hypothesis of the book, which is towards a clearer articulation of the aural dimension, that 'cloud of forgetting', where God is truly heard. Such is the true legacy of scripture. The ear that is of God is of the earth: The Rilkean *Ein Ohr der Erde*, is 'Earth's ear. To it alone she talks this way. If you insert a jug, she feels who you are interrupting what she wants to say.'[21] The ear is God's wonder-worker without tools. Meister Eckhart makes a visual observation about the celestial and the terrestrial eye that works equally well for the ear:

The ear by which I listen to God is the same ear by which God listens to me.

21. Rainer Maria Rilke, *The Sonnets to Orpheus*, trs Stephen Mitchell, New York: Simon & Schuster, 1996, p 101.

Theosony – the metaphor

Most of our language, theological or not, is metaphorical. Rudolf Otto very early on introduces the concept into theology with this classic claim: 'Only from afar, by metaphors and analogies, do we come to apprehend what it [the *mysterium*] is in itself, and even so our notion is but inadequate and confused.'[1] In Christianity, the 'word' is a metaphor, which in the context of this volume is that the triune God is not any particular word. The Christian word-metaphor is instructive and useful particularly when it points towards the listening process required; the listening act, which is a listening beyond the power of the human word. It is the likeness of the act of 'word' itself, which is the salient point, not any particular word but the experience of the word-beyond-word which transforms and reveals. There is another theological significance and validity when the metaphoric utterance 'word' appears; the 'Word' of God clearly refers either to the written word of God in scripture or to the Word made flesh in Jesus Christ. In other words, 'word' in theology has more than one literal meaning.

It is like the *sound* of a word, which of its essence has to be heard of and listened out for. Scripture, on the other hand, is not called the 'Language of God'; neither is the Son of God referred to as 'the incarnated Language of God'.

Scripture abounds in figurative speech which is a literary device in which language is used outside its literal sense: God is the good shepherd, people are the flock, 'the voice of the Lord flashes forth flames of fire (Ps 29:7). 'Metaphor in language – the prime mover ...'[2] is the key that unlocks the imagination. 'Sound', 'silence' and 'God' are three very distinct terms that, in one sense, defy and resist combination. But lining them all up in the

1. Otto, *The Idea of the Holy*, p 34.
2. Steiner, *Real Presences*, p 182.

metaphor of 'the Sound of God' releases a new understanding of divine presence. The world of sound in its turn assumes a religious dimension and a new self-understanding in the process.

Theosony uses metaphors of its own and applies these to God analogously. There are three basic metaphoric elements in theosony. Firstly, there is the ear itself, both in human and divine terms, referring to the human ear, the ear of the incarnate Son of God, and the Divine Ear. Secondly, there is the voice (also meaning 'sound' in scripture). The human voice, the voice of Christ and the Voice of God which is one and the same as the sound of the human, the sound of Jesus and the Sound of God. Thirdly, there is the metaphor of silence.

'We are here confronted with a unique characteristic of aural perception, which can only be described metaphorically by words from the realms of other senses. Talking about the rise and fall of tones is using a metaphor, and nothing more.'[3] In referring to the particular imaginative language that one addresses to and listens for in Christianity, praying is always in the language that comes naturally but it evolves from and transcends all human language. Our 'father' as opposed to our 'mother' tongue is more a language of pure sound. Simone Weil expresses this succinctly: 'the words we exchange with him do not matter, but only the *sound* of his voice, which assures us of his presence.'[4] Thus hearing conveys immediacy and immersion. Biologically, as already explored, the inner ear perceives sound not only by means of the outer ear but also directly from vibrations within our skull, and we feel sound.

Theosony, tuning into God's self-unveiling through the various facets of the sense of hearing, is intoned through the *imagination*. This Development proposes theosony as one of the constructs of imagination that is integral to any human participation in the creative act of God. Imagination and the senses intersect in God-made-man. The vital creative activity of prayer disturbs, awakens and nourishes the imagination. The ear of the imagination harbours the unimaginable sound of God's timbre. John O'Donohue describes the soul-work of the imagination: 'The

3. Zuckerkandl, *Sound and Symbol*, p 86.
4. Weil, *Waiting on God*, p 38. Italics mine.

imagination is the creative force in the individual. It always nego-
tiates different thresholds and releases possibilities of recognition
and creativity that the linear, controlling, external mind will never
glimpse.'[5] The work of prayer is negotiating alternative imaginative ways of catching echoes of the sound of God. Angelus Silesius
(Johann Scheffler) puts it like this: 'Nothing is without voice: God
everywhere can hear / Arising from creation his praise and echo
clear.'[6]

Every believer lives and prays out of the world of the imagination. To pray is to imagine. Rilke defines the artist in spiritual
terms as one 'who develops the five-fingered hand of his senses ...
to ever more active and more spiritual capacity.'[7]

Imagining, forming mental images of what is not perceived by
the senses is the work of imagination. This faculty reproduces images already stored in the memory and these images can be
aroused through associated images; new heretofore-unknown
images emerge through a combining of former experiences.[8] The
scope and focus of the process of imagination permeates all aspects of human existence and as Happel states, cannot 'be relegated to one area of human life'.[9] Religious imagination, through its
multifaceted, interdisciplinary constructs, acts as mediator of
meaning and understanding of religious experience. Symbol, narrative, myth and iconography – both visual and aural – make
sense of the totality of religious experience.

Imagination liberated discovers relationships between things,
creates symbols and finds new meanings. A theosonic imagination
of intimacy discovers harmonious concordances between God and
God's creation. In auditory, as opposed to visual terms, theosony as

5. O'Donohue, *Anam Chara*, p 145.
6. Angelus Silesius: *The Cherubinic Wanderer*, p 51. In a footnote to this
couplet, Josef Schmidt states that this notion of echoing or resounding God
was a very popular concept in sixteenth and seventeenth century poetry,
'in fact, a whole subgenre "echo-poems" developed from it.' Fn 35, p 51.
7. Rainer Maria Rilke, *Where Silence Reigns: Selected Prose by Rainer Maria
Rilke*, trs G. Craig Houston, NY: New Directions Books, 1978, p 55.
8. See *American Dictionary*, p 603.
9. See Stephen Happel, 'Imagination, Religious' in *The New Dictionary of
Theology*, p 508.

imagination allows God to sound the divine in the soul in whatever way possible. Theosony as imagination is present in silence as much as its sound. The hidden, mysterious, yet intimate Divine Ear of God awaits the silent song of the imagining one. Imagination, according to the artist M. C. Richards, is 'singing to a wide invisible audience.'[10] For Farmer, imagination and memory go hand in hand as 'transcendent capacities .... Memory is the basis of all systematic knowledge, and memory and imagination together make possible that foresight and creativeness without which man with his puny physical equipment would never have survived, still less evolved into civilised life.'[11]

10. M. C. Richards, *Imagine Inventing Yellow*, NY: Station Hill Literary Editions, 1991, p xii.
11. Farmer, *Towards Belief in God*, pp 66, 67.

Theosonic Scriptural Events

'What ... remains unconnected or incomplete on the story level finds a resolution in the act of hearing.'[1]

Six arguments for preferring the Gospel of John

The first reason is threefold: this gospel is the Gospel of the Word, the author's hearing of Christ is clearly God's word (Jn 1:1, 14). The passage from death to eternal life is in the very act of listening (Jn 5:24).[2] Secondly, the particular *language* through which Jesus is heard in this narration is literary, poetic and rhythmic. These stylistic techniques are different from the other synoptics and according to Raymond Brown are semipoetic.[2] Such language is different from 'prosaic human communication ... The Johannine Jesus comes from God, and therefore it is appropriate that his words be more solemn and sacral.'[3] In words appropriate to this book, the auditory point here is that this language is post-cosmic and post kerygmatic. It is a language that in its difference actually sounds strangely familiar. Thirdly, this composition is highly dramatic in tone.

The author possesses rich literary skills and his linguistic genius operates on four different levels. He carefully and correctly communicates his insight into this Eternal Word to the listeners / readers. In so delineating his story and thoughts about Jesus, his own self-development is portrayed and, in turn, that of the reader and through him the ultimate formulation of God's revelation in human words, albeit poetic and rhythmic, is accomplished. Through the linguistic interchange between John and his audience, human language becomes the sound of God. Cosmic sounds are mere reflections of the sound of God (Jn 3:8). The literary, dialogical

1. Kelber, *Teaching Oral Traditions*, p 338.
2. Raymond E. Brown, *An Introduction to the New Testament*, p 333.
3. Ibid, p 333.

nature of the fourth gospel makes clear that it was intended, although primarily read, to be spoken, acted and heard.

The story of Jesus Christ according to John as a work of dramatic art demands a whole new approach to listening and hearing the Word. Stephen Smalley makes the dramatic analogy: There is a prologue (Ch 1), Act 1 (Chaps 2-12), Act 2 (Chaps 13-20) and an Epilogue (Ch 21).[4] In any drama, it is the plot and the characters themselves that interest the listener. The author is known only through the silent biography that filters through. The biographer here is never actually mentioned by name. This dramatic gospel lends itself to a reading, a listening and an interpretation which is 'surely not historical but literary.'[5] The proof of the literary rather than the historical nature of the text is, according to Rudolf Schnackenberg, in the unique turn of phrase of John's Christ. In the words of the Johannine scholar, Francis Moloney, 'This gospel is not written to tell us about the faith experience of the people "in the story" but to challenge the faith of the people who are "reading the story", who are to ask, "Where do I stand?"'[6] This is the reader-response approach to this story about what God has done for Jesus and what Jesus has done for God. In the words of Schnackenberg, John's 'rendering of Jesus' words are ... so full of images and parables ... The whole diction is transposed to a higher plane ... enriched with new concepts ... characterised by highly significant formulae ... and by dualistic-*sounding* contrasts.'[7] Whether John believed his own stories to be factually true is not the important point one feels, on reading this poetic, dramatic work; what is important is the power of the gospel as God's self-revelation through Jesus. The message of the text is solely concerned with God's self-revelation in a Word: God's Word spoken loudly and clearly on earth through the name of Christ.

4. Stephen S. Smalley in 'John, The Gospel According to' in *The Oxford Companion to the Bible*, p 373.

5. John Ashton, *Understanding the Fourth Gospel*, Oxford: Clarendon Press, 1991, p 511.

6. Francis J. Moloney, 'Johannine Theology' in *The New Jerome Biblical Commentary*, p 1425.

7. Rudolf Schnackenberg, *The Gospel according to St John*, three volumes, Kent: Burns & Oates, 1992, vol 1, p 21. Italics mine.

According to Wijngaards, 'St John's gospel portrays Jesus as the *voice* of God …'[8] 'He whom God has sent speaks the words of God, for he gives the Spirit without measure' (Jn 3:34).

The second reason brings up the Christian bias of this volume and is twofold. In the fourth gospel, Jesus, the Nazarene, takes the title role. Secondly, as everyone 'who has ears to hear' can hear the sound of God, so too, in the gospel according to John, no one is deprived of God's loving friendship. As Raymond Brown writes: 'For John there are no second-class citizens among true believers; all of them are God's own children in Christ.'[9] As the drama unfolds, Christ is sometimes the revealer of the kingdom and Word of God, sometimes, particularly through his death and resurrection, the glory of that same kingdom and Word. Thomas Brodie proposes that this gospel is an invitation from Jesus to his hearers to 'move to a new level of understanding … the level of the holy'.[10] This new spiritual awareness is from the spirit, which is 'mind-surpassing'.[11] Yet it is not ear-surpassing; this realm of the spirit is audible: 'The wind blows where it chooses, and you *hear* the sound of it …' (Jn 3:8.). This is a listening compendium; the sacred play presents the central figures in varying roles of listening: for instance, listen and learn (Jn 6:45), listen and obey (Jn 12: 48), the truth is in the listening (Jn 18: 37).

In the drama of John, Jesus is the central character. The evangelist is eager to present the reader/listener with a logo-centric Jesus Christ right from the first words of the prologue. Jesus Christ is the Word of God made flesh who desires to reveal and articulate the message of the kingdom of his Father. This he does through the medium of human language. Raymond Brown puts it thus: 'The Johannine Jesus used the language of this world to

8. John Wijngaards, MHM, *Experiencing Jesus: Scripture, the Witness of Saints and Mystics, and a Life of Prayer show the Way*, Notre Dame, Indiana: Ave Maria Press, 1981, p 29. Italics mine.
9. Brown, *An Introduction to the New Testament*, p 378.
10. Brodie, *The Gospel According to John*, p 19.
11. Ibid, p 19.

refer to the realities of the world from which he came.'[12] John presents Jesus as the human link, the bridge between God and humanity.

Thirdly, the gospel according to John is a *symbolic, auditory, metaphoric* statement from beginning to end. This gospel is the symbol of God's word in human speech; such a wordy medium is vital in humanity's understanding and intimate conversing with the triune God. Brown defines the words of the Johannine Jesus as 'the earthly used to symbolise the heavenly.'[13] Rahner agrees: 'The revelation of God, whatever its origin, must in the end be translated into human speech, if man is not to be completely taken out of his human mode of existence by it.'[14] Through the hearing of the human word, the human being enters the time capsule, which travels through the years in time and space to the moment when God's revelation was originally spoken aloud out of the silence of the universe. Sound is the weak but indispensable way in which God can be heard.

The fourth gospel is relevant to this present work as it can be described as feminine in the full sense of the meaning of this word, grammatically and biologically. In the Exposition of the First Movement, various theories about the feminine qualities of the human ear were raised, suggestions which are not simply pertinent to women but refer rather to a dimension in all human experience. Every soul must endeavour to keep the perfect equilibrium between the masculine and feminine, the yin and yang aspects and that sense of balance resides in the aural. So the Good News according to John is particularly inclusive of the feminine: Christ is the embodiment of the *logos* that ancient feminine wisdom, (Greek *'gnosis'*, *'sofia'*.) These three words, in the principle Western source languages of Hebrew, Greek and Latin are usually defined as feminine in gender.[15] John's resurrection story, the longest of all the gospel narratives, centres on one woman's need for and

12. Brown, *An Introduction to the New Testament*, p 378. Italics in original.
13. Ibid, p 378.
14. Rahner, *Hearers of the Word*, p 158.
15. See Huston Smith, *The World's Religions: Our Great Wisdom Traditions*, San Francisco: HarperSanFrancisco, 1991, p29.

conversion to faith, a conversion which is aural. It is significant that this version of the first reunion with humanity is with a woman who has absolutely no status or position in society. Mary Magdalen's faith abides in her love (Mk 16:1) and loyalty (Lk 8:2), two attributes to be striven for by male and female alike. Perhaps the noblest profession of belief in all of the New Testament is uttered by another woman, Martha (Jn 11:27). One word 'yes' is not sufficient to convey the depth of her belief, which Jesus calls into question; she qualifies it by this, that and the other. Jesus is the Messiah, the fulfilment of all scriptures' promises. He is the Son of God, human and divine; he is 'the one coming into the world' (Jn 11:27), the One yet to come in glory. Three Trinitarian titles spoken and heard summarise the pinnacle of all Christian thought, male and female.

Fifthly, the gospel according to St John appeals to the *emotions*. Although the emotional is arguably present in all the gospel stories, the Johannine narrative is full of emotion and as such is simply and unavoidably moving for the reader. The emotional is unavoidable rather than arbitrary. The underlying message to every Christian is about bowing down one's ears, listening graciously to the voice of God in the moment. According to several biblical critics, this theophanic moment, told by the fourth evangelist, is particularly persuasive and poignantly emotional. C. H. Dodd calls the appearance of the Man of Suffering (Is 53:3) to Mary Magdalen as 'the most humanly moving of all the stories of the risen Christ.'[16] Raymond Brown goes further to define it in terms of authenticity. 'This longest and most meaningful account', he writes, 'is also perhaps the most faithful to the original and oldest story, which testifies to the appearance to one woman only.'[17] She is the sole witness here, yet despite the lateness of the witnesses, Brown believes that 'the tradition of the appearance to Magdalene may be ancient.'[18] Secondly, this is a supreme example of the term 'to play something by ear'. Playing something by

---

16. C.H. Dodd, *The Interpretation of the Fourth Gospel*, London: CUP, 1970, p 441.
17. Raymond Brown, *The Gospel According to John*, vol 2, p 1003.
18. Ibid, p 1003.

ear means to act according to the situation. All prayer is about saying and hearing what is best, and what is moving, at that moment in time. Mary's intimate conversation with Jesus appears to follow no definite agenda, plan or structure; they are both being perfectly true to the situation. The mysterious message of the Magdalen moment is this: To play the vital loving role in an encounter with the triune God by ear is to open oneself to the emotional workings of the Spirit who always promises a truth in sound.

Finally, the gospel according to St John concerns *the religious, revelatory experience*, which is the essence of Fundamental Theology. The author of a book on this theme, Gerald O'Collins, claims that the 'communication of experience sums up what the gospel intends.'[19] A three-level experiential exposé, according to O'Collins: it traces the personal experience of Jesus more than the other gospels; Christ is never alone in the presence of God and Jesus reveals the glory of God at all times. The hidden treasure in John's gospel ranges from the finite, cosmic, sound of nature, such as the wind, through the finite sound of the voice of Jesus Christ, to the infinite silent Voice of God. In summary, this gospel of St John is 'a story of what Jesus has done for God.'[20] It is the story of all of the lives of the Christian human race in listenership, and it is the story of the true believer's response in the shadow of that listening. *'Every major motif in the gospel is directly linked to the concept of revelation'*, John Ashton stresses.[21]

19. O'Collins, *Fundamental Theology*, p 97.
20. Francis J. Moloney, 'Johannine Theology' in *The New Jerome Biblical Commentary*, p 1420.
21. Ashton, *Understanding the Fourth Gospel*, p 515.

'In the beginning was the WORD...'

What is important here is the subtle but certain distinction between Jewish and Greek interpretation of the Word. The Greek *logos* carries an intellectual, inner power; *däbär* for the Jew is dynamic, inviting and demanding.

Däbär is persuasive and effective. In the gospel of John, the Jewish concept of *däbär* meets the Greek concept of *logos*. *Logos* – the Word of God – is the word-possessed, creative, incarnate power of God through Jesus Christ. John fuses Hebrew and Greek tradition and the thought of Philo of Alexandria, who first whispered the connection between *däbär*, *logos* and the Jesus of Nazareth. *Logos* embraces *däbär* as an invocation eliciting a response from the hearers and listeners. Charles Davis summarises the varying interpretations of the Greek *logos* and Hebrew *däbär* which he states, although translated as 'word', are not precise synonyms.[1] There are two meanings to the word *däbär* in ancient Jewish thought: speech/word and creative action;[2] similarly, the Greek *logos* is both word and also the essence, the precise meaning of a thing.

Defining the concept of *däbär*, Barclay writes: 'A word was more than a sound expressing a meaning; a word actually did things.'[3] In other words, a word carried within its sound an actual transformative personal experience. 'Actions speak louder than words' is a contemporary truism. However, in the Jewish mindset, actions and words speak equally loudly, distinctly and effectively. Charles Davis defines such implications: 'The Hebrews

1. See Charles Davis, 'The Theology of Preaching' in *Preaching*, ed Ronan Drury, Dublin: Gill & Son, 1962, p 6.
2. See J. Barr, *The Semantics of Biblical Language*, London: SCM Press, 1961, pp 107-160 on the whole area of biblical etymology. Specifically on *däbär*, see pp 129-140.
3. William Barclay, *New Testament Words*, London: SCM Press, 1971, p 185.

were more concerned with words as conveying a call, an invitation or command; a word was something addressed to the will, *demanding a decision from those who heard it.*'[4] The Word of God for
every Israelite is an invitation to a divine/personal encounter
which is also, at one and the same time, a conversion. A word, according to Davis again, 'carries an action capable of effecting what
the word expresses.'[5] This is important in contemporary Christianity where words are only half-alive; the husk is there, but the
kernel is lost. The question is how to restore the other half.

The imperative here is that verbal energy is not the prerogative
of a particular race or a certain time or discipline. In philosophy, one
classic text on the distinction between different modes of utterance
is a book containing a series of talks given by the English philosopher, John. L. Austin entitled *How to do Things with Words.*[6] His definition of utterance is important in this particular theory of theosony
and relevant to the concept of *däbär*. It is the 'performative utterance'
which is the elusive, yet tangible event that happens '*at the moment of
uttering being done by the person uttering.*'[7] To declare something is not
to question the truth or the falseness of it, it is, in the very saying, an
active accomplishment. Austin defines the inherent power of the
spoken word, the performative, as a '*force*'.[8] Speech is forceful as the
source of being of the utterer: 'written utterances are not tethered to
their origin in the way spoken ones are.'[9] The study of declared utterance and achievement, neglected in philosophy is now being
reckoned with, according to Austin: 'For some years we have been
realising more and more clearly that the occasion of an utterance
matters seriously, and that the words used are to some extent to be
"explained" by the "context" in which they are designed to be or
have actually been spoken…'[10] Utterance and feat in theology, the

4. Charles Davis, 'The Theology of Preaching' in *Preaching*, ed Ronan
Drury, Dublin: Gill & Son, 1962, p 6. Italics mine.
5. Ibid, p 6.
6. J. L. Austin, *How to Do Things with Words*, eds J. O. Urmson/Marina
Sbisà, Cambridge MA: Harvard University Press, 1962.
7. Ibid, p 60.
8. Ibid, p 100.
9. Ibid, p 61.
10. Ibid, p 100.

original significance of *däbär*, is no longer significant beyond the written documentations of its existence once upon a time.

The theologian, Gerhard Von Rad, speaks of the 'word of power' which he suggests is universal and 'is in no way something peculiar to Israel.'[11] Jews, along with other ancient tradition, used the expression – the word – as a reality of both thought and will. Yet 'once pronounced, it continued to possess its own life, full of efficacy and even (in certain ancient texts) of magical force. This same thing was true of the word of God.'[12] Once simply spoken by the prophets and pronounced in the Law, it created the common denominator between the ideal of the covenant and God's salvific plan for history. 'By the word of the Lord the heavens were made ... For he spoke, and it came to be' (Ps 33:6, 9). Barclay makes an essential link between the saying and the doing: 'Always we must remember that in Jewish thought God's word not only *said* things; it *did* things.'[13] God's Word is still active and at work and freely given to humanity: God does things for humanity through the word. In short, the Jewish understanding of the spoken / sounded word surpasses the oral and aural sound to effect a religious experience.

In Greek philosophical discourse, *logos*, the noun, conveys numerous meanings referring to 'speech,' 'word,' 'thought,' 'the science of,' 'the underlying reasons, the principles and methods of a particular thing,' 'the meaning of a thing'. It was a very popular, much-loved little phrase common to the literary genres of poetry and prose.

Logos, as a noun cognate with a verb, also has an interesting range of meanings. Liddell and Scott cite three broad categories of connotation: the first centring on the image of picking up, gathering in, choosing for oneself; the other two denotations are specifically concerned with saying and speaking, covering a wide range of verbal functions from commanding, oration, exclamation and

---

11. Gerhard Von Rad, *Old Testament Theology*, Vol 2, London: SCM Press, 1975, p 82.
12. Thierry Maertens, *Bible Themes – A Source Book*, Vol II, p 11.
13. Barclay, *New Testament Words*, p 185.

reproaching.[14] Therefore, this Greek verb – *legein* – can mean 'to pick up', 'to gather', 'to choose for oneself' 'to pick out' which are essentially receptive, interiorising gestures. It also signifies 'to tell' and 'to speak'. Yet the many meanings of the Greek term make no reference to the act of listening. The ear picks up sounds around it and gathers them in for oneself. The ear makes sense of the sounds it hears with a very different rationale to other senses. But, on the other hand, as Fiumara states, 'There could be no saying without hearing, no speaking which is not also an integral part of listening, no speech which is not somehow received.'[15]

How did the Greek philosophical ideal of *logos* come to be adopted so freely and easily by Christianity? Heraclitus of Ephesus first used this word in pagan Greek thought. Philo (c.20BCE-50CE), an Alexandrian Jew, took up the story and integrated biblical monotheism into a school of mystical thought which emphasised the scriptural *logos* as the Divine word mediating between the unknowable God and his creation. Philo was, according to Bernard McGinn, 'the first figure in Western history to wed the Greek contemplative ideal to the monotheistic faith of the Bible'.[16] Integral to the mystical thought of Philo, for whom the scripture revealed the meaning of life, was this notion of *logos*. He used the term over a thousand times.

What emerged as a Christian interpretation of *logos* was a process of inculturation from the matrix of a two-stranded society and culture: the Jewish influence of Second Temple ritual (515 BCE-70CE) with its late Temple sacred books such as the apocalypses and the Hebrew Bible, well developed by the second century BCE; and Hellenistic philosophical discourse.

Greek-speaking Judaism had no difficulty with textual borrowing. *Logos* in the evangelist John's terminology came to embody God's word. Friedrich Heiler describes how 'the profoundest con-

---

14. Liddell and Scott, *A Greek-English Lexicon*, Oxford: Clarendon Press, 1843, 1958 ed, p 1035.
15. Fiumara, *The Other Side of Language*, p 1.
16. Bernard McGinn, *The Presence of God: A History of Western Christian Mysticism: The Foundations of Mysticism: Origins to the Fifth Century*, Vol 1, NY: Crossroad Publishing, 1992, p 35.

templative experience of the ancient world entered into Christianity, where it was purified and completed'.[17] Jesus Christ was the *Logos* – the true incarnate *theophania theou* or manifestation of God. Jesus Christ as Word combines the Greek Platonism and Stoicism of *logos* with the Hebrew *däbär*. *Logos*, the inherent rational principle upholding creation, is aligned with the Jewish notion of the creative, active, saving Word of God.

When John, the Evangelist, takes up the word *logos*, it is to focus on Christ, both as the living incarnation of God's word on the one hand, and the everlasting source of God's teaching on the other (Jn 3:34; 12:49, 50b). John merges the two testaments in one tome. The message is the ultimate explication of God's intervention in the course of human history. There is also a convergence between the *pneuma* of John's gospel and the wind that blows in Isaiah. That wind comes full circle to be recognised through its sound and voice.

George Steiner draws the connection between the Hellenistic philosophical concept of *Logos* inherent in John and the verbal, *albeit* visual, primacy of Western civilisation. 'It is appropriate that he [John] should have used the Greek language to express the Hellenistic conception of the *Logos*, for it is to its Greco-Judaic inheritance that Western civilisation owes its essentially verbal characteristic.'[18] This Word is the healer of creation, restoring order through its perpetual sound and redirecting all ears towards the Father. In the words of the psalmist, 'my ears you have opened' (Ps 40:6). Now the Word whispers the Word.

Christ makes the inaudible God audible through the *Logos*. What does this say of the triune God as silence? God is the pinnacle of silence; Jesus breaks the duration of this silence to and for humanity. For von Balthasar, 'God's language is first and foremost his own; the event of his incarnate Word, Jesus Christ. God speaks in his flesh.'[19] John's prologue equates Jesus Christ, Son of

17. Friedrich Heiler, 'Contemplation in Christian Mysticism', in *Spiritual Disciplines: Papers from the Eranos Yearbooks*, Pantheon, NY: 1960, p 192.
18. Steiner, *Language and Silence*, p 30.
19. Hans Urs von Balthasar, *Truth is Symphonic: Aspects of Christian Pluralism*, trs Graham Harrison, San Francisco: Ignatius Press, 1987, p 59.

the Father with this *Logos*. Christ is the everlasting, eternal Word.
John paints the entire horizon of creation out of this Word. In the
space between the letters of the word of St John, the ear and the
eye meet in pure praise; the canvas of light meets the concerto of
sound in the human expression of divine revelation. 'Then God
said' (Gen 1:3) – the creation words – but no one listened until the
Logos became flesh. Put another way, humanity only half listened;
it was defective hearing until the Jesus of Wisdom appeared. In
the hearing of Jesus of Nazareth, the Word of God is no longer half
heard but is fully obeyed in and through his message of the kingdom of God.

Paul and Augustine's concept of *logos* propose a religious experience that is auditory, hence theosonic. Werner Kelber suggests that 'Paul links the word primarily not with content, but
with the *effect* it has on hearers.'[20] *Logos* is no longer an abstract,
philosophical, rational concept; it lives in its sound. Through the
power of this Word incarnate, the world is suspended and sup-
ported. The *logos tou theou* in Pauline literature is a metaphor that
seizes the hearer's ears in its sound through the very power of the
words spoken and in the moment of their utterance.

Augustine, in his spiritual autobiography, refers to his reading
(aloud, undoubtedly) of neoplatonic philosophy around the
Platonist concept of *logos*. However, he writes, 'but I did not read
there that the Word was made flesh, and dwelt among us. God …
has given him a name which is above all names … and that every
tongue should confess that the Lord Jesus is in the glory of God
the Father.'[21]

To summarise the concept of *logos* in the gospel of John, the incarnated person of Jesus Christ assumes a new vocabulary more
akin to the language of Hellenistic circles. The response of faith inherent in Johannine thought is through the ear. In the words of
Smalley, which vindicate the prominence of the gospel of John in
this work: 'John is anxious that readers should … "hear" his
words. Verbs of … hearing are important in John and are close in

20. Kelber, *The Oral and Written*, p 145. Italics mine.
21. Ibid, p 169.

meaning to the activity of believing.'[22] This is a word to be heard and not confined to books. The word is an aural relationship between God and humanity. William Barclay concludes that *logos* 'means *a spoken message*.'[23] Hearing and listening is faith in the unimaginable *sui generis* language and *logos* of God. 'As a human word may be intimate and distinct (it is intimate insofar as it reflects a person – proceeds from a person's body and spirit – yet, because it goes out from the person, it is distinct), so the Word, in relationship to God, is intimate yet distinct.'[24] A theosonic reading of the fourth gospel is one that deciphers the rhythm of the Word. *Logos* is an echo of *däbär*; 'Word' is the echo of God.

22. Stephen S. Smalley, 'John, the Gospel According to,' in *The Oxford Companion to the Bible*, p 373.
23. Barclay, *New Testament Words*, p 179.
24. Brodie, *The Gospel According to John*, p 136.

Hearing the Risen Christ
Jn 20:11-18; [Lk 24:13-32]

... one word
He spoke – His heart a torrent in release!
For Jesus murmured 'Mary', and she heard
What gave her back her happiness and peace.[1]

The ear is more resilient than the eye. Scripture carries the same message from chapter 27 of the first book of scripture to chapter 20 of the last gospel: the ear is to be trusted in recognition and revelation. Isaac did not trust his ear in the end and missed the mark (Gen 27:1-40); Mary of Magdala trusted hers and was saved. The Lord attracts her attention, makes her 'obedient' to him, through the grain of his voice.

The conversion-conversation between the recently risen Lord and the anguished lover is the truth of the recognition moment. By the grain of his voice, Mary is surprised, provoked, challenged, shocked and transformed. She is born anew by the truth of the timbre of his voice sounding her name. Paul Newham writes about the sound of one's own voice: it 'enables us to hear reflected an audible expression of our own image, our own sense of self.'[2]

Reflecting back to the prologue of John's gospel, the word preceded the light; the mystery of recognition was in a word. The very human sound of this voice of wisdom is midwife to a new life for Mary Magdalen. Christ's voice of wisdom, wise beyond words, speaks to Mary's heart. This wisdom which is infectious is, Huston Smith believes, 'an intuitive discernment that transforms, turning the knower eventually into that which she knows.'[3]

1. Taken from *Poems of St Thérèse of Lisieux*, trs Alan Bancroft, London: HarperCollins, 1996, p 74.
2. Newham, *The Singing Cure*, p 218.
3. Huston Smith, *The World's Religions*, p 29.

Mary not only hears the spoken word, but also in the tradition of *däbär* and *logos*, *acts* upon the hearing of that word. As von Balthasar puts it, 'she is given just as much *sense* experience as she needs so that the Lord ... can send her as a messenger to the brethren. The spark of experienced presence suffices to transform empty absence into an absence that is brimful.'[4] The sense experience is purely aural; the greeting that transforms is the sound of the name. It is a moment of recognition, 'the greatest recognition scene in all literature',[5] Barclay believes, which in turn actualises Mary of Magdala's own possibility and self-understanding. What is essential here is not what actually 'happened' but what actually passed in the silence between them.

David Tracy's definition of a classic, already partially quoted, suggests that: 'What we mean in naming certain texts, events, images ... persons, "classics" is that here we recognise nothing less than the disclosure of a reality we cannot but name truth ... some disclosure of reality in a moment that might be called one of "recognition' which surprises, provokes, challenges, shocks and eventually transforms us.'[6]

The drama of Magdalen has three acts. There are four characters: two angels, the Risen Christ, Mary of Magdala. Act one witnesses Mary, weeping outside the tomb. The angels hear her, converse with her and question the source of her grief. She is, we must presume, silent then, at least silent enough to hear them. Then on hearing, not on seeing them, she replies. 'The angels make no [visual] impression on Mary. She is not seeing correctly.'[7] Mary of Magdala is not seeing properly in her distraction. Her visual sense is numbed in tears. But she is hearing perfectly well to understand and respond to the interrogation of the two angelic figures.

Act Two is the scene of the mysterious voice from the garden. That icon of nature of a piece of ground which brings forth growth, nourishment for both body and soul, a garden, is central to the life-cycle of Christ, as John's narrative constantly, particu-

4. von Balthasar, *Truth is Symphonic*, p 133. Italics mine.
5. Barclay, *The Gospel of John*, p 312.
6. Tracy, *The Analogical Imagination*, p 108.
7. Brodie, *The Gospel According to John*, p. 565.

larly as the locus of both the Crucifixion and the new burial tomb.
(John 19:41) This is the freshly tilled garden of Eden where the
new Adam is the green-fingered Christ who possesses the natural
ability to bring all to full growth through salvation.

The Risen Jesus enters centre-stage. The Magdalene fails to
recognise her Lord either by his appearance before her or by the
sound of his voice as he asks the same question. Sight, and indeed
sound at this stage, deceive her into 'supposing him to be the gar-
dener' (Jn 20:15) who has carried her Lord away. But she was not
entirely missing the mark in thinking that Jesus was the grounds-
man; R. H. Lightfoot summarises: 'In the obvious sense of the term,
and as she used it, she was mistaken; but she also, like Caiaphas
(11:49) and Pilate (19:5, 14), spoke more truly than she knew.'[8] So
the voice from the garden is the sound that thrills Mary and she
runs to her companions to tell them whom she had encountered.

The climax to the story unfolds: Mary is named through the
voiced sound of her name by the one whom 'God ... highly exalted
... and gave him the name that is above every name' (Phil 2:9). The
risen Saviour is not simply calling any name; he is keenly aware of
the power of the spoken word that carries an intimacy within it
between namer and named. This is a profound moment; echoed-
intimacy unfolds and Mary knows again; she hears the identical
sound she already knows. Walther Eichrodt writes 'knowledge of
the name is more than an external means of distinguishing one
person from another; it is a relation with that person's being.'[9]
Naming once again, as it did in the God / Christ event, evokes true
conversion. 'She turned and said ... Rabbouni! (which means
Teacher)' (Jn 20:16). Marrow interprets this title, which appears
in three of the four gospels, as 'a cry of faith, not just a dramatic
anagnorisis.'[10] (*Anagnorisis* is a Greek word for 'recognition'.)

This was the aural turning point. From this moment of hearing, she has 'life in his name' (Jn 20:31). Hearing and listening cor-

8. R. H. Lightfoot, *St John's Gospel: A Commentary,* Oxford: OUP (1956),
1972, p 322.
9. Eichrodt, *Theology of the Old Testament,* Vol 1, p 207.
10. Stanley B. Marrow, *The Gospel of John: A Reading,* NY: Paulist Press,
1995, p 359.

rectly is to have an abundance of health in soul and body. 'Blessed are those who have not seen and yet have come to believe' (Jn 20:29). Hearing is believing and believing is witnessing to that belief. Hers is the privilege to announce to the disciples 'that he said these things to her' (Jn 20:18).

What is critical is, in Augustinian terminology, that 'then having turned with her body, she supposed what was not, now having turned with her *ear*, she recognised what was.'[11] 'In the end, according to Schnackenburg, 'the risen one assumes a form … appropriate for those to whom he wants to reveal himself.'[12]

Schillebeeckx adds his interpretation of the Magdalene intimate recognition: 'Spiritual contact with Jesus, ruptured by death, has been restored: they can once more address each other in intimate, personal terms, death notwithstanding.'[13] David Tracy describes the moment of recognition as an encounter with art: 'In our actual experience of the work of art, we move into the back-and-forth rhythms of the work: from its discovery and disclosure to a sensed recognition of the essential beyond the everyday; from its hiddenness to our sensed rootedness; from its disclosure and concealment of truth to our realised experience of a transformative truth, at once revealing and concealing.'[14]

Another biblical drama of aural resurrection recognition has strong resonances here in another early biblical recognition tale: the narrative of the Emmaus story. Only Luke narrates it and in true Lucan tradition, he emphasises the place of Jerusalem as the locus of resurrection. The walkers start out from Jerusalem. Jesus reveals himself visually to the two walking disciples deep in conversation – 'but their eyes were kept from recognising him' (Lk 24:16). The aural experience precedes and prepares the new revelatory optic when they recognised him in the breaking of bread (Lk

11. St Augustine, *Tractates on the Gospel of John*, The Fathers of the Church, trs John W. Rettig, vol 92, Washington DC:The Catholic University of America Press, 1995, tr 121.2, p 58. Italics mine.
12. Schnackenburg, *The Gospel according to St John*, Vol 3, p 317.
13. Edward Schillebeeckx, *Jesus: An Experiment in Christology*, (1974), London:William Collins, p 345.
14. Tracy, *The Analogical Imagination*, p 114.

24:31). The Risen Christ is to be heard in every single human word that has been breathed into being by God the Creator if one only knows how to listen. In the space between their words, God is hidden ready to emit the perfect note. In the very act of talking about the Son of God, God begins to perform. The poet, Patrick Kavanagh, paints the many theosonies: 'He's great, he's God, he ran through the streets telling/Everybody that would *listen*.'[15] Cautiously, Rahner adds, '[t]hough admittedly he does accost many on the way who never notice it.'[16] 'You shall indeed hear but never understand,' (Mt 13:14).

Yet another gospel narrative which tells of Jesus appearing firstly to the beloved of Magdala, Mary, relates how she had been healed by Jesus of seven demons which plagued her earlier life (Mk 16:9). Jesus knows the power of psychic energy that uttering a personal name carries. He knows instinctively and culturally that 'the name denotes the essence of a thing: to name it is to know it, and, consequently, to have power over it.'[17] Mary is not being called by any combination of convenient sounds. God speaks to Mary, and in turn to every human being, with the one word that cuts to the quick. For Mary, it is the sound of her own name that brings her to the truth.

15. Patrick Kavanagh, 'The Son of God', 9, 10, *Patrick Kavanagh: The Complete Poems*, ed Peter Kavanagh, Newbridge: The Goldsmith Press, 1972, (1992), p 271.

16. Rahner, *Theological Investigations*, Vol 7, p 170.

17. de Veaux, *Ancient Israel: Its Life and Institutions*, p 43.

Naming and names

Just as it is helpful to draw attention to the cultural understanding of the Hebrew and Greek uses of 'word', so too an exploration of the rich meaning which naming implied in antiquity and scripture will strengthen the argument that deplores its absence in contemporary society. There is a transformative power in the sound of one's name which was revered and respected by the Hebrews and is evident in scripture. Scripture tells us that it is God who named all of creation into being. Even after the fall, God still continued to name. 'For primitive man the name is not merely a means of denoting a person, but is bound up in the closest possible way with that person's very existence, so that it can become in fact a kind of *alter ego*.'[1] Una Agnew goes so far as to suggest that one's name is undying, not liable to perish and celebrated through all time: 'To be named, biblically speaking, is a pledge of immortality. It is a supremely mystical and creative event, since naming can invoke the hidden power of the named.'[2] Ancient Israel was keenly aware of this inherent mystery which words can carry, particularly one's name-word. Von Rad assures us that 'in everyday life ... certain words were thought of as having power inherent in them, as for example, people's names.'[3] For the women of the early east, the first step of the life-journey of creating an intimate relationship with one's baby is her naming of it. There can be a sacred ritual in bestowing or calling a name, because to reiterate, in the words of Maertens, a name 'expresses the nature of the being that bears it.'[4]

Many traditions rely on maternal experience to dictate the name of the unborn. For instance, North American Inuit pregnant

1. Eichrodt, *Theology of the Old Testament*, Vol 1, p 207.
2. Agnew, *The Mystical Imagination in Patrick Kavanagh*, p 37.
3. Von Rad, *Old Testament Theology*, ii, p 83.
4. Thierry Maertens OSB, *Bible Themes – A Source Book*, Vol 2, p 405.

mothers in childbirth would speak out several names during the final stages of birthing. The name sounded out with the very second of life outside the noisy womb was the name that remained:birth-moment and birth-name are one and the same.

In the Old Testament narratives, mothers are in the majority as name-givers. Apparently, out of the forty-six accounts of namers, twenty five were mothers, eighteen were fathers and three were either women friends or midwives. The first birthing story is when Eve gives birth to and names her son. Seeing him first, she cries out in pride, relief and thanksgiving to the Lord: 'I have produced a man with the help of the Lord (Gen 4:1). 'Cain' means 'I have produced'. The name bestowed on this newly born child embraces, in a word, the experience of conception, pregnancy and birth. The tapestry of mother-son bonding is embroidered in the single thread of the name Cain which is a pun or a play on words 'probably to be explained as kaniti is, "I have gotten a man-child".'[5]

Leah, daughter of Laban who deceitfully gave her in marriage to Jacob, named at the moment of birth her four sons with deep sighs which are wordplays for each name: first-born Rueben (That is See, a son)[6] has two etymologies – 'Because the Lord has looked on my affliction' (Gen 29:32) and he 'will love me' (29:32). 'Because the Lord has heard' (29:33) is the wordplay of the name Simeon. The name of the third son, Levi, means 'to be united' and the fourth son is named Judah from Leah's exclamation 'I will praise' (29:35). 'The names of Leah's children are given popular etymologies in each case corresponding to her utterances at birth.'[7] The conflicts and antagonism between Leah and Rachel are immortalised in these four names.

Jacob, the father of these birth-named sons, was also named at the moment of birth because of the extraordinary event of his delivery. 'Jacob was so called because, while still in his mother's womb, he grasped the heel, 'aqeb', of his twin (Gen 25:26), whom he had displaced, 'aqab' (Gen 38:29).'[8] His name-giver is ambiguous,

5. *Dictionary of the Bible*, McKenzie, p 114.
6. NRSV f, p 26.
7. *A New Catholic Commentary on Holy Scripture*, p 27.
8. de Veaux, *Ancient Israel, Its Life and Institution*, p 44.

as are the name-givers of his twin brother. Those who attended this delivery named the first born 'Esau' which means hairy because his tiny body was 'like a hairy mantle' (Gen 25:25). Jacob is the heel-grabber, which is the essence, the meaning of his name. Even from the womb, the struggle of the twins began. With the cunning help of his mother, Jacob dons gloves of kid skins and deceives Isaac into believing and trusting the sense of touch; had Isaac trusted his ear, the blessing of the first-born would not have gone awry. The sound of the name is ultimately more reliable than the name in itself. The name assumes a life of its own.

A personal name, therefore, in antiquity, was irretrievably linked to the meaning and being of the person. Christianity is a religion that thrives on the invocation of the name of Jesus. Jesus Christ is a theological title that Christians inherit. Being a Christian is a constant echo of the confession of belief eloquently spoken by Martha in the fourth gospel: 'Yes, Lord, I believe that you are the Messiah, the Son of God, the one coming into the world' (Jn 11:27).

To die without being named, that is, without being baptised, was to be condemned to limbo, the threshold existence on the borders of heaven and hell. Christians distinguish between family names and the Christian name given one at baptism. Christians are christened in Christ and receive a new name. Thierry Maertens is clear that in biblical culture the calling of another's name is a sign of intimacy: 'To name a being meant in a certain way to affirm one's capacity to know, to possess him.'[9] When God calls by name, redemption is at hand; the sounding of one's name is the summons: no name, no salvation. This is the promise of the listening prophet Isaiah: 'Do not fear, for I have redeemed you; I have called you by name, you are mine' (Is 43:1).

Scripture records how names can change or be changed by others during the course of one's lifetime. Jesus said: 'You are Simon son of John. You are to be called Cephas' (which is translated Peter) (1:42). The New Revised Standard Version of the Bible carries a footnote on the etymology of this name: the Aramaic word (*kepha*) and the Greek word (*petra*) meaning 'rock'. God re-named

9. Thierry Maertens OSB, *Bible Themes – A Source Book*, Vol 1, p 21,

Abraham and Sarah (Gen 17:5, 15). In Deutero-Isaiah, the Lord
promises a new name to the New Jerusalem that will be uttered
from the mouth of the Lord in acknowledgement of obedience
and loyalty (Is 62:2). The Spirit of God is to present the obedient
one with a white stone on which is written the name, which is
secret to everyone except God and the stone-holder (Rev 2:17).

Eastern tradition talks with the same imagery about the effect
of the name. The Sufi devotee Hazrat Inyat Khan writes: 'The effect of a man's name has a great deal to do with his life, and very
often one sees that a man's name has an effect upon his fate and
career.'[10] Tame writes that in Hinduism 'a name is not an arbitrary
reference number, but an actual mathematical formula of ratio
and vibration upon which the creation and sustainment of the ...
living being is based.'[11]

God named everything into creation through sound. Naming
and sounding the name are synonymous. The sound of the name
is the meaning of the name. In ancient Israel, 'The Israelites ... described God as creating everything by speaking (Gen 1:1-2:3) ...'[12]
Moses, the liberator and lawgiver of the Israelites, listened obediently to the voice of Israel's deity from the burning bush calling
out his name twice. Standing barefoot on the holy ground, the
true name of God is revealed aurally to Moses. 'I am who am' (Ex
3:14); my deeds, my acts are my name. According to Frederick
Denny, 'Yahweh, as name and theological concept, affirms both
God's eternal reality and his reliable presence with his covenant
people, Israel.'[13] That divine name 'in the most eloquent, liberat-
ing and liberated song in Israel'[14] is the *leit-motif* of the Moses aria
of the sea of freedom (Ex 15: 1-19). Miriam, who is held by many to
be probably the true composer, also sings the praises of the Lord
through the sound of the name (Ex 15:21).

The depth question that this work on theosony asks is: What is

10. Inayat Khan, *The Mysticism of Sound and Music*, Vol 2, p 254.
11. Tame, *The Secret Power of Music*, p 176.
12. Schneiders, *The Revelatory Text*, p 37.
13. Frederick Mathewson Denny, 'Names and Naming' in *The
Encyclopedia of Religion*, Mircea Eliade, Vol 10, p 301.
14. Brueggemann, *The Prophetic Imagination*, p 25.

it in the sound of this name that energises and animates? Walter
Breuggeman alludes to two energising traits which resounding
the divine name meant to these two choir-leaders: directness and
the primeval. 'There is something direct and primitive about the
name in these most primal songs of faith and freedom.'[15] In short,
the Hebrews, who had the entire Jewish scriptures off by heart,
lived in the sound knowledge of the name and deeds of God. The
Jesus of the fourth gospel proclaimed the name of God.

The Names of Jesus and Mary
The name 'Jesus' represents the Hebrew and Aramaic *yesu'a*
which is a late form of the Hebrew *yehosu'a*. It is a 'theophoric',
that is, a name obsessed with and possessed by God, embracing
some divine name or title of God in its make-up. The category of
theophoric names, according to Roland de Veaux, in ancient
Israel was 'the most important category of names'[16] To be given
the name of Jesus is to be called 'Yahweh is salvation'. Angelus
Silesius, the German mystic who converted to Roman
Catholicism in 1653 was convinced of the power of Jesus. 'The
name of Jesus is an oil poured out and spilt. It nourishes and
shines, the soul's own woe it stills.'[17]

Jesus is true to his name; he is the saviour who carries the
authority of God. The ancient East valued the mystery of names.
Jesus lived by his saving name. His followers and disciples fol-
lowed suit: the name of Jesus carried status. According to Kelber,
'[I]n early Christian culture, speakers who spoke in Jesus' name
could function as carriers of his authority. The name itself was endowed with wonder-working power.'[18]

The name Mary is also derived from the Greek names: 'Maria'
or 'Mariam'. Again it is a Hellenistic derivation of the Hebrew
'Miryam'. The etymology of this name is uncertain but it has been
suggested that it could be derived from the Egyptian 'mrjt' which
means 'beloved'.[19] Barbara Thierring claims that Mary is a title,

---

15. Breugemman, *The Prophetic Imagination*, p 25.
16. de Veaux, *Ancient Israel: Its Life and Institutions*, p 45.
17. Angelus Silesius, *The Cherubinic Wanderer*, p 87.
18. Kelber, *The Oral and Written Gospel*, p 20.
19. See *Dictionary of the Bible*, McKenzie, p 580.

not a name.[20] The appellation refers to a role which women played
in antiquity when ascetic orders like the Therapeutae 'celebrated
the Exodus as a drama of salvation, with two choirs, one by men
led by a man representing Moses, the other of women led by a
Miriam.'[21] Mary of Magdala and Mary of Nazareth could well
have been singers in their own lives untold of in the gospels, using
their voices to pray to God.

The Name of all Names and No Name

It is interesting that in naming and calling out to God, Jesus Christ
used the metaphor of the Father or Abba/Father, an affectionate,
intimate 'pet name' and urged every Christian to prayer to 'Our
Father' (Mt 6:9). Every Christ believer is privileged to nominate
God 'Father'. Denny uses a superlative to describe this phenomenon: 'Father has remained the most characteristic Christian
appellation for God, used especially when the speaker draws near
to him in prayer, worship and praise. All other names for God,
whether inherited from the biblical tradition of the Jews or gener-
ated within the Christian movement, have been tempered by the
intimate personal dimension that Jesus emphasised.'[22] The name
for God in the Irish language is simply *Dia*. Prayer as dialogue becomes *Dia-logue* – a nearest and dearest conversation between
God's *logos* and the praying one who is known by and in the image
of that divine word. But for the early Hebrews, this Divine presence is called by many names: sometimes *El Shaddai* (the murky
one), sometimes *Elohim*, other times, *Jehovah* and then the unspeakable *Jahweh*.

   The goal of the true Christian is beyond oneself; the name of
God is the essence, the destination of that journey beyond oneself.
Karl Rahner reflects: 'It could be the case the word alone is capable
of giving us access to what it means.'[23] The Father is the space in
between. Thomas L. Brodie puts it like this: '"God" tends to ex-

---

20. See Barbara Thierring, *Jesus the Man*, London: Corgi Books, 1993, p 120
21. Ibid, p 120.
22. Frederick Mathewson Denny, 'Names and Naming' in *The
Encyclopedia of Religion*, p 301.
23. Rahner, *Foundations of Christian Faith*, p 44.

press the deity as distant; "Father", the deity as involved in human life.'[24] The names of God and Father are the ultimate reconciliation between grace and nature. John's prologue ... begins with a heavy use of 'God' (1:1-2:6,12-13), but the name tapers out and, after the word becomes flesh, is largely replaced by 'Father' (1:14). The prologue's final verse uses both names, in effect combining and contrasting them ... Because God is unnameable and above all names; God is possessor of every name and no name. According to Rudolf Otto, '[n]ames have a power, a strange power of *hiding* God.'[25] Angelus Silesius in his mystical verse has this to say: 'Indeed one can name God by all His highest names / And then again one can each one withdraw again.'[26]

Scripture recalls how the sound of the name of God dispels the darkness of the night. 'From out of the sound of his name, the morning darkness dims to lay bare his name. For lo, the one who forms the mountains, creates the wind, reveals his thoughts to mortals, makes the morning's darkness, and treads on the heights of the earth – the Lord, the God of hosts, is his name' (Amos 4:13).

The psalmist foretells the great Christ event: 'O Lord ... how majestic is your name in all the earth!' (Ps 8:1). Through Jesus Christ, the echo of God's name is sounded once and for all: 'The naming of God ... is not simple ... It is not a single tone, but polyphonic',[27] Ricouer suggests, using sonic imagery. All scriptural literary genres name God. God's name is the common denominator of all scripture.

The theosonic implications of naming in contemporary theology are about the sound, the sounding and the hearing of the name. It is in the actual act of speaking and listening to one's name that a religious experience can occur; the sound is where the connection between the sound of the voice in the naming and the transformative power meet. A theosonic experience of naming is where the inner name of the soul hears the outer sound of the name and

24. Thomas L. Brodie, *Genesis as Dialogue: A Literary, Historical and theological Commentary*, NY: OUP, 2001, p 8.
25. Otto, *The Idea of the Holy*, p 221.
26. Angelus Silesius, *The Cherubinic Wanderer*, p 115.
27. Ricoeur, *Figuring the Sacred*, p 224.

recognises it for the first time. The name of the soul and the name of the body are one; the secret access to the recesses of one's God and one's own being is the intimate, vital invitatory naming by the Supreme Best Shepherd. The sound force of a name holds the real meaning of God's love 'poured into our hearts through the Holy Spirit who has been given us' (Rom 5:5).

Good Shepherding

Good shepherding begins and ends with the power of obedience that the grain of the shepherd's voice casts upon his flock. Chapter 10 in the fourth gospel gives three 'good shepherd parables' spoken by Jesus. Raymond Brown writes that Mary Magdalene's conversion 'is accomplished when Jesus calls her by name – an illustration of the theme enunciated by the Good Shepherd in 10:3-4: He calls his own by name, and they know his voice. Mary is sent to proclaim ...'[28]

The symbol of shepherding is one of the most persistent in scripture. Sheep and goats are the most frequently mentioned domestic animals in the biblical world as indeed are lambs, which are young sheep less than a year old. Scripture abounds with numerous references to these roaming animals, valuable for their fleece and flesh. Particularly in the Jewish scriptures, sheep-related references are largely literal and provide intimate insights into the life of the sheep herder and the animals' gregariousness, for instance how sheep live together in flocks. The Suffering Servant of the Lord in Isaiah is like a sheep prone to wandering, submissive and defenceless (Is 53:6, 7). Another faithful servant of the Lord, David, also famed for his harp skills and psalm compositions, is chosen by God as he tended his ewes. He showed such a *forte* in the sheepfolds that God chose him to be shepherd of Jacob, father of all nations and his own Israel. 'And he chose David his servant and took him away from the sheepfolds. From the care of the ewes he called him to be shepherd of Jacob his people, of Israel his own possession' (Ps 77:71, 72).

This metaphor is immediately implicated with the oral and aural; it is the sound of the familiar voice that brings the hearers to

28. Brown, *An Introduction to the New Testament*, p 359.

safety. Everything is in the sound of that voice and in trusting that sound, 'he restores my soul. He leads me in right paths for his name's sake' (Ps 23). As von Balthasar summarises: 'God is the Shepherd of Israel: in this image authority and life are perfectly identical at their source.'[29] The shepherd must keep before him the power in his voice to convey to the sheep a sense of direction. The true sheepfolder of old is one who is at one with his own voice and sound because we know that in Hebrew and in Greek, *phone* stands for both 'sound' and 'voice'.[30] He must 'gather the lambs in his arms, and carry them in his bosom, and gently lead the mother sheep' (Is 40: 11).

To name God 'the true Shepherd', to name humanity 'the lost sheep' is the perfect theological symbol of the Old Testament. 'Give ear, O Shepherd of Israel' (Ps 80:1) is the psalmist's heartfelt plea for God's saving grace in the midst of devastation. You who are the Supreme Shepherd must now listen to the sound of your flock bleating in disarray. Here is a plea for compassion. Jesus is God's answer to the chaotic flock. According to Karl Rahner, Jesus using the allegory of good shepherding 'only derives its true meaning from these preceding words: "I am".'[31] Because Jesus is there and real to every human being, identifiable in the comforting sound of his voice, there is no possibility of being lost. The voice is not just any sound; it is the sound of salvation and perfect existence. It is a grace unimaginable but concrete in its sound if only humanity learns to discern the grain of the divine voice. The truth of 'I am', which must echo 'I am who am', is the message of Christian faith, a faith dependent on and originating in hearing and the hearing comes from Christ (Rom 10:17).

---

29. Von Balthasar, *Truth is Symphonic*, p 142.
30. See Lightfoot, p 117; Schnackenburg, p 373; Francis J. Moloney, p 99; for just three of the many commentaries which state this duality of interpretation.
31. Rahner, *Theological Investigations*, Vol 7, p 174.

'The wind/spirit/breath ...
you hear the sound/voice of it' (Jn 3: 8)

T he Greek word *pneuma* can refer to any of three realities: 'spirit', 'wind' and 'breath'. In the Hebrew scriptures (and apparently, in the Aramaic language) this trilogy of meaning existed also. 'Spirit' conventionally, according to C. H. Dodd, is 'applied primarily to the wind ... and to the breath of living beings ...'[1] The Divine or Holy Spirit of God was the breath of God's creative and redeeming involvement with the universe. Israel's experience of this Spirit is spoken first and foremost by the prophets. Listen to the prophetic word – life and power reigns. 'Once one has ... heard, one is no longer the same.'[2]

Wind, the air in motion across the surface of the world, is a miraculous phenomenon that much of humanity regards as unsurprising. Weather vanes, also called weather cocks, are the flat pieces of metal that move steadily to and fro in tandem with the direction of the wind, and are still seen fixed on many a church spire. Their message goes largely unnoticed now. Symbolically, the cock indicates the direction that the wind is coming from and going towards for humanity, who is on the ground looking up. The cock is also an audiocentric symbol. The moment of cock-crow ushers in the new day and was the warning sound of betrayal for Judas. One very beautiful hymn of praise of St Ambrose sings it all: *Praeco diéi iam sonat, noctis profundae pervigil, nocturna lux viantibus a nocte noctem ségregans.* (A sound divides the darkest night, the crowing cock brings in the day; his night-time cry marks out each hour heartening travellers on their way.)

Breath and breathing are equally mysterious and miraculous in their life-giving and sustaining work. Air received into or evicted from the lungs is essential to the sound or sounds uttered through

---

1. Dodd, *The Interpretation of the Fourth Gospel*, p 213.
2. Schneiders, *The Revelatory Text*, p 17.

the mouths of living creatures. In short, breath is the life-giving force of humanity; the wind is the pulse beat of nature. The sound of the breeze is the living voice of nature. Walter Eichrodt articulates this richness of both wind and breath in the lives of our scriptural ancestors: 'No wonder, then, that in the blowing of the wind and in the rhythm of human respiration, ancient Man detected a divine mystery, and saw in this element in Nature, at once so near to him and yet so incomprehensible, a symbol of the mysterious nearness and activity of the divine.'[3] It is a different auditory wisdom that tuning into nature promises and the poet recognises wistfully the sin of not listening more: 'I know that I have heard spoken/A different wisdom as/The tree was shaken/ Above the parlour grass … I should have listened longer.'[4]

It is interesting to observe how Johannine commentators ignore the auditory phenomenon of the breathing wind that has a clear sound and voice (Jn 3:8). Of all the commentaries consulted,[5] only two refer to the reality of the sound. These commentators are Rudolf Schnackenburg and Francis J. Moloney. Schnackenburg refers to Nicodemus as a 'hearer' of Jesus, firstly; second, he writes that the 'central idea is that wind is also a mystery as to its origin and goal, but it still remains a reality, perceptible by means of its sound ('voice'), recognisable through its effects.'[6] Moloney makes a passing reference to the sound and voice, not in the context of hearing, but more relevant to the double meaning of wind and Spirit: 'Sound' of course also represents 'voice' thus the 'sound' of the Spirit-filled wind is at one and the same time the very 'voice' of the Spirit.'

In short, the interpretation of this short parable, a sonic image from nature, suddenly assumes a spiritual meaning: the raging wind represents the work of God through the Holy Spirit. This is a wind, a simile Raymond Brown opts to call it, to be heard and trusted by all who choose to hear. (Incidentally, the commentary

3. Eichrodt, *Theology of the Old Testament*, Vol II, p 46.
4. Patrick Kavanagh, 'Different Wisdom' 1-6, *Patrick Kavanagh: The Complete Poems*, p 65.
5. I consulted twenty-five in all.
6. Schnackenburg, *The Gospel According to St John*, Vol 1, p 373.

on this verse by Raymond E. Brown uses visual images throughout, which are disturbingly incongruous.[7]) What is constant and enduring is that each ear is 'activated by one and the same Spirit, who allots to each one individually just as the Spirit chooses' (1 Cor 12:11). The Spirit chooses the ear into which to breathe the message of God and it is a Breath which 'blows where it chooses and you hear the sound of it' (Jn 3: 8). Rudolf Schnackenburg defines this process, cited above, as both mysterious and real at one and the same time: The effects are in and through the listening.

This Nicodemus scene 'is the first of the important Johannine dialogues'[8] or conversations. The message is that in order to be 'reborn' into and enter the kingdom of God, one must hear the sound of the Spirit/Wind that blows the *metanoia* required for such an entry. This aural, free-spirited wind was what Jesus was hinting at in his night-time discourse with Nicodemus, when he compared the Spirit with the wind.

The pharisee, Nicodemus, visits Jesus in the *darkness* of the night. Rudolf Schnackenburg correctly warns against using this fact to imply his shady character. For whatever reason, the author of the fourth gospel sees fit to indicate night-time activity. What is important here is the biological fact that even in the darkness, the vocal message or communication is orally and aurally unimpaired. The night-time is the time of hearing and listening. There is a symmetry between every darkness and every secret thought about God. The German Christian poet, Novalis, wrote a poetic cycle about the symmetry between the world, Sophia, and the resurrected Christ. In the depths of the night, the portress of heaven steps out of 'ancient stories, bearing the key to the dwellings of the blessed, silent messenger of secrets infinite.'[9]

Macquarrie highlights the dynamic albeit invisible nature of the Spirit: 'The breath is the invisible though none the less palpable

---

7. Brown, *The Gospel According to John*, p 141. 'for although we can see the effects of the pneuma ... all about us, no one can actually see the *pneuma* (wind) that causes these effects. p 141. Italics mine.
8. Ibid, p 341.
9. Novalis, *Hymns to the Night: Spiritual Songs*, trs George MacDonald, London, Temple Lodge Publishing, 1992, p 11.

characteristic that distinguishes a living man from a dead one; the
breeze is the equally invisible force that stirs around man in the
world and that manifests itself in many effects there.'[10] Breathing
can be heard although not seen. Breath has less unpredictability
about it than has the wind. The 'breath of life' of the one truly alive
is more keenly directed and accurate. Breathing, like the wind and
indeed listening, is invisible. To live is to breathe. All humanity is
'the breath of life' (Gen 6:17). John O'Donohue makes this point
about Christian Trinitarian understanding: 'In the Christian tradition, the understanding of the mystery of the Trinity ... suggests
that the Holy Spirit arises within the Trinity through the breathing
of the Father and the Son.'[11]

The Spirit / breath / wind blows to be *heard* in the present, not in
the past nor in the future (Jn 3:8). It is the Spirit that initiates, nurtures and sustains a theosonic conversation between scripture and
reader. It is not an automatic, a given, for the reader. In fact, the
harder the task of interpretation, the more attentive and active is
the Spirit. The power of the Spirit comes alive through its graced
sound 'which is present and does transform all those willing to
listen.'[12] Here is an incarnation of the Spirit where spirit meets
flesh in the flesh of the ear. It is Jesus telling humanity once again
how to pray.

Moreover, it is the Spirit in *sound* and not in the silent visual
word that gives life. The Spirit of God is know-how and experience. '[O]ur competence is from God, who has made us competent
to be ministers of a new covenant, not of the letter but of the spirit;
for the letter kills, but the Spirit gives life' (2 Cor 2:5, 6, italics mine).
Although its source and destination are unknown, what is clear is
that it sounds and can be listened to. 'One must believe in the wind
without understanding its workings; he [Nicodemus] must do
likewise with the spirit (the same Hebrew word – likewise in

10. John Macquarrie, *Paths in Spirituality*, London: SCM Press, 1972, p 41.
In an entire chapter in this book on the concept of the Spirit, he does not
refer to the aural element although he quotes and comments on the
Johannine *logion*, 3:8 on p 42.
11. O'Donohue, *Anam Chara*, p 69.
12. Tracy, *The Analogical Imagination*, p 43.

Greek – means 'wind' and 'spirit').'[13] Belief in the Spirit may lack
understanding of its workings, but belief is guaranteed aurally.
The source and destiny of the wind is vague and hidden. The reality, the fact, the presence of this spirit is its *sound*, which is immediately aural. 'It is the Spirit, given to the one who believes, whose
voice is heard in and through the believer whose origin and destiny, like that of Jesus, is hidden in God.'[14] The boisterous wind is
the supreme *symbol* of the Holy Spirit. In order to be 'reborn' into
and enter the kingdom of God, one must hear the sound of the
Spirit/Wind that blows the rebirth and transformation of the
metanoia required for such an entry. Once this Spirit is heard, it
brands the listener with a name on a white stone, which is the secret pin-number, that releases true identity (Rev 2:17). The sonic
wind and the naming stone suggest a theology of nature as sound.
The Creator is the primal music that co-relates in every sound and
in the name of every living thing. A stone is silent because God
wants it to be so. Only God alone hears the *actual* timbre of every
human voice. The God of Creation is a listening God. There is a
secret sonic quality in every voice and there is another hidden
name for every human being which God alone knows and it is
auditory. God is sound for us: the real world is the one that has its
beginning in the promising sound of God. Being in the centre of a
cromlech, a circle of standing stones, is to know the sound of the
silent stone voices. Stones, rocks and pebbles are as audible as
they are responsive; the degrees of reception rely on the hearer
and the be-holder. The miraculous unseen and unheard power of
God in sacred stone is the measure of the dream of Jacob's ladder.
When the dreamtime ladder leaves no trace, the stone pillow that
witnessed the sound of the Lord endures. Jacob names this stone
in the name of the Lord. Humanity and divinity are one in the
stone and have been since. A sonic theology of nature, therefore,
implies the freedom of the sacred to be heard and listened to in
any form. Moreover, such a theosony of nature trusts in the *forte* of

13. Raymond E. Brown, *The Gospel and Epistles of John: A Concise
Commentary*, Collegeville, MN: The Liturgical Press, 1986, p 33.
14. Schneiders, 'Born Anew', p 193.

human nature to recognise the sacred, solemn aural expression. Nature's mode of extraordinary aural, sonic and silent expression are precious resources in an epistemology of theosony.

Summary

The symbolic Gospel of John is not, unlike the synoptics, simply symbolic of the kingdom of God. It is a poetic, dramatic symbol of the Christian event, the living Christ himself and the events of his life, which were aural and oral. Faith relies on hearing Christ and his word, according to this Gospel. Three Johannine excerpts were presented through the course of this section, three symbolic references to humanity as the flock who listen to the voice of the Good Shepherd (Jn 10: 3, 16, 27). Concluding on theosony in the John gospel, these two trilogies – of fourth gospel and Good Shepherd – are mirrored by three further audiocentric citations from the fourth gospel. One contains an educational message: 'Everyone who has heard and learned from the Father comes to me' (Jn 6:45). Another contains a cautionary note: 'The one who … does not receive my word has a judge' (Jn 12: 48). The third quotation of Jesus is his true promise of hope and salvation in the act of hearing: 'Very truly, I tell you, the hour is coming when the dead will *hear* the voice of the Son of God, and those who *hear* will live' (Jn 5:25).

CHAPTER FOUR

Theosony and Silence

Give yourself the opportunity of silence and begin to develop
your listening oin order to hear, deep within yourself, the
music of your own spirit.
— *John O Donohue, Anam Chara*

'Words, after speech, reach
Into the silence ...'
— *T. S. Eliot, Four Quartets: Burnt Norton V*

Introduction

When a man is silent, he is like man awaiting the creation of language for the first time ... In the silence, man is as it were ready to give the word back to the Creator from whom he first received it. Therefore there is something holy in almost every silence.[1]

The introductory quote by Max Picard insists on both the interconnectedness and the sacred nature of all silence and sound. He penned this little book, still today a classic on the experience and singularity of silence, in 1952 and of it, Gaston Bachelard had this to say: 'Particularly, if we were to describe how silence affects not only man's time and speech, but also his very being, it would fill a large volume. Fortunately, this volume exists. I recommend Max Picard's *The World of Silence*.[2]

This chapter seeks to define silence because, in silence, the human word and God meet and are at one. In the Middle Ages, the word 'symphony' (from the Greek meaning 'a sounding together') referred to any consonant combination of two notes. In the 'symphony' of God's self-communication, silence and sound are the two main themes or subjects. The aim of this introduction, fragmentary in style, is to explore the wide-ranging connections between these two themes and to chart the same extent of indifference to silence in Western theology. Silence, like sound, is a reality of God's self-disclosure to humanity. Ambrose Wathen avers that 'silence is essential for the life of intimacy with God to which man is called.'[3] More specifically, silence is a linguistic idea which reflects a more solitary, personal expression of divine reve-

---

1. Max Picard, *The World of Silence*, Chicago: Gateway Edition, 1952, trs Stanley Godman from *Die Welt des Schweigens*, Switzerland: Eugen Rentsch Verlag, 1948, p 33.
2. Gaston Bachelard, *The Poetics of Space*, p 182.
3. Ambrose G. Wathen OSB, *Silence:The Meaning of Silence in the Rule of St Benedict*, Washington DC: Cisterican Publications, 1973, p xi.

lation. Simply, silence primarily permits the space for humanity to pray. To know the experience of silence is to be able to put words on it. But this phenomenon of silence in Western Christianity has been undervalued and passed by.

Theological scholarship has ignored any serious discussion of silence, as it has on the area of listening and hearing. Here follows a selected theological literary review of silence.

The second edition of *The New Catholic Encyclopedia* carries no entry under silence in its recent publication. Interestingly, however, the previous edition of 1967 includes two short contributions on silence: one on 'Silence, Practice of,' by N. Lohkamp, the other on 'Silence in Worship' by G. Mensching.[4] Both articles merely scratch the surface but, on the other hand, the authors still emphasise the necessity of the practice of silence for spiritual growth. As Mensching puts it: 'In the communication of the individual soul with God … there is a preparatory silence. If God is to speak, man must be silent.'[5] Yet, the most recent edition includes no separate entry for silence. Even within the comprehensive section of articles on all aspects of the liturgy,[6] including music, gesture etc, there is no specific entry on the liturgical role of silence. So it would appear from this inconsistency that the realm of silence is actually diminishing in Roman Catholic theology.

There are two very valuable contributions on the theme of silence in reference sources. Mircea Eliade's *The Encyclopedia of Religion* has a three-page article by Elizabeth McCumsey, making two important points: the primacy of silence in religion, on the one hand, and the paucity of literary sources in the area on the other. She opens with a statement that silence 'is one of the essential elements in all religions,'[7] but in relation to further reading suggestions, she concludes that 'books devoted to silence are few.'[8]

4. *The New Catholic Encyclopedia*, Vol XIII: 'Silence, Practice of,' by N. Lohkamp, p 213; 'Silence in Worship' by G. Mensching, p 213.
5. *The New Catholic Encyclopedia*, 1967 ed, Vol 13, p 213.
6. See *The New Catholic Encyclopedia*, 2003 ed, Vol 8, pp 671-729. There are over one hundred pages in this liturgical section.
7. *The Encyclopedia of Religion*, ed Mircea Eliade, Vol 13, p 321.
8. Ibid, p 324.

Secondly, the *Dictionary of Fundamental Theology* has an entry by one of the editors, Rino Fisichella: 'Theologians have neglected silence'[9] is the first sentence. In their 'keenness to become scientists, they have relegated this essential medium for theological thought to the realms of mysticism and spirituality, so running the constant risk of falling short of their purpose.'[10] A cross-reference to an article on 'language' is relevant here. Contributed again by Fisichella, he warns theologians not to be afraid of counting silence as one of the components of their theological language: 'silence is both the source and the end of any theological language when confronted with the revelation of the trinitarian mystery of God.'[11]

Of the series of six *New Dictionaries*, published by Michael Glazier, originally intended to 'take stock of the remarkable developments in the church and in theology',[12] only two of the six make any reference to silence at all. *The New Dictionary of Theology* contains no article on silence. Neither does *The New Dictionary of Catholic Social Thought*, *The Concise Dictionary of Early Christianity* and *The Liturgical Dictionary of Eastern Christianity*. The two source references are the *New Dictionary of Catholic Spirituality* and the *New Dictionary of Sacramental Worship* and the quality of these entries do nothing to compensate for the lack in the others.

The first gives a short but perceptive contribution by Bob Hurd who highlights what he calls 'the dark side of silence'[13] in the life of the Catholic Church. This is a silence that represents repression and he sees Vatican II's liturgical reforms as a step in the right direction in remedying this repression. In the second, published in 1990, the emphasis on the role of silence is within the liturgical context. Three snippets of Michael Downey's article reflect the importance of silence: 'Silence is a vital dimension of

9. *The Dictionary of Fundamental Theology*, p 1001.

10. Ibid, p 1001.

11. Rino Fisichella, 'Language' in the *Dictionary of Fundamental Theology*, p 603.

12. See Editorial Preface both in *The New Dictionary of Theology*, p v, by Joseph Komonchak, and in *The New Dictionary of Catholic Sprituality*, p vii, by Michael Edward Downey.

13. Bob Hurd, 'Silence' in *The New Dictionary of Catholic Spirituality*, p 884.

liturgical prayer … that dimension which enables the person and community to be brought more fully into the mystery of Christ's presence … a necessary dimension of all liturgical activity.'[14]

A Dictionary of Liturgy and Worship edited by J. G. Davies, allows W. Jardine Grisbrooke to call for more areas of silence 'for in an age of far too little silence they could be of great devotional and psychological value.'[15] *The Modern Catholic Dictionary* includes a two-sentence entry calling silence 'the conscious effort to communicate with God … a precondition for recollection of spirit or the perceptible effect of being recollected.'[16]

The Oxford Companion to Christian Thought, *The Oxford Dictionary of the Christian Church*, the three-volume *Encyclopedia of Biblical Theology* and the international theological encyclopedia, edited by Karl Rahner among others, *Sacramentum Mundi*, four significant theological reference books, contain no reference to silence.

In summary, of the sixteen major reference sources consulted, only seven contain any specific reference to silence. Of these seven, three articles were cursory and bordering on the superficial. Yet, the paradox remains: two of the three references call for a greater attention to the role of silence in worship and accentuate its essential capacity in theology.

As already stated, Western Judaeo-Christian tradition has tended to be word-heavy and logo-centric. Christianity, along with Judaism and Islam as religions of the Word, stand in stark contrast to the primarily silent, spiritual traditions of the East. Indeed, the 'retreat from the word' – borrowed from the title of an essay written by George Steiner in 1961 – had little or no effect on Christian religious values. Having acknowledged the rational preponderance of verbal analysis in theological speculation, very little of that verbosity centred on the religious dimension of silence. This lack of attention to silence is not just applicable to theological discourse. Silence, after-all, Elizabeth McCumsey reminds us,

14. Michael Downey, 'Silence, Liturgical Role of,' in *The New Dictionary of Sacramental Worship*, p 1189. Italics mine.
15. W. Jardine Grisbrooke, 'Silent Prayer' in *A Dictionary of Liturgy and Worship*, ed J. G. Davies, London: SCM, 1972, p 349.
16. *Modern Catholic Dictionary*, ed John A. Hardon SJ, p 505.

'lies behind the words, supports the rituals, and shapes the way of life, whatever the words, rituals, and way of life may be'.[17] Guardini summed up the situation aptly: 'The topic [silence] is very serious, very important and unfortunately neglected; it is the first presupposition of every sacred action.'[18]

17. Elizabeth McCumsey, 'Silence' in *The Encyclopedia of Religion*, ed Mircea Eliade, Vol 13, p 321.
18. Cited by Silvano Maggiani OSM, 'The Language of Liturgy', in *Handbook for Liturgical Studies: Fundamental Liturgy*, Vol II, ed Ansgar J. Chupungo, Collegeville, MN: The Liturgical Press, 1998, p 244.

Towards a phenomenology of silence

M ax Picard makes the connection between listening and silence: 'Listening is only possible when there is silence in man: listening and silence belong together'.[1] Etymologically, 'phenomenon' comes from two Greek inter-related words: *phainomenon* which means 'that which appears' and *phainem* which means 'to bring to light' or 'to shine'. Experiencing silence 'brings to light', 'shines' on aural sensory perception. Silence is the source and the destiny of every sound as well as every listening. John O'Donohue summarises this point: 'All good sounds have silence, near, behind, and within them.'[2] Sounds, listening and silence are a trilogy of human and religious experience; hence the relevance of silence to this book and the argument for devoting the entire introduction here to the subject.

Silence is an original, primary, human event like birth and death. To be in this still inner world is to quietly listen and hear. Out of listening silence, an obedient response is revealed. 'Silence is always in a state of listening …'[3] Listening is always in a state of silence. Silence, like the phenomenon of listening, is always obedient, waiting for sound to set it in motion. William Wordsworth describes the poetics of his own solitude: 'obedient as a lute/That waits upon the touches of the wind.'[4] Silence waits obediently and freely for the touch of sound. Silence is not a spectator; it participates in the work of the ear.

Silence is a positive reality that is a powerful means of self-expression. An intimate knowledge of silence is integral to human meaning and is synonymous with human existence. Silence brings self-understanding back to the being who chooses and

1. Picard, *The World of Silence*, p 174.
2. O'Donohue, *Anam Chara*, p 70.
3. M. F. Sciacca, *Come si vince a Waterloo*, Milan: Marzorati, 1963, p 183.
4. William Wordsworth, The Prelude, Book Third, 136-139, p 108.

creates it. The hush of stillness is the great self-challenger. In the great space of stillness, limitations and expectations are exposed and confronted. 'Man does not put silence to the test; silence puts man to the test.'[5] Theologically, an awareness of God puts silence to the test; silence nourishes the possibility and potentiality of God for humanity that has long since lain like a dry withered leaf.

Silence rehabilitates. To choose stillness is ultimately to desire personal, wholesome self-transformation. It is an opportunity to listen. John O'Donohue makes the connection between the trilogy of sound, listening and silence with some personal advice: 'Give yourself the opportunity of silence and begin to develop your listening in order to hear, deep within yourself, the music of your own spirit.'[6] In the space of silence, the inner contradictions that work against well being are addressed and healed.

Yet silence is a contradiction in terms, in that to try to define or articulate it, one has to break it, interrupt it, and surprise it. Picard states this paradox emphatically: 'In no other phenomenon are distance and nearness, range and immediacy, the all-embracing and the particular, so united as they are in silence.'[7] Such earthly inaudible sound and silence are the essence of Theosony. The inner sound of silence resides in the caverns of the imagination. If truth be told, silence is the ability of sound to be creative and resourceful. Silence is a whole other world of imagined sound. In the stillness of silence, the imagination forms the conversation space with God. On the other hand, the imagination can run riot, noisily filling the gap where God is waiting; silence is then knocking on the door of the deaf one.

Other disciplines are aware of the transformative nature of *listening*; there is an attention being paid to *silence* in other areas of research. Indeed, it is also the case in both listening and silence that theology has much to gain from such commentaries. Philosophy, psychoanalysis and musicology are just three disciplines from which observations are drawn here.

5. Picard, *The World of Silence*, p 1.
6. O'Donohue, *Anam Chara*, p 72.
7. Picard, *The World of Silence*, p 2.

In *philosophical discourse*, Gemma Fiumara's theory on silence proposes 'the creation of a co-existential space which permits dialogue to come along.'[8] Philosophy is recognising the silent power. Such insights as Fiumara's have immense potential in a theological context: 'Silence … can be a very fertile way of relating, aimed at the inner integration and deepening of dialogue … letting the deeper meaning and implications of that relationship emerge.'[9] Silence is as essential to listening as breathing is to existence. It is also the locus which allows for and enhances a *response* to that which is heard in silence. Silence is the *maieutria*, the mid-wife, to true response.

In *pyscho-analytical* discourse, the listening work of the psychoanalyst is in the essential reading between the spoken words of the analysand. 'The psychoanalyst has to learn how one mind speaks to another beyond words and in silence.'[10] In theological discourse, however, the essential function of sacred silence is to propose and win the motion of a theosonic listening, which is dialogical and reciprocal in any triune divine/human relationship. The realm of silence is a theological listening and, in turn, an answering to the sound of God.

Some *musical* observations are appropriate at this juncture. The contemporary classical music composer, John Tavener claims that the 'Voice' of the Holy Spirit speaks in the silence of contemplation. 'In a series of recent eschatological works I feel that finally I have begun to find "The Voice". I know now that it is not a matter of finding what to say, but of how to be silent and to hear the Spirit speaking in this silence.'[11] (I met this composer in 1993 in London and then he spoke at length on this Spirit-filled silence from out of which had emerged his then most recent work, an opera entitled *Mary of Egypt*.)

It is another contemporary composer, John Cage (d. 1992), who highlighted the positive notion of silence. One of the leading figures of twentieth century avant-garde music, Cage recalls that in

8. Fiumara, *The Other Side of Language*, p 99.
9. Ibid, p 102.
10. Reik, *Listening With the Third Ear*, p 146.
11. Tavener, *The Music of Silence*, p 90.

1951, on entering and remaining for some time in a sound-proof, anechoic, six-walled studio space, two deafening sounds overwhelmed him: a high-pitched sound which was his own nervous system and a lower pitched drone which was his blood circulation.[12] The consequence of this particular Cagian experiment is to prove that there is no such reality as the complete absence of sound.

Cage was an avid devotee of Indian religion, eastern philosophies and Zen Buddhist tradition, and all cultures where chance elements and the role of silence in personal awareness are paramount. Cage's innovations, particularly in the 1950s, dispelled any understanding of silence as merely absence of either sound or speech as outdated, narrow and inadequate. Silence is not the absence of sound, he held. '[T]ry as we may to make a silence, we cannot.'[13] In short, the realm of silence is a positive ground or horizon of sound.

John Cage illustrated this point in a composition entitled 4'33 composed in 1952. John Stanley goes so far as to label this work 'notorious'.[14] (Actually Cage's music in the fifties was met with much hostility and rage and at one performance in New York of a work *Atlas Elipticalis* in 1964, the orchestra sabotaged the event and many of the audience walked out.) The piece is loosely intended for any number of performers and any random combination of instruments gathered together on a concert-hall stage in silence, for the duration of time, which is the title. This work of art again proves that an ambience of complete absence of sound is impossible to create and sustain. The listening ear is never silent; it is open to the ambient sonic demands all around. Stanley, nonetheless, accurately summarises the influence and effect thus: 'Presumably a Zen-inspired composition, its "music" consists of any audible sound from the audience or outside, and the emphasis is thus shifted from "understanding" to "awareness".'[15]

---

12. John Cage, *Silence*, p 8.
13. Cage, *Silence*, p 8.
14. John Stanley, *Classical Music: The Great Composers and their Masterworks*, London: Mitchell Beazley, 1994, p 246.
15. Stanley, *Classical Music*, p 246.

I would argue that the piece, *4.33*, is more in the realm of the religious, the spiritual than the musicological. I believe that there are at least five issues called into being through this piece, which are deeply theological. One has to do with losing oneself in silence. Another has to do with the power of the listening context. A third highlights an experience that is new, unexpected and surprising. The fourth is the fact that each listening is different and unique to every person in every situation. The final point that this piece offers to religious experience is the power of the listening silence to break down barriers. Some cursory remarks on the five points are relevant albeit tantalising, in that the scope of this present work only allows for superficial speculation, with in-depth explorations and correspondences postponed.

1. In the so-called silence, an existential silence, one can no longer lose oneself in rational external sound. Humanity in such existential silence digs deeper below the layer of understanding to the level of self-enlightenment.

2. Then there is the distinction to be made between first-hand and second-hand, even first-ear and second-ear hearing here: In the actual performance context, the ritual of being in physical attendance is the spiritual/religious act; in the second-ear context, in listening to a recording, the power ceases to exist or at least is greatly diminished. The theological overtones are both on an aural and a silent level: being present to the Sound and the Silence which reveals God is being present to the actual moment which is not disembodied.

3. John Cage seeks to convey in sound, precisely timed, the message that the hidden, the unexpected, the surprising, the improvised in human existence is revealed through a certain kind of listening within a certain time frame. Since all sound and hearing is the graced sound event of God's self revelation, then the message for theological speculation translates into a new kind of listening which has to do with stillness, silence and time.

4. No two silent harkings to the inner voice of God's self-disclosure are the same. No two listenings to Cage's silence are identical either. The praying/listening moment changes each time and is different for everyone; one must become comfortable in

the improvisatory silence, that is, a silence that is on the spur of the moment, open and free to the stirrings of the Holy Spirit. Simply, it is playing silence by ear.

5. John Cage sought to eliminate the marked distinction between 'art', the 'concert-hall' and 'being' and 'living'; the role of a listening silence can break down the barriers between 'theology', the 'church', 'humanity' and the triune God. Such 'silent' listening, as Cage experimented with, has enormous theological implications and possibilities.

These few, by no means exhaustive, interdisciplinary reflections, drawn from philosophy, psychoanalysis and music, have much to propose to a theology and a theory of theological listening; in the hush that holds the self-communication of God for humankind is the peace of connectedness and loving response. In short, a true two-way conversation with God is the calm, the pure stillness of becoming fully alive to the world and to the Holy Spirit.

In summarising the mutidimensional ontology of silence, three points arise. The first is that silence is the positive ground or horizon of sound. It is an infinite commodity in that it surrounds all sounding. Within the realm of the silent, the meaning of the sound is processed long after the sound has ceased. It is a definitive state of activity. The ancient Chinese proverb, 'The sound ceases but the sense goes on' summarises true silence. A listening in the silence is irretrievable. According to Seamus Heaney, 'the silence breathed / and could not settle back.'[16]

Secondly, sound and silence are in the strict relationship of cause and effect: sound is nourished and nurtured by silence. '[S]ounds ... "sound" because silences are in function.'[17] There could be no sound without silence and no true silence without sound. 'We perceive sound only because there is an un-manifested state of absolute silence, the state from which all sound originates.'[18] Words are sustained by silence. Silence is the natural milieu of sound and sound is unimaginable without silence. Silence and sound are not opposites, but are paradoxically and

16. Heaney, *Station Island*, p 61.
17. Sciacca, *Come si vince a Waterloo*, p 26. Quoted in Fiumara.

fundamentally correlatives, bound together in mutual or complementary relationship. In iconic, ironic, metaphor, they form a dip-
tych; two sides of a coin of human listening and being. The optical
image conveys this aural insight. They create an inseparable duality. Thus, stillness and its corresponding resonance simply 'are'.
Silence is the *cantus firmus* of life; all sound merely interacts with
the constant vibrating silent hue of nature.

Finally, Cage proposed a musical paradigm of silent self-consciousness. Here is a silence that gives access to self-consciousness
but also heightens awareness of circumambient cosmic and inci-
dental sounds. 'Hectoring, guilt-making, fantasising, narcissistic
wool-gathering just do not hold up day after day against the
silences that invade prayer. They fall into their own silences. The
silences swallow them up.'[19] In other words, the fact of silence is a
given in life and theology, as is the sense of hearing; it is crucial that
its neglect is acknowledged and ways of inserting silence and hearing back into theology are explored and practised. Suggesting an
ontology of theological silence, therefore, is to refer to that quiet
state as the first principle or category involved in sound.
Recognising and then experiencing the presence of God in auditory
terms means arguing for the existence of the God of sound founded
on the assumption that silence is a discoverable property in the very
concept of that auditory and silent religious experience. The ground
and source of all the multidimensional facets of the religious auditory and silent experience is in the *a priori* existence of God. It is the
heart of our being – a strange, aural race, Emily Dickinson held.
'And Being, but an Ear, / And I, and Silence, some strange Race /
Wrecked, solitary here.[20]

18. Randall McClellan, *The Healing Forces of Music: History, Theory and
Practice*, Rockport, MA: Element, 1991, p 3.
19. Ann and Barry Ulanov, 'Prayer and Personality: Prayer and Primary
Speech' in *The Study of Spirituality*, eds Jones / Wainwright / Yarnold,
London: SPCK, 1986, p 28.
20. Emily Dickinson, *The Complete Poems*, London / Boston: Faber and
Faber, 1970, p 129.

Silence and Divine Discourse

S peech, that is patterned, structured verbal sound, is complete in relationship with the silence that gives rise to and contains it. Ambrose Wathen summarises this point: 'Words do not exist without silence, for silence is an essential part of intelligible sound and without silence there would be no language.'[1] Any act of speech breaks the silence and resurrects it again on cessation. 'One can hear silence sounding through speech. Real speech is in fact nothing but the resonance of silence.'[2] Joanne Daly believes that silence and discourse are naturally in equilibrium, which is aural terminology: 'Silence is not the enemy of dialogue, but its natural counterpoise.'[3] Silence keeps discourse balanced.

What is uppermost here in this theology of listening is to make the radical, surprising connection between the Word of God and the Silence of God. Reflecting on God begins with a listening in the silence of the temple of one's own thoughts. Teresa of Avila speaks of this silent experience gracefully: 'Every way in which the Lord helps the soul here, and all he teaches it, takes place with such quiet and so noiselessly that, seemingly to me, the work resembles the building of Solomon's temple where no sound was heard. So in this temple of God, in this his dwelling place, he alone and the soul rejoice together in the deepest silence.'[4] Teresa is surely the patron saint of silence through this infinitely rich phrase. In true silence, she believes, all things are accomplished despite the ambient sounds. Her model is Solomon's temple,

1. Wathen OSB, *Silence:The Meaning of Silence in the Rule of St Benedict*, p xii.
2. Picard, *The World of Silence*, p 11.
3. Sister Joanne Daly, 'Out of the depths', in *Sisters Today* 38, 1967, p 195.
4. Quoted from *The Collected Works of St Teresa of Avila*, trs Kieran Kavanaugh and Otilio Rodriguez, 2 vols, Washington DC: Institute of Carmelite Studies, 1976, 'The Interior Castle' 7.3.11, Vol. 2:441-442.

miraculously and silently built when 'neither hammer nor axe nor
any tool of iron was heard in the temple while it was being built (1
Kings 6:7). Teresa of Jesus' message of silence is one of marvellous
fidelity to God which is ultimately a cosmic stillness where this
Divine voice is heard. Her anthem is: 'But the Lord is in his holy
temple; let all the earth keep silence before him!' (Hab 2:20).

Philosophically speaking, Fiumara portrays the mental leap
between word and silence: 'The thoughtful mind out of silence
bursts forth in the relentless concert of the logos-in-progress.'[5]
Words once spoken out of the silence fade into another silence
from out of which meaning and understanding gradually emerge.
T. S. Eliot's meaning of words, spoken and heard, and eventual
silence implies dynamism, movement and success in establishing
communication: 'Words, after speech, reach / Into the silence …'[6]
Words along with silence reach out to God.

Paradoxically, most reflection resides within the interior silent
castle of the mind precisely because we are at a loss for words to
break out of the silence. This is particularly true about the name
above all names, which is God. Once spoken, the rest is silence.
Karl Rahner is aware of this paradox. Writing about the ineffable,
elusive power of the word of God, he says that the word 'God'
'means "the *silent* one" who is always there, and yet can always be
overlooked, unheard …'[7]

The dilemma for the Christian believer, Hans Urs von
Balthasar holds, is that 'everything is decided by the question of
whether God has spoken to man – about himself, of course, and
then about his intention in creating man and his world – or
whether the Absolute remains *silent* beyond all earthly words.'[8]
Karl Rahner expresses a similar quandary in the form of prayerful
questioning: 'Is your silence … really a discourse filled with infinite promise, unimaginably more meaningful than any audible
word you could speak to the limited understanding of my narrow

5. Fiumara, *The Other Side of Language*, p 95.
6. T. S. Eliot,' Four Quartets: Burnt Norton, V', *Collected Poems, 1909-1962*,
London: Faber and Faber, 1963, p 194.
7. Rahner, *Foundations of the Christian Faith*, p 46. Italics mine.
8. Von Balthasar, *Christian Meditation*, p 7. Italics mine.

heart …?'[9] These theologians, the most important of the few commentators on the role of listening and silence in theology, conjoin
the aural and the silent in God's self-disclosure. The silence of
alert attentiveness and reply in this essentially aural theology are
complementary. Since the essence of Christianity is the self-communication of God's Word to humankind, through his incarnated
Son, then theological praxis must concern itself with silence and
discourse. For Ambrose Wathen, silence is about communicating
with God. In this vital conversation, 'man must listen and so be
silent, and when man wishes to respond, he must use silence as
well as words to make himself intelligible.'[10] Silence and sound
listening are inseparable. Silence is the shore of the ocean of
sound.

   In all human discourse, a listening silence is present. For Max
Picard, 'When two people are conversing with one another, however, a third is always present: Silence is listening'.[11] This is noteworthy in the theology of listening. God's self-revelation can be
disclosed in the very silence between the divine/human discourse. The triune God communicates with humanity from the
depths of stillness and sound. The inner being of the Trinity demands a vocality, an expression and a silence.

   It is like the supreme mantra in the Hindu tradition: *Om* is
formed from three letters, a diphthong merges 'a' and 'u' and with
'm' in a trinity which is one sound only. In Christian tradition,
God and Jesus are the diphthong; the silence of the Holy Spirit is
the 'm'. In this Christian trilogy of silence, the past, present and
the future is to be heard. All that is beyond the triad of hearing, listening and silence, God fills and goes way beyond. Silence can
speak and can be the grace of God freely and lovingly bestowed.
Silence can also be the heart of the soul that reveals the friendship
with oneself.

   David Tracy hints at the importance of silence in religion.
'Silence may indeed be the final and most adequate mode of

9. Karl Rahner, *Encounters with Silence*, trs James M. Demske, London:
Burns & Oates, 1975, p 21.
10. Wathen, *Silence*, p xiii.
11. Picard, *The World of Silence*, p 8.

CHAPTER FOUR   193

speech for religion.'[12] God alone reveals the silence which is mind-
fully heard in an eternal, two-way dialogue. Furthermore, Picard
confirms that 'in the human mind, silence is merely knowledge of
the *Deus absconditus*, the hidden god'.[13] The God who freely reveals
will be known not only in names but also in silence. This silence
does not reduce God to absence or mere emptiness, but is the fullness, which is a Trinity of Persons. It is almost as if the Trinity is not
composed of just three parts but of four: the fourth is the silence
that reveals the triune God to the universe and wherein cosmic
sound disappears. Human silence, which human ears can perceive, arises out of the silence that cannot be heard yet which is
drawn back to the world by an organic momentum. The Word is
the fruit of the silent seed of divine / human encounter. To taste the
full fruit is to taste the revelation of God in and through the dialogical Trinity. This still place of God is where the human being can
encounter a symbol or sign that expresses and directs attention towards the presence of God. In the silent revelation of God's Word,
human experience is touched and endowed with a discipline of
love. For Mark Patrick Hederman, 'every word of revelation has a
margin of silence.'[14] That being the truth, in fundamental theology,
which focuses on divine revelation, discourse and silence, must be
inclusive in the discussion. In theology, one cannot survive, indeed exist, without the other.

Silence and divine discourse are the concern of discipleship.
The listening disciple's mind is silent, patient, virtuous, listening,
receptive and responsive. *Nam loqui et docere magistrum condecet,
tacere et audire discipulum convenit* – Speaking and teaching are the
master's task; the disciple is to be silent and listen.'[15] The follow-
er's tacit inner ear mirrors the absolute silence from out of which
God's Word breaks forth.

It is a discipline acknowledged and imposed even by the pre-
Christian philosopher-mystic Pythagoras who imposed on new

12. Tracy, *The Analogical Imagination*, p 174.
13. Picard, *The World of Silence*, p 14.
14. Mark Patrick Hederman, *Anchoring the Altar*, Dublin:Veritas, 2002, p 13.
15. *The Rule of St Benedict*, ed Timothy Fry OSB, Collegeville, MN: The
Liturgical Press, 1981, p190/191.

disciples five years of total silence. The primacy of sound, its definition and organisation is an important aspect of the Pythagorean legacy. The discovery of the numerical basis of all musical concordances is attributed to him. It could be speculated that he was keenly aware not only of the paradox but also of the synonymous nature of both silence and patterned sound, which is music. Nine hundred years later, Ambrose of Milan cautioned that: 'It is more difficult to know how to be silent than how to speak.'[16] For the disciple who submits to or chooses this discipline of yearning, it carries its own infinitely creative risks also.

The discourse with God, which is of the essence of all theological reflection, is integrated and deepened in the space of silence. The realm and practice of silence is just one other manifestation of God that embraces the word and implicates the ear. Von Balthasar puts it succinctly: 'Interior silence carries the word that sounds, justifies it and gives it efficacy.'[17] To access the quiet voice of God, silence must be tempered or heightened. It is not a suppression of sounds but an appropriate shaping of expression that empowers listening to the intonation of God.

Every human being moves toward the silent mystery of God before which all sounds disintegrate and fade. In this Divine silence, the human encounter and quest is as ever for 'one who was always here before I was.'[18] God is the silent one, who when heard and addressed in prayer begins to sound. For the praying listener, there is ' a time to keep silence and a time to speak' (Eccles 3:7, Sir 20:1-8). In the Book of Job, the underlying theme is one of God's silent timing. God remained silent until Job in his own time handed sound over. When Job fell into silence, God could be heard.

There is a time, therefore, for silence that is, at one and the same time, a time for listening. The two-roomed *locus silentiae* or space of silence waits to realise the message of God's grace in what appears to be a void, which can never be anticipated or prepared for. The prayer of the silent one is defined by Thomas Merton as

16. Ambrose of Milan, *Three Books on the Duties of the Clergy*, quoted from *The Encyclopedia of Religion*, p 323.
17. von Balthasar, *Word and Revelation*, p 171.
18. von Balthasar, *Christian Meditation*, p 85.

the 'attentive, watchful listening of 'the heart.'[19] The wisdom of silence in scripture is a 'famine of the word' (Amos 8:11-12). So here is the full cyclic pattern of prayer: the listening to God which of its essence craves for silence and the prayerful response to God also has the same hankering. Silence, therefore, is the prayer base of the triangle, which reaches up to the summit of God. From this prayer-filled base of still calm the cloud of alienation lifts. It is as if the realm of silence is the vertical, where heaven meets earth; being in the listening space of the base of that silent triangle is the horizontal, where silence penetrates the human body through the human sense of hearing. Max Picard makes a similar analogy: 'The word and therefore man is in the centre between two regions of silence … the lower human silence … and the higher silence of God.'[20] But this stops short: God's silence is not only wedded to the human world and experience, there is the primeval silence of God. This divine silence of the imagination is the poetry of God because 'poetry is the language of silence.'[21]

19. Thomas Merton, *Contemplative Prayer*, London:DLT, 1975, p 33.
20. Picard, *The World of Silence*, p 232.
21. O'Donohue, *Anam Chara*, p 67.

Silence – 'A Virtue, have it if you can ...'

Avirtue in its widest sense of meaning is, according to Karl
Rahner, 'any perfectly developed capacity of man's spiritual soul, or the development itself.'[1] To claim that silence
is a virtue is to suggest the transformative nature of silence and its
theological possibilities. A virtue is, according to Paul Wadell, a
'characteristic way of behaviour which makes both actions and
persons good and which also enables one to fulfil the purpose of
life ... conversely, a lack of virtue constitutes a deprived nature
and a diminished self.'[2] Of its very nature, a virtue grows and increases through repeated behaviour and reveals both the character and subsequent action of oneself. Therefore, as Wathen suggests,
'silence is a moral virtue.'[3]

Virtues are transformative. On repeated practice, a process of
change can occur, what Thomas Aquinas terms, a 'modification of
a subject' which is the primary proponent of a Christian virtue
ethics.[4] Wadell finds: 'That is why virtues are central to Christian
spirituality.'[5] Through the decision to become silent, one can, if
one chooses, allow oneself to be open to a transformation filled
with, and by, God's self-communication.

Transformative silence, therefore, takes its place beside the
three categories of virtues: the three theological virtues defined

1. Karl Rahner, 'Virtue' in *Encyclopedia of Theology: A Concise Sacramentum
Mundi*, ed Karl Rahner, London: Burns & Oates, (1975), 1981, p 1794.
2. Paul J. Wadell, 'Virtue' in *The New Dictionary of Catholic Spirituality*, p
998. On a minor note, it is interesting that no entry under 'virtue' appears
in *The New Dictionary of Fundamental Theology*, eds Latourelle/Fisichella,
1994.
3. Wathen, *Silence*, p xiii.
4. See St Thomas Aquinas, *The Summa Theologica of St Thomas Aquinas*, trs
Fathers of the English Dominican Province, London: Burns Oates &
Washbourne Ltd., 1923, Pt 1-11, q 49, a 2, p 282.
5. Wadell, 'Virtue' in *The New Dictionary of Catholic Spirituality*, p 998.

by Paul in the First letter to the Corinthians (13:13), faith hope and
love; the natural cardinal virtues which are prudence, justice, tem-
perance and fortitude; and the eschatological virtues as labelled by
James Walter as gratitude, humility, vigilance, serenity and joy.[6]
In this latter taxonomy of 'virtues', a theosonic silence is at home
in its alliance with 'serenity' and 'joy'.

Exercise of the virtue of silence allows for full potential to be
achieved. The goal is ultimate human excellence. The virtue of
silence is teleological: from Aristotle to Thomas Aquinas, the
realm of silence targets the good. Silence can be a process by virtue
of which God shapes us gradually in love. It is a conversion
through the grace of God's loving silence. After all, as Tracy summarises, 'the only God there is, is the God who is love.'[7]

The quality of the virtue eventually becomes the quality of
oneself. Choosing to don the robe of silence is to court *conversion*. It
is argued, therefore, that the aural sense can be a central force in
one's conversion. Paul Wadell claims that men and women move
to their end through the virtues, but the movement is not a change
of place but a change of person, which is why conversion is a fit-
ting name for what the virtues do.'[8] In this context, when one
acquires silence, obedience and humility, one becomes silent,
obedient and humble. 'That is why virtues – and vices too – are not
ornaments of the self but the deepest expression of oneself.'[9]
Silence is virtuous because, as in all the virtues, it is not what is
done but how it is done. Donning the silent cloak is not enough.
One must walk in silence. The important union between the virtue
of listening, silence and obedience draws this discourse to a close.
'No sooner did he hear than he obeyed me' (Ps 18:45).

A final word here on the concept of monastic silence since it
was in the context of Benedictine monastic silence that Placid
Spearritt referred to silence, along with obedience and humility,

---

6. James J. Walter, in his article on 'virtue' in *New Dictionary of Theology*,
p1083. Perhaps it is within this category that silence – allied to serenity –
finds its rightful place.
7. Tracy, *The Analogical Imagination*, p 431.
8. Wadell, 'Virtue' in *The New Dictionary of Catholic Spirituality*, p 998
9. Ibid, p 998.

as one of the 'great trilogy of *monastic* virtues.'[10] As has already been pointed out, the concept of 'obedience' is aural etymologically; to be obedient is simply to listen keenly to one another or to God. Therefore, in monastic virtue, two of the trilogy are virtues of aurality.

Elizabeth McCumsey presents silence entirely in monastic terms – environmental, communal, personal and mystical. Even mystical silence cannot be defined apart from the articulated mystic's experience. 'Even the silence of the mystic is an expression of a meaning produced by a speaker.'[11] Monasticism so finely tuned and articulated by St Benedict in his Rule, which 'became almost the sole norm of Western monasticism',[12] highly values both the aural centred virtues of hearing and silence. Choosing silence is about self-transformation. Ambrose Wathen holds that in monasticism 'one thinks in silence, one reflects in silence, one meditates and contemplates in silence.'[13] Benedictine silence is at one and the same time a virtue of obedience. The retreat from speech as Benedict understands it 'is one of penance and self-discipline … a method of avoiding sin …'[14] Placid Spearritt states that 'silence is the second of the monastic virtues …'[15] The first is 'obedience' which is the subject of Benedictine Rule, Chapter 5, although it forms a consistent thread throughout the entire Rule. However, it is more accurate to say that both silence and obedience are conjoined, neither being first or second; silence is the *primus inter pares* – a first among equals. It is obedient to itself in its listening and response. 'Connected with listening … silence is integrally related to obedience … Silence is the necessary prerequisite for obedience.'[16] One must obediently listen; one must obediently search out silence. If one or other experience is absent, the timbre of the Divine Voice of revelation is muffled beyond any comprehension

10. See Spearritt, 'Benedict' in *The Study of Spirituality*, p 152. Italics mine.
11. Tracy, *The Analogical Imagination*, p 175.
12. *The Rule of St Benedict*, ed Timothy Fry OSB, p 113.
13. Wathen, *Silence*, p xii.
14. Love, 'Listening to Silence' p 6.
15. Spearritt, 'Benedict' in *The Study of Spirituality*, p 154.
16. Wathen, *Silence*, p 31.

or understanding.

On the other hand, there is a dark side to silence and discourse, a darkness which words and language share: hearing words and silence can become distorted in perception and interpretation. Writing about language philosophically, Leslie Kane puts it simply: 'Language ... often serves to perpetuate barriers of misunderstanding.'[17] I had a conversation with a Benedictine writer, Fr Vincent Ryan, about the widespread notion before the Vatican II reforms, of day and night silence in monasticism. He highlighted this negative element and he was quite clear that this malevolent abuse of silence was good riddance where silence can confuse and become the centrepiece in a clash of communication. Furthermore, he recalled that silence was a necessary punishment for sin; the most extreme penalty or sanction was a total silence even from oral participation in the daily monastic offices. A silence can be persuasion to turn from speech on account of fear or adversity; to simply shut up for the sake of avoidance of consequences. So too silence can be abused and misunderstood in relationships carrying a variety of meanings including dismissal, exclusion and total refusal. Silence can, in this regard, be a vice if it is enforced or fearfilled. So cultivating a healthy silence means quelling an addiction to superfluous noise, babble and much more.

---

17. Kane, *The Language of Silence*, p 19.

Silence – The book-ends of Scripture

Silence is like a pair of bookends supporting each end of the
scripture's book row, holding upright and together the silent
message of *Deus Semper Major*. The entire tome of Judaeo-
Christian scripture is one long conversational story between
Creator and created which emerged from silence. God is the silent
one, the hidden one of the Jewish Testament. God, the conversation partner of the Old Testament, keeps bringing the conversation back to covenantal memories that are both aural and visual.
The purpose now is to make the point that within scriptural silence, God's Voice has always been revealed. In other words,
through an understanding of the concept of silence in scripture,
God is Word and Silence uniquely revealed and uttered in the fullness of the Trinity. This revelation is both sonic and silent. Hans
Urs von Balthasar refers to the incarnate Word of Jesus Christ as
'the wordless but still resounding Word.'[1] Out of the completeness
of the Trinity, God utters the incarnate Word that is a symbol of creation. 'All utterable words are enveloped by an aura of silence and
of the silent One, for he is more than utterable.'[2]

The Old Testament silence of God is also about seeing. 'Do not
hide your face from me' (Ps 27:9). Silence is the hidden sight and
sound of God. God's face and sound are synonymous in both the
Old and New Testaments. 'I will hide my face from them' promises
the Lord to Moses (Deut 31:17). But in the eternal covenant of love,
God owns that moment when he hid his face from them (Is 54:8)
when he was silent in their defence. This silence holds in it deep
healing after punishment. 'For I have hidden my face from this
city … I am going to bring it recovery and healing' (Jer 33:5-6).
Through this silence of the hidden face, therein lies wholeness

---

1. Von Balthasar, *Christian Meditation*, p 41.
2. Ibid, p 82.

and healing which has to be found in the absence or presence of sound.

God is to be *both* seen and heard. 'Do not hide your face from your servant ... make haste to answer me' (Ps 64:17) the psalmist cries in a prayer for deliverance from persecution which demands visual and aural assurance. God of my eye is also God of my ear. And again, another of our afflicted psalmist forebears calls for and endorses the exact theosonic circle: God is called upon in prayer (Ps 102:1) he must not hide his face, i.e. be silent before our cry (v 2); God must aurally incline to us (v 2b); and God must be *maieuteria*, the midwife, to us all as yet unborn in the praise of the Lord (v 18).

Psalm 30 also sanctions that sense of the hidden God who dismays, hiding in sight and sound (Ps 30:7b). Dismay from both verbal and visual concealment is breath taking: it is death itself: 'When you hide your face, they are dismayed; when you take away their breath. They die' (Ps 104:29).

A silence, an absence of spoken words, befalls Ezekiel in isolation. He cannot go to speak to his people to try to convert them. The very sound of the voice of the Lord in Ezekiel's ear is the latchkey for these rebellious house of Israel which will open the mouth of Ezekiel and will 'let those who will hear, hear; and those who refuse to hear, refuse ... (Ezek 3:19). From out of this silence revelation is born. In short, God's silence is God's saving presence: 'For God alone my soul waits in silence' (Ps 62:1). God is my saviour in silence: 'from him comes my salvation' (Ps 62:1b). God's silence is the key that is lying around to unlock the bolt of the door through which humanity goes to God and God comes to humankind. Not only does a key give access to another space; it also protects and secures that space. Once admitted therefore to 'stand in the house of the Lord, in the courts of the house of our God' (Ps 135:2), the key of silence secures and controls the entrance into that mysterious, graced divine presence.

John Rybolt claims that the author of the Book of the Wisdom of Solomon, although depicting a movement from peace to mourning, 'sets the stage carefully ... when the personified word

of God appears.'[3] 'When peaceful silence lay over all, and the
night had run half of her swift course, your all-powerful word, O
Lord, leaped down from heaven, from the royal throne' (Book of
Wisdom 18:14-15). Von Balthasar links this 'all-powerful word
with the Word made flesh in John.'[4] This scenic description resonates with another passage from The Apocalypse: peaceful silence
reigned in heaven, not on earth, not for half the *night* but for '*about*'
half an *hour* (Rev 8:1). Such celestial silence is beyond all human
imagination; even John of Patmos lost all conception of time in its
midst of the stillness.

In the unfolding of scriptures, sound and silence are constantly
revisited as the *loci* of God's self-communication. A divinely decreed and ordained plan of salvation which God had prepared
through the 'still small voice' of Elijah was first heard out of the
not-so-peaceful silence of Horeb. For the Christian, as Max Picard
writes:

> Since Christ the Divine Word came down to men from God,
> the 'still small voice', the way of the transformation of silence
> into speech was traced out for all time. The Word that ap-
> peared two thousand years ago was on the way to man from
> the beginning of time, and therefore from the very beginning
> there was a breach between silence and speech. The event of
> two thousand years ago was so miraculous that all silence
> from time immemorial was torn open by speech. Silence trem-
> bled in advance of the event and broke in two.[5]

Silence marks the embryonic reality of God's incarnate Son, a
fact that David Tracy describes as 'the not-yet always present in
the always-already reality disclosed in Jesus Christ.'[6] In the silence
of the Marian womb, the Word of God is muted for the appropriate gestation period. Hans Urs von Balthasar writes that 'the birth
is preceded by nine months ... of deepest silence, so that, in so far

3. John Rybolt, 'The Book of the Wisdom of Solomon' in *The Collegeville Bible Commentary*, p 720.
4. Von Balthasar, *The Glory of God*, p 117.
5. Picard, *The World of Silence*, p 15.
6. Tracy, *The Analogical Imagination*, p 430. He eloquently plays on this paradoxical idiom on pp 429-431.

as the event whereby "the Word becomes flesh" occurs precisely at the conception, the act of the Word's becoming man means an act of becoming silent.'[7] True theologically, but in biological terms not so, since hearing is well developed in the womb at about five months of pregnancy. However, this does not detract from these marvellous conclusions of Von Balthasar. This new silence embraces the mystery of the triune God. Silence precedes the historical and prophetic word. For Angelus Silesius, silence is a stillness that is filled with the will of God. 'Nothing resembles naught than to be silent, still: For silence nothing seeks but what he wills, my will.'[8]

The ultimate word of God in the incarnation of Jesus Christ in turn transforms into a new silence of the eschatological kingdom of God – *Basileia tou Theo*. One aural theosonic symbol is the silence of the Cross into the transformed prayer of the Holy Spirit. As Jesus Christ resolutely embraced the silence of the Cross, the moment of silence is the birth of the new Creation. Now the silent God shatters his own silence in the new song of victory over darkness and death. Golgotha, aptly named by Mircea Eliade as 'the summit of the cosmic mountain',[9] is the everlasting symbol of silence. 'Man lives between the world of silence from which he comes and the world of the other silence to which he goes – the world of death.'[10] For Christians, therefore, the world yet to come is one of divine silence, to be embraced at the summit of each one's cosmic mountain. On the other hand, according to Gelineau the absence of the Sound of God means death because 'if he no longer speaks and is silent we should take the initiative to cry to him in order that he should reply, for silence is death.'[11]

Words and deeds of Christ issue from his own still integrity of silence, which is his openness and oneness with God, all human beings and the entire cosmos. It is, at one and the same time, an

7. Von Balthasar, *The Glory of the Lord: A Theological Aesthetics*, VII, *Theology: The New Covenant*, p 143-144.
8. Angelus Silesius, *The Cherubinic Wanderer*, p 67.
9. Mircea Eliade, *The Sacred and the Profane: The Nature of Religion*, Orlando, FL: Harcourt Brace Jovanovich, 1987, p 39.
10. Picard, *The World of Silence*, p 25.
11. Gelineau, 'The Path of Music', p 137.

obedient listening and humble response. The incarnate God-man, who is the fullness of the Father's Word, lived in word and died in silence to return that ultimate divine Word to that same Father. In Jesus Christ, God's silence ceases.

The Symphony of the divine begins with the theme of creation. An awareness of the world is an awareness of oneself through the evocation or 'vocation' of God. Every word he speaks, every act he makes, is God's Word in all its human guises. 'The concrete, spoken (or *silent*) Word cannot be detached from the Word that he himself is. And this Word ... does not intend ... to reach us, perhaps up to our physical or spiritual ear, but to let his words ... touch the inmost core of our person.'[12] Yet Jesus' words and gestures are his silence also. '... there is no Word or gesture of Jesus of which we could say: that has nothing to do with me.'[13] Therefore, every silence of Jesus has to do with all Christian believers. His obedient silence is the guarantee of cosmic salvation. Salvation is the trust of the Son of God in silence. 'For God alone my soul waits in silence, from him comes my salvation' (Ps 62:1). Human silence represents the vast oceans of existence while the Incarnate silence in contrast is the *terra firma*, infinitely smaller but filled with the sound ground of God's silent self disclosure.

Throughout the pivotal moments of Christ's profound silence before his accusers, his silent patience, grief and suffering, radically become first person experiences. Darkness and solitude evoke the fact and act of christological silence (Mk 1:35, Mt 14:23). That same darkness and solitude evoke the fact of a death and resurrection in that same silence. 'Yes, in solitary, silent, vague darkness, the Awful One is near.'[14]

---

12. Von Balthasar, *Christian Meditation*, p 35. Italics mine.
13. Ibid, p 36.
14. Otto, *The Idea of the Holy*, p 221.

Summary

ilence is the eternal note that is the everlasting silence of God. In the cumulative levels of theosony, the realm of silence is the third note; the first being cosmic sound, the second being speech or self-aware communication, in the theosonic symphony which is fully heard and performed by Jesus Christ and conducted by the Holy Spirit, under the baton of the triune God. In Christ, silence and sound are consonantly combined. According to Thomas Carlyle, 'Speech is of Time, Silence Eternity.'[1] God's self-revelation is one of both word and silence. God's story unfolds in the spoken and the unspoken. There is no turning a blind eye to God; there is no turning a deaf ear to God. Karl Rahner speaks theologically: 'The absolute being of God appears as a being that speaks or remains silent, in other words as the God of a possible revelation through his word, because he is the God of a necessary revelation through speech *or* silence.'[2] Taking this statement to be absolutely true, the question recurs again and again: how can humanity experience these divine sonic and mute expressions?

The religious experience, which is silence, is about being what Karl Rahner terms a 'free listener'.[3] Listening freely is being 'attentive to the speech or the silence of God in the measure in which he opens himself in free love to this message of the speech or the silence of the God of revelation.'[4]

In the divine/human encounter, the silent space is threefold: on the one hand, it is the space of *listening* to the voice of God; on the other hand, it is the vital non-verbal *communication* space wherein the praying human *responds* to that voice; in third place is

---

1. Thomas Carlyle in *Sartor Resartus* Book III, Chapter III quoted in Kelsey, *The Other Side of Silence.*
2. Rahner, *Hearers of the Word*, 1969, p 94.
3. This is the title of Chapter 8 in *Hearers of the Word*, p 94.
4. Ibid, p 108.

the capacity of silence to overcome, to camouflage and hush up
the sounds that side-track and draw true being away from true
conversation which is with the triune God. To return to Rahner
again, 'what man always and essentially hears is the speaking or
the *silence* of a free God who subsists in himself alone.[5] Silence is
the space between the said and the saying. Stillness effects the
true dialogue with the ineffable Divine Other. It is a philosophical
consideration also according to Fiumara: 'Only when we know
how to be silent will that of which we cannot speak begin to tell us
something.'[6] Theosonic silence, therefore, is both a radical listening and a simultaneous response to the triune God who is best revealed out of the mists of silence. The greatest deficit of the aural
and the silent is that it can hear but it cannot see. But in the dialectic between silence and darkness, stillness and shade are not comparable; one hears in both sound and silence, one cannot see in
darkness, but one can hear in silence. In the words of the seventeenth century mystical poet, Johann Scheffler, better known as
Angelus Silesius: 'God far exceeds all words that we can here express / In silence he is heard, in silence worshipped best.'[7]

God's self- revelation is not only in sound and listening but is
also of necessity in silence. 'To you praise is silence, O God' (Ps
65:2). The triune Godhead's hidden nature captivates and over-
comes his own people in silent sounds that transcend human creation. The religious experience of silence and sound are, for von
Balthasar, a 'dimension of this Word that cannot be detected by
human ears.'[8] 'Heard melodies are sweet but those unheard are
sweeter' in Keats's memorable lines.[9]

Sacred silence is absurd, limitless and ineffable. God as silence
is ineffable. In the threshold of prayer where the spirit of God
speaks to humanity, silence is the underlying principle. Even, as
Rahner simply says, 'if God does not speak, man's spirit hears

5. Ibid, p 92, Italics mine.
6. Fiumara, *The Other Side of Language*, p 101.
7. Angelus Silesius, *The Cherubinic Wanderer*, p 49.
8. von Balthasar, *Christian Meditation*, p 44.
9. John Keats, 'Ode on a Grecian Urn', II, 11, 12, *John Keats: The Complete Poems*, ed John Barnard, London: Penguin Books, 1973, (1978), p 344.

God's very silence.'[10] Silence is prayer itself; in other words, it is a noiselessness communicating the sound of God which largely eludes language and dismisses it. From out of the silence emerges slowly an aural manuscript of the inner voice of God, which becomes the perfect facsimile of human response. In the attempt to probe the depths of Divine / human encounter, Word yields to the Word in silence. 'Silence is the nature of God; but in that nature ... everything is word and silence at the same time.'[11]

Relinquishing the world of words and sounds, the God-seeker bridges the hiatus between heaven and earth. The lacuna is silent. By a subtle play of silent light and silent shade, God shows in silent relief. In the experience of listening silence, Christians truly listen before Jesus, with Jesus and after Jesus. Karl Rahner answers the swarms of questions raised in a revelation of silence thus: 'Perceiving the silence of God can also be an answer, made meaningful by listening, because man can become what he must be even through God's silence.'[12] Silence and listening permit going beyond thought and knowledge into God's surpassing love; this is an epistemology which is made of silence and listening. This Exposition was towards the role of silence in that epistemology; Then theme One of the Development attempts to integrate both concepts in defining theosony as religious experience. The realm of poetry can suggest these interactions of dynamic sound, listening and silence in silent relief; interactions according to George Steiner, which 'are actions of the spirit rooted in silence. It is difficult to speak of these, for how should speech justly convey the shape and vitality of silence?'[13]

> Words move, music moves
> Only in time; but that which is only living
> Can only die. Words, after speech, reach
> Into the silence. Only by the form, the pattern,

10. Rahner, *Hearers of the Word*, p 92.
11. Picard, *The World of Silence*, p 230.
12. Rahner, *Hearers of the Word*, p 174.
13. Steiner, *Language and Silence*, p 30.

Can words or music reach
The stillness, as a Chinese jar still
Moves perpetually in its stillness.[14]

14. T. S. Eliot, Burnt Norton V, *The Complete Poems and Plays of T. S. Eliot*, London: Faber and Faber, 1969, p 175.

CHAPTER FIVE

Theosony and Religious Experience

To speak of God, the theologian must have experienced
God and been taught by God. What we can expect of the
theologian is an intelligent and self-conscious faith that
combines the sympathetic understanding of an insider
with the detachment of an outsider.

Gerald O'Collins SJ, *Fundamental Theology*, p 6.

We had the experience but missed the meaning,
And approach to the meaning restores the experience

T. S. Eliot, *The Dry Salvages*

Theosonic Religious Experience

The aim of all religions is to reveal an understanding and presence of the Divine in all its manifestations, even where there is no conscious adherence to divine Revelation. Fundamental theologians argue strongly on behalf of religious experience. Jean-Pierre Torrell welcomes 'the renewed place given to *experience* in theology' and which 'must be of concern first and foremost to fundamental theology'.[1] The multi-faceted experiences of God in the world, in life, are, according to Dermot Lane, 'some of the basic elements that make up fundamental theology',[2] which Gerald O'Collins sees as embracing 'the reality of faith, the nature of human experience and the role of reason.'[3] The *sine qua non* of any such exploration must be a personal awareness of the Divine presence in our world, that '*numen praesens*,'[4] which motivates the fundamental theologian to reflect on the nature and act of religious experience.

It is through real, personal experience of God that revelation becomes apparent. John Henry Newman uses the apposite metaphor of 'voice' to draw the primary distinction of the discipline of fundamental theology, the difference between where we come in and where God comes in, between prayer and revelation. 'As prayer is the voice of man to God, so revelation is the voice of God to man.'[5]

The true doctrine of divine Revelation is 'the personal self-

1. Jean-Pierre Torrell, ' New Trends in Fundamental Theology in the Postconciliar Period' in *Problems and Perspectives of Fundamental Theology*, eds.= René Latourelle/ O'Collins, trs Matthew J. O Connell, NJ: Paulist Press, 1980, p 20. Italics mine.
2. Dermot A.Lane, *The Experience of God: An Invitation to do theology*, Dublin: Veritas, 1981, p 3.
3. O'Collins, *Fundamental Theology*, p 21.
4. Otto, *The Idea of the Holy*, p 11.
5. Newman, *A Grammer of Ascent*, p 314.

communication of God to people in the history of salvation which reaches its fullness in the person of Jesus Christ'.[6] Self-communication of divine love through Jesus Christ is a personal faith invitation to the human being to enter into a new life of fellowship with him. The Fathers at Vatican II were keenly aware of the necessity to widen the boundaries of credibility with regard to such revelation. They emphasised the anthropological aspect of this Christian revelation. 'God's revelation would have no meaning for us if it was not also revelation of the meaning of human existence'.[7]

To have a religious experience is to be mysteriously transformed at some level. Karl Rahner holds that 'mystery ... is the underlying substrate which is presupposed to and sustains the reality we know'.[8] He elaborates on this *a priori* disposition of humanity to receive revelation as 'a certain prior apprehension which transcends every particular concrete reality'.[9] David Tracy approaches the paradox from another angle: 'When religious persons speak the language of revelation, they mean that something has happened to them that they cannot count as their own achievement.'[10] This is the paradox of religious experience: it is and has to be my experience; and at the same time it is and has to be entirely God's doing. Otherwise it is an invention of my subjectivity.

How does the religious experience of God's self-revelation transform us? In the words of Donald Maloney, 'God's communication of himself ... affects our consciousness, affects the way we experience ourselves and our relationships to the world around us'.[11] There has to be some antecedent interior grace, which Dermot Lane believes, 'develops from within nature'.[12] The duality of religious experience is the revelation of God on the one hand

6. Lane, *The Experience of God*, p 48.
7. Henri Bouillard, *The Logic of the Faith*, Dublin: M.H. Gill, 1967, p 23.
8. Rahner, *Theological Investigations*, 11, Chapter 6 'The Experience of God Today', London: DLT, 1974, p 155.
9. Ibid, p 155.
10. Tracy, *The Analogical Imagination*, p 173.
11. Donald, G. Maloney SJ, 'Revelation and Experience' in *Doctrine and Life*, Dublin: Dominican Publications, March 1975, p 196.
12. Lane, *The Experience of God*, p 33.

and on the other the recognisable 'experience' of the one so graced. David Tracy's insight is important here: 'Experience of grace ... is as large as the Christian experience of life. It is experience of man's capacity for self-transcendence, of his unrestricted openness to the intelligible, the true and the good.'[13] The fundamental truth being proposed here is that of all the existential prevenient sites where nature prepares for the event of revelation, the human ear is the most sensitive and theologically attuned. What Dylan Thomas calls 'the round Zion of the water bead / And the synagogue of the ear of corn'[14] was constructed by the creator with such biological complexity, such physiological ingenuity, that it can go way beyond itself in its operational capacity as a purely sensory organ. As already expounded in detail, whereas the eye ceases to be effective when it enters alienating atmospheres like fog or darkness, the ear continues to function in every situation and all through the night. The natural grace of the ear held into the alienating atmosphere of silence, far from rendering us impotent provides the positive and the negative combination which allows the electricity of divine energy to percolate through. The ear is the acoustic chamber, which allows the voice of God to sound, almost as a seashell placed against it can echo the sounds of the ocean. The object is the seashell, yet the inherited sound is that of the roaring sea, the sound which the seashell has imbibed from the echo of the sea and continues to resound long after the shell is separated from the sea. The truth of the divine sound is not confirmed until it changes the religious experience in an attunement in keeping with the true potential of human hearing. Initially, the listening is false because theosony, the sound of God, is actually hidden and drowned out by the quotidian, everyday sound of living. Discerning the aural distractions that deflect one's attention to theosony is the theological application of being 'all ears'. In this obedient theosony, the listening becomes an organ of religious experience, religious being. To recall Dylan Thomas once more: 'Shall I let *pray* the shadow of a sound.'[15]

13. Bernard Lonergan, *A Third Collection: Papers by Bernard J. F. Lonergan SJ,* ed Frederick E. Crowe SJ, Mahwah: Paulist Press, 1985, p 32.
14. Dylan Thomas, *Collected Poems 1934-1952,* London: J. M. Dent, p 101.
15. Ibid, Italics mine.

God's self-disclosure is always a two-way revelation: on the one hand, it is the self-manifestation of God to humanity, and on the other, it is an experienced communication from our side. Theological reflection, specifically on the epitome of such religious theosonic experience is of primary importance to fundamental theology.

Karl Rahner, *Doctor mysticus* of the twentieth century, has hinted at such reflection and there are two quotations that are important here. Firstly, he argues, that the true Christian either misses or makes the mark in the choice to be receptive, to experience or not. The mystique of mysticism is forever dispelled. 'The devout Christian of the future will either be a mystic, one who has 'experienced' something, or will cease to be anything at all'[16] is his radical prognosis. Secondly, this experience is all about a certain kind of hearing – a theosonic experience. The true believer is one who 'does not hear "something" in addition to himself ... but hears himself as the self-promised word in which God sets up a listener and to whom he speaks himself as an answer.'[17] It is what Steiner would call 'that which comes *to call on us* ... spontaneous visitation and summons.'[18] In aural terminology, Zuckerkandl's articulation of this certain kind of listening wins the day. 'A world of the purely audible opens a domain in which the ear is lawgiver ... the existence of such a domain confers an entirely new dignity upon the audible world as such ... we should speak rather of the gift the Creator bestowed upon the visible world – the gift of sharing in the audible, in the dignity of being audible ... The phenomenon is unique.'[19]

A brief critical word on theology's approach to religious experience draws the first half of this section to a close. Within the documented theory of Western religiosity, so-called ordinary human experience of God was little acknowledged and therefore scantily charted. Apart from the separate, yet conjoined area of mystical encounter with the Divine, a theological empiricism (from the

---

16. Rahner, *Theological Investigations*, Vol 17, p 15.
17. Rahner, *The Practice of Faith*, p 81. Italics mine.
18. Steiner, *Real Presences*, p 179.
19. Zuckerkandl, *Man the Musician*, p 87.

Greek for 'experience') was held to be an unproductive approach towards articulating God's self-communication to the believing one.

Karl Rahner pioneered a phenomenological approach to human experience of the Divine. One should not be silent about experience because of language limitation, 'be silent about it [experience] on the grounds that we cannot speak "clearly" about it.'[20] The sense of hearing must be examined as the locus for a two-way revelation, which involves the mysterious conjunction of antipodean opposites. The auditory becomes the catalyst of a new creation, a relational entity which, according to David Tracy, means 'being caught up in and by the power of this manifestation to the point where they both radically participate in the whole while yet, with equal radicality, are distanced from the whole.'[21] It is both distant yet near, fleeting yet permanent, *pianissimo* yet *fortissimo* (the superlatives of the musical terms, *piano* and *forte*). It is the attraction of opposites, which is the essence and fascination of Divine loving relationship. 'Surely this commandment ... is not too *far* away ... the word is very *near* to you; it is in your mouth and in your heart' (Deut 30:11,14).

This is why the second subject under discussion in this section is the religious experience of divine revelation that is specifically aural as suggested by the word 'theosony'. Theosony can be a positive, human capacity to communicate with the triune Godhead. Humanity sounds back at God. Finally, this section ends with Karl Rahner's aural phenomenology: the hearer must hear out of his or her own prior experience of giving ear to God.

O'Collins knows that 'we are and will be what we experience'.[22] We are always more than that too and theosony is beyond the one sense of the ear. But hearing can make us fully alive, can change the register of our human experience and excavate our archaeological capacity for Divine relationship: such is the primary hypothesis of this present work. Since every life experience for the Christian is the *locus* where God is revealed, then every religious

---

20. Rahner, *Theological Investigations*, II, p 159.
21. Tracy, *The Analogical Imagination*, p 173.
22. O'Collins, *Fundamental Theology* p 35.

experience is about an intimate relationship with God and a deepening self-awareness. The aural experience that permits God's
self-communication is intrinsically a religious experience. Every
experience proceeds from prior experience. There is a cumulative
element where every experience increases and expands incre-
mentally.

Cardinal Newman's perception of human experiences is that
'enough for himself ... he can only bring his own experiences to
the common stock of psychological. He knows what ... satisfies
himself ... if, as he believes and is sure, it is true, it will approve itself to others also, for there is but one truth.'[23] The apparatus in
this case is the ear through which the incarnate word offers humanity, freely and lovingly, access to God. 'But those who do
what is true come to the light' (Jn 3:21). God created the Word;
Christ sounds the Word and the Holy Spirit is the persistent recurring whisper that is never silent – *et vocem eius audis.*

How does one discern the aural experience of truth? The message can be heard, according to Rahner, '*only if* he has not restricted
the absolute horizon of his openness to being in general ... only if
he has not removed in advance the possibility of the word of God
addressing him as he pleases, of meeting him in the form he desires to assume.'[24]

Keenly attending to the presence of God in our day-to-day
lives is alighting our own humanity and guiding that humanity to
flourish in the earshot of God. The ear will ensure that the fire does
not burn out; otherwise there is nothing to guide. The message of
the Good News stays the Good News however it is experienced.
Theosony is about both the sacred in the act of listening and the act
of listening in the sacred. This accumulation ultimately enhances
and intensifies the sacred encounter that is to be understood and
acknowledged in the future.

David Tracy defines a relationship of encounter. 'There is no
ready-made recipe available before the encounter of the subject
matter to guarantee success.'[25] Relationship with God cannot be

23. Newman, *A Grammar of Assent,* p 300.
24. Rahner, *Hearers of the Word,* p 108.
25. Tracy, *The Analogical Imagination,* p 429.

bought 'made and all' (a saying of my grandfather's coined for a
suit of clothes which he bought in a shop as opposed to one either
made by himself or fashioned by a local tailor). Theosony is giving
'true welcome, into one's own small granary of feeling and understanding'[26] to an aural and oral relationship with God. There is no
standard religious experience. Experiences for each and everyone
are, George Steiner, believes, 'patterned singularly to his own receptive and communicative internality'.[27] All auditory responses
are potentially theosonic, the sound of God if only one can listen
in and through the internality. Given that fact, therefore, the crucial point is to define and identify the received, in this case aural,
communication with God, which is distinctly through the ear.

Cultivation of aural experience through skill and discernment,
'adapting our muscles, our nerves, our cerebral cortex, to respond
to [a system of symbols] accurately and precisely,[28] is the elusive
strategy of the praying one. No two experiences stand isolated or
alone. Each aural experience is in direct relationship with former
experiences and lives insofar as it will act as midwife to the experience that is to come.

The vocation, the invitation to listen and respond, is not re-
mote or vague. It is direct and dynamic. The experience of listening, generally, is, Fiumara states, 'a positive experience (even if it
is sad), since it is one of the most "direct" that humans can have.
And when the event is "unthinkable" – something absurd or incomprehensible – we cannot summon the words we need to talk
about it.'[29] Merton, musing on silence, touches on something similar when he says that 'if you dare to penetrate your own silence
and risk the sharing of that solitude with the lonely other who
seeks God through you, then you will truly recover the light and
the capacity to understand what is beyond words and beyond ex-
planations because it is too close to be explained: it is the intimate
union in the depths of your own heart, of God's spirit and your

26. Steiner, *Real Presences*, p 161.
27. Ibid, p 184.
28. Lonergan, *Third Collection*, p 127.
29. Fiumara, *The Other Side of Listening*, p 123.

own secret inmost self, so that you and he are in all truth'.[30] The Word of God is close to one's own experience and sense of solitariness; God is truly in the deep silent caverns of the heart.

Aural religious experience, as it occurs at a particular instance in time and space, is a moment of personal encounter, an occurrence of something specific; the level of awareness of such experiential moments and the subsequent understanding and interpretation, will vary from experience to experience. No authentic religious experience will go unnoticed or unregistered. It is from the woven chain of each single, sacred experience that the total encounter with the Divine evolves. Here again an anthropology is explicit; the inmost self can communicate with the loving God through the human senses.

In summarising the diversity of humanity's experience of God's self-disclosure, the articulations of three people are important here, a poet and two theologians. For Angelus Silesius (Johann Schleffer), the sound of the heart in tune with God is unimaginably sweet. 'There is no sweeter tone heard in eternity/Than when my heart with God resounds in harmony.'[31] There is melody, rhythm and harmony, the three fundamental elements in Western classical music, at the disposal of the imagination through these words. Furthermore, they harmonise with the olfactory experience of the psalmist: 'How sweet are your words to my taste, sweeter than honey in the mouth!' (Ps 119:103). Secondly, Rudolf Otto held that all human beings potentially possess this sense of religious experience: 'This inborn capacity to receive and understand, is the essential thing. If that is there, very often only a very small incitement … is needed to arouse the numinous consciousness'.[32] Through the receptive aural experience, the numinous is heard. There is a specifically religious, 'graced' dimension to all human listening. Anthropology embraces theology through the senses. Thirdly, the imaginative listening which is a potential pos-

---

30. Thomas Merton, *The Hidden Ground of Love: The Letters of Thomas Merton on Religions Experience and Social Concerns*, selected and edited by William H. Shannon, New York: Farrar, Straus, Giroux, 1985, p 158.
31. Angelus Silesius, *The Cherubinic Wanderer*, p 95.
32. Otto, *The Idea of the Holy*, p 61.

session of the human being must be accompanied by the Rahnerian notion of 'good will'. The sound of God 'must always count on the "good will" of the hearer. For what he is supposed to hear is not what is contained immediately in the concept itself.'[33] Finally, the God-experience of self-disclosure is a three-fold activity of the imagination that is absurd, ineffable, and precisely 'too deep for words'; it is a positive, persistent experience nonetheless.

---

33. Rahner, *Foundations of Christian Faith*, p 26.

A threefold classification of Theosonic Religious Experience in Scripture

The aural experience of divine self-communication recorded and transmitted through scripture falls into three broad theosonic varieties.

Cosmic theosony is an anthropomorphic, metaphorical attentiveness to the voice of the ambient world from out of which a consciousness of God's presence emerges. Birds, fowl, beasts, wind through trees, sound in falling water, sing the praises of God. God created these sounds to reveal the ingenuity and generosity of the divine love. 'Did you call me / Or was it the wind / On my ill-carpentered window?'[1] If you cannot hear me, listen to the sounds of the universe around. No human being could even imagine the totality of those sounds.

Kerygmatic theosony incorporates a clear message or confrontation. Fully cognisant of the variety of meaning which this technical theological term evokes, I use it here in accordance with the following definition by the founder of 'literary criticism', William Beardslee: Kerygmatic is 'the style of … proclamation, whereby the hearer … is personally confronted.'[2]

Then, *Silent* theosony, 'the sound of sheer silence' (1 Kings 19:12), is the paradox of 'My Beloved … the silent music, the sounding solitude.'[3] Silent theosony resonates with the mystical state of silence, which is a form of mysticism, 'hesychasm', first practised by fourteenth-century Mount Athos monks. Silent theosony is a quiet, (the literal meaning of the Greek 'hesychasm')

---

1. Patrick Kavanagh, 'The Call', 1-3, in *Patrick Kavanagh: The Complete Poems*, p 64.
2. William A. Beardslee, *Literary Criticism of the New Testament*, p 84.
3. St John of the Cross, *Spiritual Canticle*, Stanza XIII. *The Complete Works of St. John of the Cross*, trs ed E. Allison Peers, Wheathampstead: Anthony Clarke, Burns and Oates, (1935), 1978, Vol 2, p 72.

or still interior state where God resounds in the ear of the heart. The mystic Meister Eckhart puts it simply: 'There we hear without sound …'[4] The one who reaches this silent state is re-calling the tradition of the hesychast who, according to Kallistos Ware, 'in an interior sense … practises inner prayer and seeks silence of the heart.'[5] Silent theosony is not manipulable: it can only be experienced. It is a mystical state that is silent, literally to the core. Elizabeth McCumsey, referring to mystical silence, puts is thus: there is 'nothing of deprivation in it, but rather a fullness beyond words. Such silence – in form so like, and in essence so unlike, everyday silence – has no place in mundane reality and therefore bewilders the mind.'[6]

Cosmic Theosony

An alertness to natural surrounding sounds can surpass all other sensual receptivity. Gerard Manley Hopkins speaks of the possibility for Divine encounter: 'All things therefore are charged with God, and if we know how to touch them, give off sparks and take fire, yield drops and flow, ring and tell of him … God's utterance of himself in himself is God the Word.'[7] God echoes in the sound of all living creatures. The power of God is heard in the thunder storm and the chiming of bells.

Cosmic theosony is a listening obediently to these distinctively human words and sounds of the cosmos. 'Listen! / There is surely something to be heard … O there is a flying word about us? For earth ears … Let us listen! / Let us listen!'[8] It is a hearing that calls forth a clarity of understanding, a keenness to the sound of the

4. M. Walshe, *Meister Eckhart: Sermons and Treatises*, Vol 2, London: Element Books, 1979, p 214.
5. Kallistos Ware, 'The Hesychasts: Gregory of Sinai, Gregory Palamas, Nicolas Cabasilas' in *The Study of Spirituality*, eds Jones, Wainwright, Yarnold, London: SPCK, 1986, p 243.
6. Elizabeth McCumsey, 'Silence', *Encyclopedia of Religion*, Vol 13, pp 321, 322.
7. Gerard Manley Hopkins, *Prose Commentary on the Exercises of St Ignatius*, Pick 1966, p 404, 16.
8. Patrick Kavanagh, 'Listen', 1, 2, 4, 5, 9, 10, *Patrick Kavanagh: The Complete Poems*, pp 31, 32.

world. It is the first step in hearing beyond and before the natural range of hearing. Re-sonating with and to the created sound of God awards the empathetic listener with an indelible emblem of the divine Other. Scriptural cosmic theosony is rich and wide-ranging. A comprehensive presentation of and commentary on the entire subject in scripture is the work of another project. This present work marks some cosmic theosonic moments from the Old and New Testaments.

First, there is the double deception story of Isaac, deceived both by Rebekah on the one hand, and all of his senses, except the ear, on the other. Isaac, old and blind, himself conceived through the word of God, blesses the wrong son because he did not trust his own ears. 'The voice is Jacob's voice, but the hands are the hands of Esau' (Gen 27). The nearly blind Isaac uses three other senses – touch, taste, and smell. As David Tracy puts it, 'the fourth, hearing, tells the truth: The voice is the voice of Jacob ...'[9] But Isaac, like Zechariah, refuses to listen and the consequences are immense. Unlike Rebekah, Isaac ignores what he hears and so is deceived. As a result of not hearing, he eats Jacob's tasty meal and gives away the first-born's blessing, rather as Esau himself had given away his first-born's birthright for a gulp of pottage.'[10] The critical moment is lost because of the 'hatta' of disobedience, the sin of not listening. On the other hand, Rebekah has a genius for listening. Thomas Brodie muses on this woman's aural brilliance. Rebekah,

> in contrast to Isaac ... is attentive and active. Above all, she still hears, and does so in the context where hearing suggests aware-ness and openness, including openness to the wider world of God's word (cf. 26:2, 5, 6). She 'hears' Isaac's instructions, and in her conversation with Jacob there is an emphasis on hearing, commanding and obeying ... Rebekah is remarkable ... by her involvement in the world of hearing and obeying.[11]

---

9. David Tracy, *The Analogical Imagination*, p 428.
10. Brodie, *Genesis as Dialogue*, p 309.
11. Ibid, p 308.

Although, it must be acknowledged, she does put her keen listening skills to less than admirable use.

Secondly, the psalms alive with and through sound are loaded with cosmic sonic imagery. Eight psalms are noteworthy here. For the psalmists, 'the earth is full of the steadfast love of the Lord' (Ps 33:5). In turn, the universe glorifies the majestic name of God (Ps 8: 9). The gibberish of childish voices is God's buttress (Ps 8:2). This auditory metaphor is reminiscent of what J. L. Austin names as the phonetic act, which is 'merely the act of uttering certain noises.'[12] This first stage of human sound chants on the glory of divine majesty and human dignity: 'Out of the mouths of babes and infants you have founded a bulwark' (Ps 8:2). Psalm 8 sings that humanity is only a little lower than God and that the human *Imago Dei* as ruler of all the universe has but one mission which is to proclaim the divine majestic name of the creator.

Psalm 29 listens to the cosmic voice of God extolling his power through the sound of nature. The voice of God thunders first and foremost for the psalmist over the waters. Here God's creation completes the circle. As Berendt puts it: '[I]t was that divine, creative voice which moved upon the face of the waters when God created the world.'[13] Then the psalmist goes on in an inspired metaphorical outburst where the voice of God 'breaks the cedars of Lebanon', 'flashes forth flames of fire', 'shakes the wilderness', 'causes the oaks to whirl' and 'strips the forest bare'. How does one describe in words the sound of flames of fire, the whirring of oaks? What human mind can imagine verbally the gentle breath of the Holy Spirit? If the Holy Spirit had a sound, would it be *like* the gentle breeze or the still small voice?

A later Psalm – 62 – makes the divine / human connection in auditory (and in silent) terms. 'The auditory element in Psalm 62 is salient,' Michael Signer states.[14] 'Once God has spoken: twice

---

12. J. L. Austin, *How to Do Things with Words*, p 95.
13. Berendt, *The Third Ear*, p 24.
14. Michael A. Signer, 'Conversation One: One Covenant or Two: Can We Sing a New Song?' in *Reinterpreting Revelation and Tradition: Jews and Christians in Conversation*, eds Pawlikowski / Perelmuter, Wisconsin: Sheed & Ward, 2000, p 18.

have I heard this' (Ps 62:11). Signer argues that God spoke one covenant, which is both revealed and concealed in the Hebrew scriptures. But the important point is that it offers two distinct interpretations of that covenant, 'one in the Oral Torah for Jews, and one in the incarnate word for Christians.'[15] This Psalm hints imaginatively at the notion of the divine voice of God who can speak all things intelligibly at once. The human voice can only say or sing one thing at a time. God, on the other hand, can 'hear ... and give ear to the words' (Ps 54:2) of every mouth and tongue in the universe. God is forever simultaneously translating. On the other hand, the mystic hears this verse, this voice of God, in dual theosonic terms. Meister Eckhart hears a true divine Trinitarian voice which faintly reverberates in every cosmic sound: 'His utterance is but one. In his words he speaks his Son and the Holy Ghost and all creatures, which are all one utterance in God ... I heard God and the creatures.'[16] In the reading of this one verse of the psalmist, cosmic, kerygmatic and silent theosony are embraced.

Enthronement psalm 98 is acoustically anthropomorphic and cosmic; the supreme methodology for praising God is for the entire world, humanity and nature alike to 'make a joyful noise to the Lord' (v 4). At the presence of the Lord, the environment assumes human sonic expressions. The psalmist invokes the ocean and its waves to roar with all its sea-life and with every single being in the world.

Yet again, St Augustine's theology is relevant on cosmic theosony. Augustine teaches humanity how to listen to the God-created world. Listening cosmically is to question the whole universe about its creator:

'And what is my God?' I put my question to the earth. It answered, 'I am not God', and all things on earth declared the same. I asked the sea and the chasms of the deep and the living things that creep in them, but they answered, 'We are not your God. Seek what is above us' ... I spoke to all things that are about me, all that can be admitted by the door of the senses,

15. Ibid, p 19.
16. Walshe, *Meister Eckhart*, p 148.

and I said, … [t]ell me something of my God'. Clear and loud they answered, 'God is he who made us'.[17]

Although this book concentrates on one particular sense, all the senses play a role in the relationship between humanity and God. This is the clear message of Augustine; the senses are created *by* God yet the senses are *not* God and can only afford a faint image of God. The five senses unite us to the cosmos; the five senses are the expression and essential mediators of religious feeling and experience. Friedrich Schleiermacher paved the way, unconsciously in sonic terms: listening to the message of God is one that resolutely resonates. This quotation has already been used but it is relevant yet again at this point. 'Your senses mediate the connection between the object and yourselves … your whole nervous system can be so permeated by it [religious feeling] that for a long time that sensation dominates and *resounds* …'[18]

Kerygmatic Theosony

Kerygmatic theosony is an aural experience that embodies a specific message or *kerygma*. It leaves little ambiguity about its content or the subsequent action to be taken. The human voice speaks, calls out, evokes and summons either to its own sound, as it seeks to communicate personally and with others, or the sound of other human voices; the human ear listens and understands on whatever level. Kerygmatic listening seeks to communicate, create and express. The use of the term 'kerygma' needs unfolding.

In a comprehensive article in the *Encylopedia of Theology*, Eberhard Simons defines this Greek word *kerygma* as 'a central reality of Christianity. It can indeed be regarded as one of the key concepts for the description of revelation.'[19] Macquarrie writes of 'the content of theology as a kerygma or proclamation of the revelatory and saving acts of God'.[20] The range of meanings out-

---

17. English translation from *St Augustine's Confessions*, Penguin, 1975, p 279.
18. Schleiermacher, *On Religion*, p 109. Italics mine.
19. Eberhard Simons, 'Kerygma' in *Encyclopedia of Theology*, p 797.
20. Macquarrie, *20th Century Religious Thought*, p 320.

lined by Simons all have to do with the oral and aural; these words are 'address', 'call out', 'summons' and 'preaching'.[21] *Kerygma* expresses the New Testament writers' 'conviction that "salvation" is essentially linked with the ... reality of the *word*: God himself in his epiphany is *word* and expresses himself as such ... it denotes both the act and the message.'[22] Oskar Sohngen links divine kerygma with hearing and vocal utterance: 'The kerygma of God's miraculous deed in Jesus Christ is also *akoê*, hearing. That music stems from the realm of the auricularia, audible things – as does the gospel – that it has a heavenly origin, and that it comes to us in the same way, namely, through the voice ...'[23] A new graced word is heard as revelation in Christian social life.

Four of the many instances of biblical kerygmatic theosony provide sufficient illustration: The silence within which Elijah hears the voice and message of God (1 Kings 19:11-18); the calling of Samuel to prophetic activity (1 Sam 3:2-12); thirdly, Jesus Christ as kergmatic theosony incarnated; finally, The Book of Revelation as the narrative of the triple theosonies.

Elijah searches on the mountain of God for the Lord who 'is about to pass by' (1 Kings 19:11). But not in the great wind, or in the ensuing earthquake and fire, is the Lord found but only in the 'sound of sheer silence'. The wind (Ex 3:2), the earthquake (Ex 19:18), fire (Ex 19:18), the trilogy of cosmic forces, have revealed God heretofore. But this is something else above and beyond nature. As Jerome T. Walsh puts it: 'Yahweh's appearance is heralded by natural upheavals, but it is ineffably more: it is a "sound of sheer silence".'[24]

Three interesting points are of significance here. The first has to do with the actual, *original sound* of the three-word symbol, the other is about the distinctive *images* – aural and tactile – thrown together in this symbol of divine revelation, and the third point refers to the actual meaning of the Hebrew word 'sound' that also means 'voice'.

21. Simons, 'Kerygma', p 797.
22. Ibid, p 797.
23. Oskar Sohngen, 'Music and Theology: A Systematic Approach', in *Sacred Sound: Music in Religious Thought and Practice*, ed Joyce Irwin, Chico: Scholars Press, 1983, p 13.
24. Walsh, *Berit Olam*, p 276.

Walsh suggests that the Hebrew 'phrase "voice / sound" is rich in *sound*'.[25] This richness has to do with the arrangements of the consonants: the order of q-d-m in one clause is inverted in the other m-d-q. This answers the question *why* it is rich in sound, but it does not address the really interesting question about the *how* it is that this one word should carry a sonic excellence which brings us to the threshold of our hearing powers. This suggests that the mysterious sound of God's self-disclosure is experienced in pure sounds, not necessarily by meaning. Could it be that this sound, and sacred sounds like it, appeal to a sixth sense, a sense that comes to life when one is experiencing the revelation of the triune God through listening and silence? To return to the topic of this oxymoron, there is a subtle combination of sensory images, which is both sonic and tactile. Sound and silence are auditory: 'sheer' is described by Walsh as a tactile word. For something to be described as 'sheer' means that it is tangible. The third point is illustrated through the diversity of translations of this trilogy: transliterations of the Hebrew phrase vary from 'the still, small voice', 'the sound of a gentle breeze' to the preferred one here 'the *sound* of sheer silence'.[26]

In the kerygmatic silent voice, God despatched Elijah to Damascus (1 Kings 19:11-19). Elijah must obey the command. This is a listening which transcends the stormy listening experience described in philosophical terms by Fiumara: 'A listening experience would actually come across like a storm and overwhelm us – silently – distancing us from the constant of the discourses that saturate our culture, ready at all times to convey the most sophisticated "philosophical" devices *against* the storm.'[27]

Samuel, after three failed calls to him by God as he lay in the temple, eventually, on the advice of his master Eli, listens intently to God who promises 'that he will make both ears of anyone who hears of it tingle': Samuel is impelled to share God's message of opposition against Eli's house with Eli himself (1 Sam 3:2-12).

From kerygmatic theosony in the Jewish scriptures, we move

---

25. Ibid, p 276. Italics mine.
26. NRSV, p 327.
27. Fiumara, *The Other Side of Language*, p 122.

to the incarnate Word of God, Jesus Christ, the kerygma in person. Twenty-seven writings of the New Testament right up to The Apocalypse comprise parables, storytelling and verbal miracles urging people to listen to the Messianic message of *Basileia tou Theou* (The kingdom of God).

The Book of Revelation is perhaps the loudest listening-centred biblical writing in scripture. It is the culmination of early Jewish and Christian Apocalypticism. Jean-Louis D'Aragon in *The Jerome Biblical Commentary* notes that some fifty-four Holy Spirit visions and sixty-seven angelic interventions reveal God's mysterious revelation to the supposed author, John of Patmos.[28] This unfolding of 'what must soon take place' is highly charged with listening – a theosonic revelation. According to Adela Yarbro Collins: The Book of Revelation is a 'narrative of a special kind. It narrates extraordinary … auditions that concern things normally … *unheard* by human beings.'[29] From the beginning of The Apocalpyse, there is a theosonic approach: one must only read *aloud* the words of the prophecy, and 'blessed are those who hear' (Rev 1:3) the voice of the pages. The focal information in the first verse is John's description of the voice of God heard on Sunday, the Lord's day, on Patmos: 'I was in the Spirit on the Lord's day, and I heard behind me a loud voice like a trumpet saying' (Rev 1:10). This is the revelatory moment for John and the allegorical reference to the trumpet sound is in keeping with biblical tradition. 'The sound of a trumpet was traditionally used to describe a theophany (Ex 19:16, 19).'[30]

Chapters two to four contain seven pastoral letters or messages to the churches of Asia Minor – each message reiterating some fourth-gospel topics. But each one of these messages issues a consistent invitation: 'Let anyone who has an ear listen to what the Spirit is saying.' Hearing the word of God is not sufficient. 'Let everyone who hears, say …' (Rev 22:17).

The opening verse of chapter eight is interesting and has al-

---

28. See Jean-Louis D'Aragon SJ in 'The Apocalypse' in *The Jerome Biblical Commentary*, p 468.
29. Adela Yarbro Collins, 'The Apocalypse (Revelation)' in *The New Jerome Biblical Commentary*, p 996.
30. Ibid, p 1001.

ready been lightly touched on in the Exposition of the Fourth Movement. 'When the Lamb opened the seventh seal, there was silence in heaven for *about* half an hour' (Rev 8:1). It was after this imaginary length of silent time that the trumpets are handed to the angels. From silence to sound, the message is clear. The scroll defining God's will (Rev 5:1) is opened out of silence to sound. The sounding of the trumpet, the key sound of theophany, causes devastation and plague. On the other hand, the sound announces the day of the Lord (Rev 11:15-19). The seventh trumpet sound in ensemble with the strong, resounding heavenly voices, seems to mirror the seventh seal, the seal of silence.

The voice John heard he clearly believed to be from heaven (Rev 14:2). The cosmic sounds of rushing water and startling thunder, all familiar cosmic sounds of theophany as noted, vaguely describe the sound. John further compares the sound to singers accompanying themselves on harps. For St John of the Cross, this singing is gentle and he makes the connection between the cosmic and the silent theosony thus: 'This voice [Rev 2] is infinite, for … it is God himself who communicates himself, speaking in the soul … He produces in the soul great delight and grandeur.'[31]

Arising from the inspiration of the Holy Spirit, John of Patmos hears the voice of an angel. Thomas Allen Seel makes the point about the 'grain' of the voices of revelatory angels who assume the role of the prophets who spoke in the Old Testament. Of the voice of the Book of the Apocalypse, Seel has this to say: 'Characteristic of revelatory vocal ψωνή (phone) is the empowered strength and clarity of its tone. While prophets in the Old Testament were able to 'speak' for Yahweh, only angels will be able to be sanctioned to carry the Godhead's message in eschatological time.'[32]

In the final pages, John the Divine narrates his theosonic and visual revelations, acknowledging the aural nature of the experience initially: 'I, John, am the one who heard and saw these things.

---

31. St John of the Cross, *Spiritual Canticle*, Stanza XIV, *The Complete Works of St John of the Cross*, p 78.

32. Thomas Allen Seel, *A Theology of Music for Worship derived from the Book of Revelation*, p 103.

And when I heard and saw them …' (Rev 22:8). This aural precedence reflects also the experience of Job and is referred to in the
course of the discussion on silent theosony. A final word, by way
of transition to the ultimate silent theosony, from St John of the
Cross about the aural religious experience of his namesake, the
narrator of the Apocalypse. Theosony, God's aural self-disclosure, appeals to the 'spiritual faculties'; it is 'silent to the sense and
the natural faculties, it is a most sounding solitude to the spiritual
faculties.'[33]

Silent Theosony

To term a theosony 'silent' is an oxymoron, a contradiction in
itself. A silent theosony is in the realm of the mystical: the space in
which to pray. Already acknowledged above, this theosonic definition was inspired by two images from the *Spiritual Canticle* of
John of the Cross. A religious listening encounter can be purely
mystical: 'Now a word came stealing to me, my ear received the
whisper of it … there was silence, then I heard a voice' (Job 4:12,
16b) is the silent audio-centric experience of Eliphaz, one of the
three comforters of Job. Here is the same oxymoron that the title –
silent theosony – refers to. In the midst of the night, the ear remains
alert to receive the sheerly silent. In the 'sound of sheer silence',
Yahweh is heard. Hearing comes before vision too for Job. In his
last words, he answers his Lord: 'I had heard of you by the hearing
of the ear, but now my eye sees you' (Job 42: 5).

The most spectacular moment of silent theosony is told of in
the Acts of the Apostles (Acts 2). The coming of the Holy Spirit
envelops all present with complete at-one-ness, redressing and
dispelling the inherited confusion of the Tower of Babel. All the
mellifluous sounds of the entire languages of the universe resound throughout the house. Here 'sound' and 'voice' in the one
word, make perfect sense to the hearer; the truth is heard as if one
eloquently said it oneself. For Silesius, the sound of two words
places him firmly in the space between chaos and the Godhead:
'Two words I like to hear, and they are *from* and *toward*: From

<hr>

33. St John of the Cross, *Spiritual Canticle*, Stanza XIV, *The Complete Works
of St John of the Cross*, p 85. Italics mine.

Babel and myself, toward Jesus and toward God.'[34] From out of
the sound of humanity's word, the Word of God is faced toward.

This Pentecostal advent of the Holy Spirit is defined as a heavenly sound. According to St John of the Cross: 'This spiritual voice
and sound was heard in the spirits of the apostles at the time when
the Holy Spirit, in a vehement torrent ... descended upon them ...
[it] is accompanied ... by grandeur, strength, power, delight and
glory; and thus it is as an immense and inward sound and voice,
which clothes the soul with power and strength.'[35]

Luke tries to describe this ineffable theosony but no cosmic
sound is adequate – no mundane images can describe the 'sound
like a violent wind' which filled the entire house where they were
sitting (Acts2:2). Symbolising the breaking in of the Holy Spirit
through a sound 'like' the wind conforms not just with the Greek
language wherein 'wind' and 'spirit' are phonetically related but
also the same Hebrew word signifies both 'wind' and 'spirit' as
has already been recognised here. In Aramaic and in Greek
'breath', 'spirit' and 'wind' are one and the same word. The author of the fourth gospel symbolises that same breath of God in
another play on words or sounds in chapter 3 of his gospel: 'The
wind blows where it chooses, and you hear the sound of it ... So it
is with everyone who is born of the Spirit' (Jn 3:8). The only reliable
faculty in religious experience is the aural, Jesus himself proclaimed. The farewell discourse of the apostle Peter in Jewish
apocalyptic imagery foretells the day when all of God's cosmic
creation will be disclosed. How will it be recognised? Purely
through the sound and the listening when 'The heavens will pass
away with a loud noise' (2 Pet 3:10).

To conclude, the experience of the silent aural is a very personal
way of being alone and open to God's self-communication.
Platonist philosopher, Plotinus, contemplating on the Good or
One tells us that it is simply the 'flight of the alone to the Alone.'[36]

---

34. Angelus Silesius, *The Cherubinic Wanderer*, p 66.
35. St John of the Cross, *Spiritual Canticle*, Stanza XIV:10, *The Complete
Works of St John of the Cross*, p 77.
36. Plotinus, *The Enneads*, London: Penguin, (1917-1930), trs Stephen
McKenna, 1991, 6. 9, p 546.

Ten aspects of theosonic alertness

To speak of theosony is to speak of human beings in their relationship with God through an obedient attention to the Voice of the triune God. Revealing the mystery of Trinity by a listening heart ultimately reveals one's own mystery as a human being. The interpretative key that unlocks the secret of theosony is, in the final analysis, to be found in a Trinitarian theology. Theosony, the listening religious experience, clears a neutral space that creates the possibility of hearing what needs to be listened for with accurate understanding and response. Theosony is a theory of aural vigilance, being on guard to the sound of the divine utterance, which is understood, in universal sounds, in human communicative speech and in the transcendental sound of silence.

Ten central themes are reiterated over the next few pages. The first has to do with what is aurally hidden and aurally revealed in the world of darkness.

1. This praying space which is aural is no way passive or docile; it is the most intelligent avenue towards divine alterfication. The discordant echoes of sin and evil can be clearly discerned along this path. It does not intend to offer a rosy, easy, surface experience. That the triune God is hidden and mysterious is an experience that most Christians encounter at one time or another in the journey through prayer life. What is hidden and mysterious also conjures up in the imagination a twilight or even darkness experience. A creative listening occurs quite naturally in a dark, night-time reality when the distractions of the visual sense are silenced. The routine of early Irish poets was one of darkness. In order to enhance the birthing of perfect phrase idiom and sound, Robin Flower imaginatively paints this way of the dark night of the poetic soul. This, he does, not merely to describe the method of the poet in quest of truth, but even more

importantly, to highlight the extraordinary importance which this creative darkness sourced in the life and soul of the Irish language: 'If the spoken Irish of today is … the liveliest, the most concise, and the most literary in its turns of all vernaculars of Europe, this is due in no small part to the passionate preoccupation of the poets, turning and re-turning their phrases in the darkness of their cubicles, and restlessly seeking the last perfection of phrase and idiom.'[1] The fierce, wild, engrossing relationship with God can favourably be tuned and re-tuned in cubby-hole darkness into the last perfection of faithful prayer. According to the night songs of the eighteenth-century German Romantic mystic, Novalis, it is in that 'holy, unspeakable, mysterious Night',[2] that the praying soul is permitted to sing: The darkness, physically and spiritually, was dispelled through sound for St John of the Cross, and the poem *The Spiritual Canticle* echoes that song. Written in 1584, it is one of the most beautiful poems ever written. 'In one of the darkest of the dark nights which he had to endure, we can imagine him breaking into a song … a song as passionately inspired and as skilfully wrought as any that has ever come from human lips.'[3] *Bis orat qui cantat* (the one who sings, prays twice), as the ancient dictum suggests.

James Joyce was conscious of this all-pervasive nature of the ear. His final masterpiece, *Finnegans Wake*, was the product of the night, he maintained, full of nighttime activity and dream language. According to his biographer, Richard Ellman, Joyce 'justified its content as a third of human life – the night third.'[4] *Ulysses*, the work of Joyce's stream of consciousness, where the mind talks to itself, is a book of the light and the daytime. 'Having written Ulysses about the day, I wanted to

1. Robin Flower, *The Irish Tradition*, Oxford: OUP, (1947), 1979, p 106. This quotation, in part, was cited in the Introductory chapter referring to another point on the connection between auditory language and the body.
2. Novalis, *Hymns to the Night: Spiritual Songs*, p 9.s.
3. E. Allison Peers, 'Spiritual Canticle:Introduction' in *The Complete Works of St John of the Cross*, Vol 2, p 1.
4. Richard Ellman, *James Joyce*, Oxford: OUP, (1959), 1983, p 703.
5. Quoted in Ellman, *James Joyce*, p 695.

write this book about the night.'[5] What is so captivating here is that when explaining the mysterious, nocturnal, language of *Finnegans Wake*, Joyce himself advocated listening to it rather than reading it. Rational understanding is the daytime work of the eye; understanding both the rational and the absurd or that which is not in accordance with reason is the full-time work of the ear.

Joyce experimented with such aural sounding in his later writing particularly. His word was primarily chosen for its sound. Joycean word-choice did not always represent the object it referred to but depended, according to Alex Aronson, 'on the sonority and intonation of the speaker's voice.'[6] On the completion of *Finnegans Wake*, 'to those who found it unreadable, he [Joyce] suggested not reading but listening to it.'[7] This great book of nighttime activity is to be listened to. David Norris suggests that at 'night in darkness ... the ear takes precedence over the eye.'[8] Of the book, Joyce himself wrote in a letter to his daughter: 'In a word, it is pleasing to the ear ... That is enough, it seems to me.'[9] According to Richard Ellman, Joyce 'defended its technique or form ... on the importance of sound ...'[10] 'The reader's Golden Rule,' according to Norris, ' is when in doubt, read aloud.'[11] In short, 'Joyce addressed the listener rather than the reader.'[12] The golden rule of scripture is also: when in doubt, read aloud.

2. Secondly, theosony has an *anthropological* purpose. It is a listening to and for the divine word that resounds throughout the mystery of human being. Yet there is a question of knowing *how* to listen, whether one is capable of right theological listening or not. As Rahner put it, 'a true philosophy of religion in the

6. Alex Aronson, *Music and the Novel*, NJ: Rowman & Littlefield, 1980, p 40
7. Norris, *Joyce for Beginners*, p 150.
8. Ibid, p 150. Italics mine.
9. James Joyce in a letter to Lucia Joyce, June 1, 1934, quoted in Ellman, *James Joyce*, p 702.
10. Ibid, p 703.
11. Norris, *Joyce for Beginners*, pp 4/150.
12. Aronson, *Music and the Novel*, p 40.

final analysis is nothing other than the command to man to
turn his ear towards his history to discover whether the word
of God has been *sounded* there.'[13] Every physical act is a spiritual
one. There is a spiritual dimension in the function and functioning of the ear. There is a spiritual quality that surrounds
the aural field if one chooses or wants to hear. Philosopher,
Gemma Fiumara writes on how to listen: 'A salient criterion to
invoke ... is the distinction between not being able to do something and not wanting to do something even though one has
the "power" to do it.'[14] That power for the Christian resides in
the Holy Spirit who is ready and able to assist the one who
wants to converse with God and who knows that the power is
there for the asking.

3. The third theme that is heard in the hermeneutics of theosony
    is the theme of *grace*. Listening to this Son of the Father and
    Word made flesh in the midst of humanity is a moment of
    grace. It is 'an openness to God's grace'.[15] This Divine gift, the
    Spirit of absolute love, gathers all human beings, if they con-
    sent, into the harmony, the oneness, the tonic of this love – 'for
    God is love' (1 Jn 4:8).

4. The fourth fact that is important in theosony is that it is really
    theo-logical, that is *speaking about and to God*. A theology with-
    out theosony is when listening becomes separated from a con-
    versation with God. The subject becomes dislocated from the
    object and the delicate links between humankind and the
    Divine presence are imperilled. Without a keen attentiveness
    to the actual experience of listening to God, 'a man at prayer is
    still only talking to himself.'[16] The subjective, the ego, domi-
    nates the relationship which is 'a reduced-by-half rationality
    (only capable of speaking) can do more than mirror itself or ig-
    nore the relationship of the other.'[17] Refusing to listen is a turn-

---

13. Rahner, *Hearers of the Word*, p 31. Italics mine.
14. Fiumara, The Other Side of Listening, p.157.
15. Charles Davis, 'The Theology of Preaching' in *Preaching*, ed Ronan
Drury, Dublin: Gill & Son, 1962, p 22.
16. Rahner, *The Practice of Faith*, p 79.
17. Fiumara, *The Other Side of Language*, p 189.

ing away from the soul-full sound of the triune God. Christ is the sounding board who enhances the power and quality of the Sound of God and who also directs the sound in the way of the human listening audience.

5. Theosony proceeds from disposition, through habit to *virtue*, a point made in the theory of silence presented here. Listening is not a virtue until it becomes so much ingrained to be truly a quality of self. That is precisely why the sacred dimension of listening expects a genuine divine/human encounter. Being receptive to the sound of God is a paradox; a listener can only hear by standing back from, and renouncing, human sound. In the understanding of Karl Rahner, revelation 'remains always an unexpected thing, in spite of all the calculating and waiting … It is the unique self-subsistent action of a free person.'[18] True faith in God must begin within that wellspring which Christians believe to be the fruit of the Holy Spirit. As Zuckerkandl eloquently summarises in a musical context: 'A god's gift comes from the inside; he opens men's hearts and unseals their lips.'[19] This gift is the gift of the Holy Spirit, and Jesus Christ is the gift bearer and supreme human archetype who opens our hearts and promises fluency in the language of God.

6. Alertness to the activity of God at once highlights a particular ignoring of its presence in contemporary theology and theological practice. This is precisely what John Cage calls for in music, that is 'an attention to the activity of sounds.'[20] Listening to God is an instance of being answerable or accountable to God that is within one's own power and free will.

7. Theosony is the language of *feeling*. Human emotions are continually aroused through sound encounters. Cage is accurate again: 'Emotion takes place in the person who has it. And sounds, when allowed to be themselves, do not require that those who hear them do so unfeelingly.'[21] Can the accomplish-

18. Rahner, *Hearers of the Word*, p 157.
19. Zuckerkandl, *Man the Musician*, p 12.
20. Cage, *Silence*, p 10.
21. Ibid, p 10.

ment of the ear manage to sound the way praying feels? It is a question of crossing the bridge between physical and inner sounding. In the words of Zuckerkandl, 'only in the most obvious physical sense do the sounds come to the listeners from outside themselves; the true source is inside the listeners.'[22] What we are trying to describe is on the threshold between the ear, on the one hand, and emotion on the other. The realm of emotions, Storr suggests, is most readily accessed through the ear. 'What seems certain is that there is a closer relation between *hearing* and emotional arousal that there is between seeing and emotional arousal.'[23] All emotion precedes conceptualisation. Theopathy, responding feelingly and emotionally to God, is conforming to the sympathetic feelings, which the ear symbolises.

8. The eighth theosony is an *active* way of listening. It is both active and passive, concrete and abstract, receiving and yet giving. It constitutes a constant underground river of sonic experience in the living encounter of the body with the world at large. 'Whoever is from God hears the words of God' (Jn 8:47). To hear these words is simply to believe. Not to hear them and accept them as true means 'that you are not from God' (Jn 8:47).

9. Theosony is an *obedience*. Obedience is the English translation of the Hebrew *sama*, which refers to the physical act of hearing. The Greek words for obedience are also related to the same words for hearing. An act of obedience, therefore, is an act of the ear. As Rick Byargeon puts it: 'If one truly hears the word of God, then obedience is inevitable.'[24] In short, 'blessed … are those who hear the word of God and obey it' (Lk 11:28). These words are forever. 'Heaven and earth will pass away, but my words will not pass away' (Mt 24:35). The sound of God through the sound-message of Jesus Christ will never vanish but will continue sounding. Kelber, in describing the continu-

22. Zuckerkandl, *Man the Musician*, p 13 concerning Gregorian chant as prayer form.
23. Storr, *Music and the Mind*, p 26.
24. Rick W. Byargeon, 'Obedience' in *Eerdmans Dictionary of the Bible*, p 981.

ity process in ancient orality writes that 'through the agency of the oral medium [the speaker's] voice carried the voice of Jesus, and Jesus continued speaking in their words.'[25] To hear Christ is to hear the loving voice of the Father.

10. Finally, theosonic alertness to God is being *absurd*, inconsistent with reason, but in no manner ridiculous or preposterous. The word 'absurd' has aural and oral connotations as we briefly touched upon in the First Movement. It takes its etymology from Latin *surdus* that means 'deaf' or 'indistinct'. 'Surd' in English is a mathematical term of a quantity not capable of being expressed in rational numbers. It is therefore irrational and often contrary to common sense. In Algebra, a surd denotes 'an algebraic root which cannot be expressed in finite terms. It lies outside the commensurable and the decidable.'[26] Again we find a plausible definition of infinite, ineffable listening to God's self-revelation. God communicates love and goodness, in this case, through the divine initiative of graced hearing. God speaks, and that very word whispered is the listener's being and existence. Vedantic scripture, the wisdom of the Yogis who were the prophets of India, have revered the Sound and Word God. In the articulation of such a philosophy, there is an aural mysticism, a mystery of sound, listening, hearing and speaking inherent. This 'new sort of naiveté',[27] as Rahner defines dialogical prayer is, simply, how that very sense of hearing is appropriated and programmed to respond to God's initiative. God hears and responds through the interior ear. In every act or function of the ear, called or not called, the sound of God is there. Humanity lives in an ear-world of God and of itself. To put it another way, being in, and knowing, the triune God in an ear-to-ear, heart-to-heart conversational discourse is a conversation with the nearest and dearest.

In short, discerning the Voice of God – theosony – is neither this nor that, neither one thing nor another, neither one word nor another, but is in all things touched by truth. Herein lies

25. Kelber, *The Oral and Written Gospel*, p 20.
26. Steiner, *Real Presences*, p 127.
27. Rahner, *The Practice of Faith*, p 82.

the guarantee of salvation and the secret is in the aural reception of the Word of God: 'You also, who have heard the word
of truth, the gospel of your salvation, and have believed in
him, were sealed with the promised Holy Spirit, who is the
guarantee of our inheritance until we acquire possession of it,
to the praise of his glory' (Eph 1:13,14).

These concepts are, in philosophical terms, meta-empirical – beyond the field of human experience. Thus, they are difficult to
articulate and to define. Yet, as Rahner states about such concepts
in verbal revelation, 'they make up the concrete reality of
Christianity.'[28] The truth of a religious aural experience is completely beyond words yet it is completely thrown back on words
to communicate even the tiniest glimmer of the experience to oneself and to others. Elsewhere Rahner remarked that 'to the extent
that it has now become evident that even supra-mundane existence can be revealed through the human word, we are now able to
say also that man is at least the one who must listen for a revelation from this free God speaking in *human words*.'[29]

The technique of listening to the Word of God in human terms
has to be approached from the realm of the imagination.
Everyone approaches God in her and his own way: 'In the end this
great matter of belief in God must be left to the reader to settle in
the intimate places of his own personal being and life. He alone
can translate the abstractions of generalised statement into the
concrete and pungent realities of living experience.'[30]

28. Rahner, *Foundations of Christian Faith*, p 26.
29. Rahner, *Hearers of the Word*, p 155.
30. Farmer, *Towards Belief in God*, p114.

Conclusion

'Theological work is always unfinished.'[1]

'Sight says too many things at one time. Being does not see itself ... it *listens* to itself.'[2]

'Hear it calling out to every creature[3] ... the collect of a new epiphany[4] ... it's time to swim out on your own and fill the element with signatures on your own frequency ...'[5]

T he central theme of this book – towards a theology of listen-ing – poses at least five primary and three secondary ques-tions:

Is all human aural experience religious?

How does one hear the Sound, the voice of God in human existence?

Does talking about the primacy of the sense of hearing in divine self-communication exclude the physically deaf?

Is Christian aural experience any different from, for example, the mystical sonic experience of the sound 'om' for the Hindu or indeed any other type of religious experience?

What is happening precisely in the aural experience of God's self-disclosure?

The answer to the first four questions is in the taxonomy of theosony: every sound ever to have existed in human history is the Sound of God, from the sound of the silent stone to the shrill

1. Gerald O'Collins, *Fundamental Theology*, London: DLT, (1981) 1982, p 20.
2. Bachelard, *The Poetics of Space*, p 215. Italics mine.
3. Seamus Heaney, *Station Island*, London: Faber & Faber, 1984, p 90.
4. Ibid, p 93.
5. Ibid, p 94.

screech of the blackbird, to the secret sound of one's voice, to the silent sound of the praying space. This is inclusive of everybody and no different from any aural or oral religious experience imaginable.

The fifth major question is its own answer: In posing the thought linguistically, the actuality of the aural experience of God's love is actualised and understood. The only meaningful way is through language, listening and silence inferred in the concept of theosony. The psalmist, in mixed metaphor, compares his own speech with the silent meditation of his heart and with what God communicates as salvation through natural imagery, seeing and hearing: 'Let the words of my mouth, and the meditation of my heart be acceptable in thy sight, O Lord, my rock, my redeemer' (Ps 19:14).

The three secondary queries are:
Is the sound of God's revelation in the dimmest, tiniest whisper of the soul, in the sheer sound of silence?
Is that sound outside of time and space, beyond all airwaves and vibrations, beyond all one-to-one conversation?
Can it be asserted that God speaks to every human being that chooses to listen?

The answer to all three is an unconditional 'yes'.

The metaphor of conversation has been one particular *leitmotif* throughout this theology of listening. A conversation is self-revelation to and with another. Yet, human language only hints at defining the self-revelation of God. For the biblical scholar, Seán Freyne, human language 'calls for a special attuning of the ear to hear that deeper voice.'[6] In stretching the human word to 'incline the ear of the heart' to God, a theosonic methodology proposes an accompanying utterance or sounding of that human word to amplify the force of that deeper voice.

Defining what this particular attunement might be has been neglected in Western Christian theology. The sublime in God is heard and not seen, perhaps because the eye is impatient. It wants to see everything within and beyond the horizon: the ear can only

---

6. Freyne, *Texts, Contexts and Cultures*, p 95.

take in one thought at a time and each meaningful thought takes its place in a pattern of what went before and what is coming next. This is what Gaston Bachelard intimates in the mixed metaphor of the introductory quote to this Finale: the visual is a babble of images, the auditory is being itself – an auditory ontology. Since listening is so intimately bound to the origins of being, something so precious must be revered, treasured and carried over into the way we listen. Although not addressing a theology of listening, Berendt concurs that it is now 'appropriate that the culture of hearing and the miracle of the ear should be rediscovered at a time when patriarchy is losing power.'[7]

Today, some thirty years after this statement, the power-loss is almost complete and now it is clearly time to restore ear-culture. The English voice therapist, Paul Newham, puts it this way: 'What reaches the audience is not the linguistic sophistication, but the phonational depth of affect.'[8] Praying to God is simply the living union of saying something and listening. The symbiosis is in the 'sonans', the sounding.

The one appropriate response that theosony presents is not so much what Jesus Christ and his message of the kingdom of God *is*, but how does one hear the hint of it, and how does one respond to its harbinger? Hans Urs von Balthasar succinctly puts it thus by way of conclusion: 'God speaks his word within man. Not only what man utters but all that he is becomes God's organ of communication. What man is and can be is only revealed in its fullness when God makes of him his alphabet, his sounding board and sense organ.'[9]

The ear is our most characteristic organ of existential reality. Like the heart, it is ever awake until it breathes its last. When the event of listening to the sound of God's self-revelation occurs within the human frame, theosony is accomplished. This accomplishment has been documented here in as far as such reflection, observation, analysis, and this one verbal recording of a spontaneous reality, are possible.

---

7. Berendt, *The Third Ear*, p 27.
8. Newham, *The Singing Cure*, p 222.
9. Von Balthasar, *Word and Revelation*, pp 108/109.

Index

Bold numerals are references to footnotes

57, 76, 84, 88, 97, 100, 102-8, 116,
133, 135, 144, 148-9, 154, 157, 174,
183, 185, 188, 192-3, 195-6, 198,
204-7, 216, 231, 236-7, 242
Richards, M. C., 142
Ricoeur, Paul, 24, 38, 97, 101, 105, 167
Riley, Bridget, 112
Rilke, Rainer Maria, 138, 141
Roman Catholic, 17, 72, 125, 165,
179, 180
Rueben, 162
Ryan, Fr Vincent, 199
Rybolt, John, 201-2
Ryken, Leland, 115
Sachs, Johnathan, 51, 115
Sacramentum Mundi, 18, **26, 36, 44,**
181, **196**
Samuel, 225-6
Sarah, 164
Scheffczyk, Leo, 26, 44
Schillebeeckx, Edward, 159
Schleiermacher, Friedrich, 224
Schnackenberg, Rudolf, 144, 159,
169, 171, 172
Schneiders, Sandra M., **22**, 43, **99,
101**, 102-4, 106, **164, 170, 174**
Science, 11, 17, 19, 22, 34, 56-8, 67,
69, 72-3, 79, 81, 151, 180
Scott, 151-2
Seel, Thomas Allen, 80, 228
Shepherding, 139, 168-9, 175
Shiphrah, 93
Shock, 47, 48, 81, 89, 101, 104, 156-7,
187
Signer, Michael, 222-3
Silence, 7, 9, 14-5, 17-20, 22, 26-7, 30-
1, 35, 43-5, 47-8, 50, 52, 63, 68, 79,
87, 90, 93, 97, 105-7, 109, 115, 134-
5, 137, 139-40, 142, 146, 148, 153,
157, 172-5, 177-207, 212, 214-7,
219-20, 222-3, 225-6, 228-9, 231,
235, 239-40
Silent theosony, 97, 105, 219-20,
223, 228-9 *see also* Silence &

Theosony
Simeon, 162
Simons, Eberhard, 224-5
Sin, 39, 44-6, 125, 171, 198-9, 221,
231
Smalley, Stephen, 144, 154-**5**
Smith, Huston, **146**, 156
Socrates, 91-5
Sohngen, Oskar, 225
Solomon, 201
Spearritt, Placid, 197-8
Spiritual Canticle, The, **219, 228**, 229,
230, 232
Spirituality, Female, 20-2, 28, 48,
71, 86-7, 93, 97, 146-7, 161-2, 166,
197, 221-2
Spirituality, Male, 20-2, 92, 97, 121,
146-7, 166
Spoken word, 37-8, 79, 87, 109-11,
114-6, 118-23, 126, 129-35, 144,
146-7 150-1, 154-5, 157-8, 163,
168, 170-1, 185, 190-1, 201, 204-5,
207, 214, 216, 218, 225, 227, 234
Stanley, John, 186
Steiner, George, 25, **31**, 47, 50, 102,
103, 104, **105**, 106, 113, 122, 139,
153, 181, 207, 213, 216, **237**
Stillness, 44, 184, 187-9, 191-3, 195-
6, 202-3, 206, 208, 220, 222, 226
Storr, Anthony, 20, 77, 110, 236
Storytelling, 113-4, 129-31, 144,
221, 227
Sufiism, 27, 164
Tamar, 93
Tame, David, 28-30, 116, 164
Tavener, John, 185
Teresa of Avila, 190-1
Theaetetus, 92
Theology, 7-10, 13, 14-23, 25, 30-6,
41-6, 48, 50, 52-3, 56-7, 66-9, 72-6,
81-5, 87-9, 96-7, 100, 102, 107, 109-
10, 114, 119-20, 122, 124, 132, 134-
7, 139, 148, 150, 163-4, 167, 169,
174, 178-81, 184-5, 187-8, 189-90,